# PARTIES AND DEMOCRACY IN ITALY

For my mother and father

# Parties and Democracy in Italy

JAMES L. NEWELL

## Ashgate

Aldershot • Burlington USA • Singapore • Sydney

Published by
Ashgate Publishing Ltd
Gower House
Croft Road
Aldershot
Hants GU11 3HR
England

Ashgate Publishing Company
131 Main Street
Burlington
Vermont 05401
USA

Ashgate website: http://www.ashgate.com

**British Library Cataloguing in Publication Data**
Newell, James L.
  Parties and democracy in Italy
  1. Political parties – Italy  2. Italy – Politics and government – 1945–
  I. Title
  324.2'45

**Library of Congress Cataloging-in-Publication Data:** 99-53153
Newell, James L.
  Parties and democracy in Italy / James L. Newell.
    p. cm.
  Includes bibliographical references.
  ISBN 1-85521-859-3 (HB). – ISBN 1-85521-863-1 (PBK).
  1. Political parties—Italy. 2. Italy—Politics and government—1976–1994.
  3. Italy—Politics and government—1994– I. Title.

  JN5651 .N46 2000
  324.245'09'049—dc21                                    99-53153

ISBN 1 85521 859 3 (HBK)
ISBN 1 85521 863 1 (PBK)

Printed and bound in Great Britain by MPG Books Ltd, Bodmin, Cornwall

# Contents

# List of Figures

# List of Tables

# Acknowledgements

First, I would like to thank the series editor, David Arter, for giving me the opportunity to write this book and also for his stimulating and enjoyable company in Madrid. I am grateful too to Dott. Giorgio Calò of Directa srl. for generously supplying the data on which Table 6.1 is based. The Italian Chamber of Deputies Library Service, and especially Dott. Francesco Avino, were more than generous with their time and patience in teaching me the intricacies involved in consulting the Italian Parliament's data bases. Staff at the Election Services Unit of the Italian Ministry of the Interior and at the *Corte dei conti* were so amazingly courteous and *disponibili* in their provision of data and documentation that, unknown to themselves, they restored my faith in humanity and thankfully helped kill off for me that dreadful old stereotype about unhelpful public servants. I gratefully acknowledge the support of the University of Salford, and especially of Martin Alexander and Geoff Harris, in agreeing to my request for a year's study leave on half pay so that I'd have sufficient time away from my normal duties to do the writing in something approaching reasonable time. I would also like to acknowledge, with thanks, the support of the University of Salford's Embryonic Research Fund in providing financial assistance towards the cost of the research on which the book is based. Martin Bull has provided intellectual stimulation over the years and has been the challenging co-author of a number of articles in the area of parties and democracy in Italy before this book came to fruition. Serena, and my other Italian relatives and friends, have provided support in a myriad different ways – intellectual, material and emotional – as have Vicky, Robin and Tom. Above all, I wish to acknowledge the unfailing support and encouragement of my parents. Of the innumerable wonderful attributes for which they will be fondly remembered, their capacity for penetrating and critical thinking was one of the most remarkable. It is to them that I dedicate this book, with my love.

# Abbreviations

| | |
|---|---|
| **ACLI** | Christian Association of Italian Workers (*Associazione Cristiana Lavoratori Italiani*) |
| **AD** | Democratic Alliance (*Alleanza Democratica*) |
| **AN** | National Alliance (*Alleanza Nazionale*) |
| **ANPI** | National Association of Ex-partisans (*Associazione Nazionale Partigiani*) |
| **CAF** | Craxi-Andreotti-Forlani |
| **CIA** | Central Intelligence Agency (US) |
| **CCD** | Christian Democratic Centre (*Centro Cristiano Democratico*) |
| **CDU** | Christian Democratic Union (*Cristiani Democratici Uniti*) |
| **COREL** | Committee for Electoral Reform |
| **CORID** | Committee for Democratic Reform |
| **C-S** | Social Christians (*Cristiano-sociali*) |
| **CU** | United Communists (*Comunisti Unitari*) |
| **DC** | Christian Democratic Party (*Democrazia Cristiana*) |
| **DP** | Proletarian Democracy (*Democrazia Proletaria*) |
| **DS** | Left Democrats (*Democratici di Sinistra*) |
| **EMU** | Economic and Monetary Union |
| **ENEL** | National Electricity Corporation (*Ente Nazionale per l'Energia Elettrica in Italia*) |
| **ENI** | National Hydrocarbon Corporation (*Ente Nazionale Idrocarburi*) |
| **EU** | European Union |
| **FDS** | 'federation of socialists' ('*federazione dei socialisti*') |
| **Fed. Lib.** | Liberal Federation (*Federazione dei Liberali*) |
| **FI** | Go Italy! (*Forza Italia*) |
| **FPTP** | 'first past the post' |
| **ICI** | Council Property Tax (*Imposta Comunale sugli Immobili*) |
| **IRI** | Institute for Industrial Reconstruction (*Istituto per la Ricostruzione Industriale*) |
| **MEP** | Member of the European Parliament |
| **MID** | Italian Democratic Movement (*Movimento Italiano Democratico*) |
| **MSI** | Italian Social Movement (*Movimento Sociale Italiano*) |
| **MSFT** | Social Movement-Tricoloured Flame (*Movimento Sociale-Fiamma Tricolore*) |

| | |
|---|---|
| **NATO** | North Atlantic Treaty Organisation |
| **NVP** | 'non-vote party' |
| **P2** | Propaganda Two |
| **PASOK** | Pan-Hellenic Socialist Movement (*Panellinion Sosialistikon Kinema*) |
| **PCI** | Italian Communist Party (*Partito Comunista Italiano*) |
| **PDUP** | Party of Proletarian Unity for Communism (*Partito di Unità Proletaria per il Comunismo*) |
| **PDS** | Democratic Party of the Left (*Partito Democratico della Sinistra*) |
| **Pld** | Liberal-Democratic Alliance (*Polo Liberal-Democratico*) |
| **PLI** | Italian Liberal Party (*Partito Liberale Italiano*) |
| **PPI** | Italian Popular Party (*Partito Popolare Italiano*) |
| **PR** | Radical Party (*Partito Radicale*) |
| **PRI** | Italian Republican Party (*Partito Repubblicano Italiano*) |
| **PSDI** | Italian Social Democratic Party (*Partito Socialista Democratico Italiano*) |
| **PSI** | Italian Socialist Party (*Partito Socialista Italiano*) |
| **PSIUP** | Italian Socialist Party of Proletarian Unity (*Partito Socialista Italiano di Unità Proletaria*) |
| **PVA** | Valle d'Aosta List (*Pour la Vallée d'Aoste*) |
| **RAI** | Italian Radio and Television (*Radiotelevisione Italiana*) |
| **RC** | Communist Refoundation (*Rifondazione Comunista*) |
| **RI** | Italian Renewal (*Rinnovamento Italiano*) |
| **RS** | Socialist Renewal (*Rinascita Socialista*) |
| **SD** | Social Democrats (*Socialdemocratici*) |
| **SI** | Italian Socialists (*Socialisti Italiani*) |
| **SVP** | South Tyrolese People's Party (*Südtirolervolkspartei*) |
| **TAR** | Regional Administrative Court (*Tribunale Amministrativo Regionale*) |
| **UD** | Democratic Union (*Unione Democratica*) |
| **UdC** | Union of the Centre (*Unione di Centro*) |
| **UDI** | Union of Italian Women (*Unione Donne Italiane*) |
| **UDR** | Democratic Union for the Republic (*Unione Democratica per la Repubblica*) |
| **UK** | United Kingdom |
| **Unità rif.** | Reformist unity (*Unità riformista*) |

# 1 Introduction: The Revolution in Italian Party Politics

Since 1989 Italian politics have undergone a revolution, and the purpose of this book is to analyse its causes and consequences. Of course, this is not a 'revolution' in the sense of 'mass action, state-breaking and state-making' and the period has indeed seen strong continuities with past political practices. But from this it does not follow that 'events in Italy to date have not been a revolution *in any meaningful sense of the word*' (Ginsborg, 1996: 35, my emphasis). After all, the once leading figures in politics *have* been disgraced and the five traditional parties of government *have* been wiped off the face of the political map. In terms of the numbers, identities and relative sizes of the principal parties, the Italian party system has undergone a transformation – a degree of change so rare that it normally only takes place under extreme conditions such as a break in continuity following the collapse of a regime (Smith, 1989: 354) or else in concomitance with a transformation of the entire constitutional order (such as the one that took place in France in 1958 (Gundle and Parker, 1996: 1)). One might want to debate the *significance* of the changes: it may well be, for instance, that the parties 'remain agents of paralysis and instability rather than unambiguous forces for change' (Bull and Rhodes, 1997: 11) and, indeed, one of my purposes in this book will be precisely to assess what vistas the transformation has, or has not, opened up. However, once it has been conceded that the dramatic nature of the reconfiguration of the party system should not be allowed to hide its limitations (or to hide change and continuity in other areas), the raw datum – the revolution in party politics itself – remains as a brute fact in need of an explanation.

As always, it is a question of balance and of the perspective one chooses to adopt. On the one hand, Italian politics show strong cultural continuities and it seems as fair to say now as it did when Ginsborg made the point, that the political changes have 'not translate[d] into the sort of cultural revolution that had rocked Italy in 1968–69' (Ginsborg, 1996: 27). The *Tangentopoli* investigations, for instance, while bringing down an entire political class, were witnessed by the bulk of the population via the medium of their television screens and, beyond intellectual circles, failed to induce any wide-spread reflection on those cultural traits of clientelism, nepotism and tax evasion in which the activities of the *Tangentopoli* defendants were ultimately rooted. In the final analysis, *Tangentopoli* could only punish past practices, not create the conditions for new ones. Furthermore, as Magatti has argued, the heightened individualism of the 1980s in a context of renewed economic growth, increasing secularization and 'deideologization', the decline of Italy's two political subcultures – the Catholic and the Marxist – and the continuing weakness of the state have all served to weaken normative constraints on individual action with the resulting creation of an environment favouring 'the spread of those illicit behaviours which find in corruption, and more generally in clientelism, the two principle ambits of their manifestation' (Magatti, 1996: 1064). This suggests that if the emergence of the Northern League profoundly challenged the then existing power relationships, nevertheless its espousal of hard work and individualism represented far less of a break with the culture of so-called *'Roma ladrona!'* than it cared to admit. This may help to explain why, on 21 January 1998, League deputies voted against lifting the parliamentary immunity of the *Forza Italia* (FI) deputy Cesare Previti, accused of having bribed members of the judiciary on behalf of the heirs of the industrialist, Nino Rovelli, to ensure that a 678 000 million lire court judgment would be decided in their favour, and why, on 25 February, League deputies voted against lifting the parliamentary immunity of Giancarlo Cito accused of having accepted, while mayor of Taranto, an 80 million lire bribe from a porterage and transport company in exchange for a public works contract.[1]

So there are plenty of cultural continuities available to give the lie to the notion that there has been some sort of qualitative break with the entire range of political habits and practices of the past. On the other hand, continuity though there may be, it is also true that politics in the 1990s were very different to what went before. In what does the difference consist? How can the change best be characterized? Succinct answers to these questions were provided by Maurizio Cotta at a recent conference held at the University of Siena.[2] In common with a number of authors (for example, Gundle and Parker, 1996; Ginsborg, 1996) he sees the period of most intense change as being concentrated in the arc of time that runs between the election of 1992 and the election of 1994 and to which the metaphor of a 'political earthquake' is widely applied (see, for example, Gundle and Parker, 1996). The earthquake, Cotta writes, had its epicentre in the 'governing parties' and in the corresponding political class.

Its essence consists in the implosion of the parties that had dominated the political system for more than forty years and in the (at least temporary) exclusion fom the political game of the highest level of the governing class as well as a substantial part of the intermediate level. This collapse of the 'heart' of the political system constitutes the necessary condition for the start of the first significant institutional change since the failure of the majoritarian electoral law of 1953 and for a profound restructuring of the party system as well as certain important political practices. The 'shipyard' of institutional reform then opens and, propelled by the referendum (of April 1993), a major reform of the electoral system is introduced. A completely new party (*Forza Italia*, FI) bursts into the vacuum left by the governing parties; an old but marginal party (the Italian Social Movement–National Alliance, MSI–AN) manages to join the game by modifying its identity; the principal party of opposition (the Democratic Party of the Left, PDS) succeeds in reversing its decade-long decline; the League's success of the early nineties is consolidated ... . Along with the change in the constellation of the principal party actors, there is a change, too, in the structure of the party system: the traditional tri-polar format hinged on a dominant (and governing) centre pole and on counterposed and excluded oppositions gives way to a bi-polar format of (centre-)left and (centre-)right and the 'governing potential' of all the parties. Certain significant practices also change: opposing and pre-constituted coalitions confront each other at elections, whereas before, coalition building (within margins pre-defined by the tri-polar party system) was strictly confined to the period following elections ... . It is clear, then, that ... the sphere of politics has been overtaken, in certain of its fundamental aspects (institutional rules, actors, modes of behaviour) by significant changes. (Cotta, 1998: 6–7)

A number of points need to be made in connection with this characterization. First, there is the issue of *what* has changed. The object of Cotta's attention in the foregoing extract is what he calls 'the sphere of politics', consisting of institutions and rules governing the management of power, political actors (such as parties) and political behaviour (such as electoral behaviour and that of coalitions). This sphere, Cotta argues, can be conceptually distinguished from 'policy' (substantive political decisions and the processes by which they are arrived at) and 'polity' (the boundaries of the political community) although the three obviously exert reciprocal influence on each other. The focus of this book is on the 'sphere of politics' or on what I prefer to call *party politics*, covering: parties and their members; voters; the behaviour of all three in various arenas; and the institutional rules prescribing their behaviour.

Second, there is the issue of timing. Although the pace of change was undoubtedly at its most rapid, and events at their most dramatic, between 1992 and 1994, the process of historical change is, of course, continuous. This creates a problem when dealing with the sort of multidimensional change we are concerned with, for, except within broad limits, it makes it difficult to assert with much conviction when the change 'really' began. It means that phenomena that for one analyst are an integral part of the change to be explained are for another, by contrast, among the major *catalysts* of the change. Again, much depends on the perspective one chooses to adopt and, in this case, on the breadth of one's focus. Therefore, while concurring with the view that the period of most striking change began in 1992 (corresponding, as it does, to the beginning of the party system's meltdown, 'an event without parallel in a modern democracy' (Gundle and Parker, 1996: 1)) I also think that a case can be made for the view that, from the perspective of the post-Second World War period as a whole, an equally significant shift of gear took place in 1989 when, in the wake of the collapse of the Berlin Wall, Occhetto announced the beginning of the transformation of the Italian Communist Party (PCI) into a non-communist party with a new name – the PDS. With that act, the party finally succeeded, after years of struggle, in beginning to dismantle the principal foundation on which post-war party politics had been erected: the presumed ineligibility of the PCI for government and the consequent *conventio ad excludendum*. With that act, Occhetto irrevocably weakened one of the principal pillars on which Christian Democratic electoral support had traditionally rested and this, in turn, was a necessary condition for the growth and consolidation of support for the Northern League. At the same time, the PCI's transformation was accompanied by an unprecedented level of internal conflict and a major party split. If this led the leaders of the governing parties to believe that they could postpone reform of those 'partitocratic' practices which weakened their own support bases, then such practices were in turn a necessary condition for the referendum of 1991, the success of which encouraged the growing 'referendum movement' to push on towards its 1993 initiative which, through a change in the electoral system, aimed to strike a blow at the heart of the governing class.

Third, there is the question of the duration of the period of change. If it begins at the end of 1989 with the announcement of the PCI's change of name, when does it end? Indeed, *has* it come to an end, or is it still ongoing? A variety of considerations conduce to the latter view. To suggest that change has come to an end is to imply a period of stability in the features presumed to have changed. This is true of few, if any, of the components of party politics for the period since the conjunctural crisis of 1992–94. At the level of rules changes, the new electoral law ushered in immediately after the 1993 election has in no sense closed the debate on institutional reform: to the contrary. On the one hand, if the law was expected to produce a coagulation of the parties and to produce a clear winner at elections, then it is now clear that it has done neither of these things. Parties continue to multiply and, if the 1994 election saw the victory of the centre-right, then the latter was composed not of one coalition but of two, and in any event fell apart after seven months. If the 1996 election saw the victory of the *Ulivo*, then this was very much a 'chance' affair which owed far more to the relative efficiency of the electoral alliances of the centre-left as compared to the centre-right than to any significant shifts of electoral support. The most salient characteristic of 'chance' events is that they are very unlikely to be repeated and not for nothing was a recent book on the 1996 election called *Maggioritario per caso* (D'Alimonte and Bartolini, 1997a). Not surprisingly, then, almost no politician regards the 1993 law as satisfactory and without need of further reform. The period has seen frequent debates on proposals for change and a number of attempts to initiate referenda on the issue. On the other hand, and more radically, the period since 1996 has seen serious efforts being made to revise the whole of Part II of the Constitution. A set of proposals was produced in the autumn of 1997 by the parliamentary commission (the *Bicamerale*) charged with producing them, but they were then blocked by parliament in the late spring of 1998. In addition to all of this, the constellation of parties making up the party system is still in a state of extreme flux.


## Explaining the Revolution

The existing literature on the changes in Italian party politics has been marked by a number of salient characteristics. Foremost among these is the debate between those who see the changes as having been heavily influenced by long-term structural factors, and who therefore incline to the view that the changes themselves come close to being the inevitable outcome of the political system's inherent weaknesses, and, on the other hand, those who argue that the changes were the outcome of specific sequences of events which could quite easily have been very different.[3] A good example of a work belonging to the former category is Massimo Salvadori's *Storia d'Italia e crisi di regime* (1994).

Salvadori's thesis is that the events of the early 1990s represent a regime crisis – the third since Unification – whose roots, like those of 1919–25 and 1943–45, can be traced to a structural feature of the regime – its character as a 'blocked political system' lacking governing alternatives. Like the liberal and fascist regimes which preceded it, the republican regime established after the Second World War was characterized by an opposition which proposed not an alternative government but an alternative political system; not an alternative within, but against, the established institutions. This consequently provoked 'ideological civil war' thus precluding the possibility of peaceful alternation in government of the opposing forces. If in order to prevent the political system tearing itself apart, the governing class had recourse to a variety of strategies – such as the 'transformist' assimilation of some of the forces of opposition (the 'opening to the left' of the early 1960s) or a recourse to *consociativismo* – precisely because the competing demands and outlooks of governing and opposition forces *were* irreconcilable, the crisis of the one would lead to the crisis of the other, bringing about a crisis of the regime itself. The crisis of the PCI at the beginning of the 1990s led the Craxian socialists to believe that the prospect was thereby opened up of the Socialist Party (PSI) one day replacing the PCI as the Christian Democrats, (DC's) main competitor – which in turn, they thought, raised their bargaining power in a *pax spartitoria* with the DC in the present. What they overlooked was that the *pax spartitoria* itself provided fuel for new forces of opposition such as the Northern League (which aimed at the creation of a new regime) that would also be assisted by the crisis of communism. Hence, as indicated by the results of the 1992 election in which *all* the traditional parties suffered more or less dramatic declines, a crisis of the forces of opposition came to coincide with a crisis of the forces of government. And, with the assumptions of the Craxi–Andreotti–Forlani power-sharing arrangement having thus been undermined, a blocked political system gave way to a blockage of the system itself.

Salvadori's 'structural' account has been rather influential and seems clearly to have influenced a number of other writers. For example, Alfio Mastropaolo (1994a) also emphasizes the significance of the *modus vivendi* crisis between the DC and the PCI for the changes; McCarthy (1996a), too, is convinced that the events of the early 1990s should be interpreted as a 'regime crisis';[4] Bull and Rhodes emphasize the importance of structural crisis when they argue that 'collapse was the inevitable consequence of the systematic abuse of power' (1997: 5–6). Of a rather different stamp are the interpretations offered by Gilbert (1995) and Ginsborg (1996).

Gilbert's focus on the chronology of recent events rather than on longer-term structural causes reflects his view that the 'Italian revolution' was not inevitable and that, on the contrary, 'chance and contingency played a large role' (Gilbert, 1995: 3). In essence, Gilbert's argument is that the parties of government made an enormous miscalculation after the end of the Cold War. With the PCI struggling to deal with unprecedented internal dissension in the search for a new identity, the DC and PSI felt that the domestic repercussions of the collapse of the Berlin Wall could only be of benefit to them. Because the Northern League did not have sufficient weight to fill the gap left by the PCI, the governing parties thus felt safe in ignoring the evidence of danger to their positions provided by the electorate's various manifestations of growing impatience with inefficiency, corruption and the outrages perpetrated by organized crime. After that, with the collapse of their vote in 1992, the explosion of *Tangentopoli*, and the murder of Falcone and Borsellino, the governing parties were overtaken by events. Nevertheless, they might have remained in power, for plenty of people had been warning them during the 1980s of the reforms that needed to be undertaken. Hence, they *could* have taken stronger action against the *Mafia*; they *could* have read more accurately the significance of the growth of the Northern League; they *could* have resisted more successfully the temptations of corruption. Instead, by the late 1980s, the parties' behaviour had become so extreme that '[w]here once Italian public opinion had been content to grumble at its leaders but vote for them time and time again, in the 1990s, citizens had no patience left' (ibid.: 4).

Ginsborg's approach is rather similar to that of Gilbert for he argues that the crisis of 1992–94 was 'constituted of very disparate elements' (1996: 19), asserting that it is 'not at all helpful' to adopt a view of history according to which the crisis 'was inevitable and merely a matter of time' (ibid.: 20) and rejecting 'mono-causal interpretations of events' (ibid.). His thesis is that the crisis can be explained as the outcome of a series of tensions or conflicts: between national economic mismanagement and the demands of European integration; between everyday political practice and an 'official morality' upholding the rule of law; between 'virtuous minorities' and the less virtuous occupants of other power centres in the 'state archipelago' (ibid.: 26); between Roman government and northern small businessmen; between the *Mafia* and the state. The important point, for Ginsborg, is that these conflicts derived not from historical constants or from Italy's failure as a regime (after all, if anything, the crisis came about because of the conflict between the failures of the system and the *virtues* of the Republic) and that they have to be seen as being as much the consequences of immediate-term specific sequences of events as of longer-term economic and social changes underlying them.

Hopefully, my own position in the debate between the proponents of 'structural accounts' and those who wish to give more weight to agency will become clear as the text unfolds. For now, suffice it to say that it is, of course, true that giving *excessive* weight to agency can be unenlightening since if, for example, 'the downfall of the political class was caused by its failure to take action which would have saved itself, the question is raised as to why it was unable or unwilling to do this' (Bull, 1996a: 133–4). On the other hand, it is not necessarily the case that the problem is solved by citing more general structural characteristics as an answer, since the question 'Why'?' can be asked indefinitely. The perspective which seems to me to be the most enlightening is the one which focuses on agency, thus recognizing that individual actors could have chosen to act differently, but also recognizing that none were powerful enough, on their own, to control the actions of others. Therefore, with each actor pursuing strategic lines of action that were individually rational given the behaviour of others, a kind of collective action problem came to be created whereby the long-run outcome (the collapse of the party system in this case) was bound to be suboptimal in terms of what was collectively rational – at least for the members of the political establishment at that time. Thus, although each actor was a free agent, there was a very real sense in which the final outcome – the collapse of the system – was, as the 'structuralists' say, inevitable. From such a perspective, the analyst's task becomes that of elucidating the lines of action pursued by the relevant actors given their circumstances, with the aim, thereby, of making intelligible both individual action and overall outcome.

A second feature of the literature on the 'revolution' to date has been its tendency to focus on the sequences of events and structural changes leading up to, and responsible for, the collapse of the traditional parties of government to the relative neglect of what came after. This has been partly due to the simple fact that in the 'rush to publish' (Bull, 1996a: 131) in the wake of the collapse there was, at the time, little 'after' to talk about. However, as Cotta (1998: 10) points out, some years have now passed since the fateful elections of 1994, and an initial survey of what has happened in the period since then is now in order. Neither is the period a short one if one bears in mind that the 'post-fascist' system which was destined to last for more than 40 years was constructed in the five-year period between 1943 and 1948. It is, of course, true that when a process of change is still continuing – as we have argued appears to be true in Italian party politics – it is difficult to analyse outcomes as these necessarily remain unknown and so can, at best, only be speculated upon (Bull, 1996a: 132). On the other hand, one must be careful not to push this argument too far: beyond a certain point, waiting for change to 'run its course' is to risk waiting forever. Moreover, change, even when it is still continuing, can have a number of interim consequences 'along the way' and there is no reason why these consequences should not be studied as outcomes on the same terms as whatever 'final' outcomes emerge once the process of change is complete (even if one has to acknowledge that the ongoing character of the change may well make the interim outcomes impermanent). Finally, if one is analysing a process of change, an exclusive focus on what comes before is bound to be incomplete: change, by definition, is a simultaneous process both of *destruction* and *reconstruction*. Therefore, its explanation necessarily requires an analysis not only of what destroyed the old but also of how the resulting fragments were, or are being, recomposed to form something new.

That said, this book does not seek explicitly to challenge existing interpretations of the changes in Italian politics; for it would seem to be a reasonable supposition that, though with differing emphases, most if not all such interpretations identify an important part of the truth.

My goal here is a different one, even though it *does* arise from what I see as a lacuna in the existing literature, especially from the point of view of those who are unfamiliar with Italian politics. Thus, if I do not wish to *challenge* existing interpretations, I do want to enhance *understanding* of the changes, and, for this to be the case, it seems to me necessary to attempt to deal with what sometimes seems to be missing from other accounts – namely, fully elaborated descriptions of the *underlying mechanisms and causal links* tying together the various factors brought together in explanatory sequences. It is not that these underlying mechanisms and causal links are not known about. However, it is only when they are made explicit that a full understanding of how we got from the 'A' of the traditional post-war party system to the 'B' of the current state of party politics becomes, in my view, possible, especially for the so-called 'non-expert' in Italian politics.

My point can best be elucidated by means of an example. In the first chapter of his book, *La crisi dello Stato italiano*, Patrick McCarthy (1996a: 11–12) adds his weight to the widely held view that a significant role in the crisis of the early 1990s was ultimately played by the weakness of the state which, in its turn, was heavily influenced by the clientelistic mode of managing power relationships. He points out that, as a systematic practice, clientelism appeared from the mid-1950s when the DC used it as a means of acquiring support and thus of escaping from the dominance of the Church. Given, he continues, that clientelism erodes legitimacy by undermining the state's capacity to act as a neutral arbiter, and given that there did not exist a potential alternative government able to put a brake on the DC, the process continued and grew. This passage provokes two comments. First, it attempts to explain the weakness of the state in part by pointing to a causal relationship between it and clientelism. An important strand of thought in the philosophy of science stresses that what is meant by 'explaining' a phenomenon is describing the underlying structures or mechanisms that link presumed causes to the phenomenon to be explained (Keat and Urry, 1975). Thus, in the present case we need to know *how* and *why* clientelism contributed to the state's weakness (as well, of course, as having a precise conception of how the two terms are to be understood). Second, McCarthy's observation about the absence of a brake on the DC being responsible for the continuation and growth of clientelism implies that there was some sort of self-generating mechanism involved in its practice which, in the absence of a brake, would allow it to spread. For a full understanding of the point, therefore, it would be helpful if this mechanism could be elucidated. The task I have set myself in this book, therefore, is that of trying to deepen understanding of how Italian politics got from A to B by paying particular attention to these underlying mechanisms and causal links.

My purpose in writing this book, then, is to try to understand better
how the ongoing process of change has come about and thereby, I dare
to hope, to assist others in achieving a better understanding. I suspect
that people who are familiar with the Italian political scene will find
little original in it. This does not bother me: no theory or investigation
can ever be entirely original, for 'while concepts are produced by the
human imagination, they are not produced in a completely free and
unstructured manner which makes anything possible'. First, they are
constrained by theoretical presuppositions and, second, they are
constrained by data gathered using such presuppositions (Wright, 1985:
20). In other words, in the final analysis no investigation can claim to
be more than a novel elaboration or development of already existing
knowledge. With this in mind, I have not aimed at making the
proverbial 'original contribution' but, rather, have sought quite simply
to enhance my *own* understanding of Italian politics – in the awareness
that the most effective way of trying to contribute to the enhancement
of the community's stock of knowledge is to attempt to enhance one's
own.

One final methodological point is in order – one that has been
suggested to me by my reading of LaPalombara's famous, but con-
troversial, interpretation, *Democracy, Italian Style* (1987). I have talked
about 'understanding' Italian politics and should make clear that I do
not use this term innocently. Human beings, as we know, differ from
the inanimate entities and processes that are the objects of study of
most natural scientists in that their behaviour is governed largely by
the meaning they attach to their action. This being the case, it is difficult
to envisage much real understanding being possible where we are not
willing to make the effort to appreciate the viewpoint of the subjects
whose behaviour we wish to study. Attempting to appreciate subjects'
points of view in its turn requires that interpretations of specific events,
patterns of behaviour and institutions be informed by as full an
awareness as possible of the context in which they are embedded and
not be 'contaminated' by the imposition of outside frames of reference.
Again, an example will serve to make the point. One of the phenomena
that (once upon a time at least) was often taken as an indicator of a
presumed instability of Italian democracy was an apparent willingness
of citizens to defraud the state through tax evasion – for example, by
failing to give, or ask for, receipts. LaPalombara points out that in
Italian culture 'only an oafish stickler will insist on being provided
with the "fiscal receipt" of commercial transactions required by law,
if he does not really need it' (LaPalombara, 1987: 50), thus suggesting
that if tax evasion is *potentially* destructive of democracy (by being
subversive of confidence in the efficacy of public authority),
nevertheless, there is something quintessentially democratic about the
collusion involved in overlooking fiscal receipts, based as it is on the

understanding that 'if the tax laws are rigorously enforced against you today, they may be equally enforced against me tomorrow' (ibid.). And, as LaPalombara goes on to point out, if this attitude is rooted in an awareness of the divergence between formal and actual rules – in an assumption that law and its enforcement is something *negotiable* – this attitude is, in its turn, rooted in precisely that high degree of tolerance which Almond and Verba (1963) and others have claimed is so essential for democratic stability. So it seems to me that the real significance of LaPalombara's work lies not in the fact that it claimed that Italy's post-war political system was both functional and popular while almost everyone else argued the opposite, or in the fact that (as the early 1990s showed) he underestimated the sincerity of the electorate's expressed dissatisfaction with *partitocrazia* (Gilbert, 1995: 19–20); rather, its significance lies simply in its warning that a full awareness of context and of actors' points of view is essential if one wishes to achieve an interpretation wherein 'the characteristic attributed to [the] foreign culture ... differs from the folklore or prejudices about the foreign country which already exist in his own society' (Scheuch, 1967, quoted by Dogan and Pelassy, 1990: 70). It seems to me that this is sound methodological advice.

## Plan of the Book

Attempting to achieve understanding, and elucidating underlying mechanisms and links, will require both chronological accounts and thematic accounts, and in Chapter 2 a largely chronological account is offered – one in which I document and explain the trajectories taken by the main party organizations and alliances from the late 1980s through to the election of 1996. Chapters 3, 4 and 5 then deal with the *de*composition and *re*composition of the Italian party system from the perspective of the three sets of causal factors most intimately responsible for the process: clientelism, corruption and the onset of the *Tangentopoli* investigations; electoral change and the emergence and growth of the Northern League; and the crystallization of a movement seeking reform through strategic use of the referendum device. In Chapter 3 I argue that *partitocrazia* – that strange overlap between the personnel of parties on the one hand and of interest groups and administrative positions on the other – sustained a predominantly clientelistic mode of managing power relationships, something which in turn facilitated the spread of corruption. If corruption was one of the principal 'structural causes' responsible for the collapse of the traditional post-war parties, then the *Tangentopoli* investigations designed to bring it to light constituted *the* principal factor responsible for precipitating the collapse. However, the investigations would not have been able to gather their considerable momentum without the decisive support of public opinion, and so Chapter 4 is dedicated to an analysis of the broad sociopolitical changes responsible for 'decoupling' voters from their traditional party-political loyalties (thus allowing them to support the investigating magistrates' moves against the leading personnel of their parties) and for bringing about the emergence and growth of the Northern League, the principal spearhead of an electoral challenge to the established parties. Meanwhile, the League's efforts were reinforced by a movement to dislodge the parties from their positions of power by means of a referendum designed to change the electoral system. A year after the 1992 elections, the parties were in an advanced state of decay and the legislature had been thoroughly delegitimized. If this fact pointed to fresh elections once the new electoral law had been passed, the new law itself provided the basic context in which the work of regrouping and rebuilding political forces then took place. Hence, Chapter 5 is dedicated to an analysis of how the new law came into being and of how it interacted with beliefs about its likely effects to produce the line-ups offered to voters in 1994.

Chapters 6, 7 and 8 are concerned with the period since 1994. If the 1994 elections put the final seal on the old parties' disintegration, then the question arises as to what extent, and in what respects, this disintegration has resulted in the emergence of a new party system: this issue is explored in Chapter 6. Since the notion of the (still incomplete) emergence of a new party system has much to recommend it, and since there are several areas of political life one would expect to be heavily influenced by the characteristics of a country's party system, therefore, Chapters 7 and 8 examine some of the principle consequences of Italy's party-system change. Chapter 7 looks at the impact of the change on institutions; Chapter 8 at the impact on policy and on the relations between parties and voters. Chapter 9 draws, from the analyses of previous chapters, some conclusions about the impact of the change on the quality of Italian democracy as a whole.

In comparison with some other texts, this one does not, perhaps, contain much mention of some of the more dramatic episodes to have coloured the trajectory of recent Italian politics. Since my intention is to convey something of the underlying causal processes that have carried this trajectory along, I preferred not to clutter the text with the recounting of episodes which, while making for a good story, seemed largely tangential to an understanding of the main thrust of change. Effective narration of the dramatic and colourful – an entirely legitimate approach to the understanding of political phenomena – requires a style of writing with which I am not familiar and has, in any case, already been very effectively done elsewhere, notably by Gilbert (1995) in his book.

# Notes

1   *La Repubblica*, 26 February 1998, p.7.
2   'Lavori in Corso: il sistema politico italiano dopo il terremoto dei primi anni novanta: polity, politics, policies', Centre for the Study of Political Change, University of Siena, 19–21 February 1998.
3   See, for example, the review article by Martin Bull (1996a) where this contrast emerges very clearly.
4   In many respects, this suggestion takes us back to the issue of *what* has changed, since the idea of 'regime crisis' has given rise to a popular view (embodied in the widely used expression 'Second Republic') that the events of the early 1990s amount to the birth of a new regime. Many writers, including this one, would deny that regime change has in fact occurred (although it *might* occur in the event of successful constitutional innovation).

# 2 The Collapse of the Old and the Birth of the New[1]

The first requirement for an understanding of party-system change in Italy, and of its consequences, is an appreciation of the basic chronology that describes the movement from the old party system to the new. This chapter undertakes this task in five stages. First we describe the basic contours of the blocked system and its dysfunctions, and then the electoral discontent to which such dysfunctions gave rise. Then, against this backdrop, we describe the evolution in the configuration of parties making up the party system as this took place through three phases, each bound by general elections: 1987–92; 1992–94; 1994 to 1996.

## A Blocked Political System

Italian party politics between the end of the Second World War and 1989 were fundamentally shaped by the Cold War. One can argue about the extent of this influence and about the precise mechanisms through which it operated, but there is no doubting the basic fact that the party system and the behaviour of its component parties reflected, to a very significant degree, the division of the post-war world into communist and anti-communist camps.[2] The development of the Cold War served to sustain the electoral strength of the two largest parties – the Christian Democratic Party (DC), on the one hand, and the Italian Communist Party (PCI) on the other. Between them, they averaged 64.3 per cent of the vote in the period from 1946 to 1992 and were the main political expressions of a profound ideological division running through Italian society – a division which, with declining intensity as the post-war years rolled by, on the one side implied a strong feeling of identity with the working class and a conviction that the latter was destined to play a central role in the process of social transformation, and, on the other side, a strong attachment to the Church and to the ecclesiastical hierarchy, an acceptance of the Church's guidance in personal, social and political matters and, hence, a fierce anti-communism.

15

That such a division became firmly rooted in the consciousness of ordinary Italians in the post-war years was largely due to the situation which came to be created as a result of the collapse of the fascist state; for the collapse of fascism and the German occupation of most of the country created a power vacuum in which the Church and the Resistance movement became the only points of reference and contact for Italians who had no other authority to turn to except the Nazis and the Fascists (Ginsborg, 1990). On the one hand, the Church, having deep roots in civil society through its parishes and collateral associations, became a rallying point for working out ideas and attitudes. On the other hand, popular backing for the Resistance, dominated as it was by the Communist Party, gave to the latter authority and legitimacy. The growth of political participation which arose from the Resistance turned the parties into mass-based organizations allowing them to penetrate down to the grassroots level throughout the country, and thus to exercise 'a profound influence over the reconstruction of social organisations and interest groups. Many such groups were in effect captured by the parties and subordinated to the dictates of their political controllers' (Hine, 1990: 68). Meanwhile, through the development of 'flanking organizations' the DC and the PCI were able to establish social networks that would serve to inculcate among members of such organizations a sense of community and appropriate feelings of partisan solidarity.[3] These strategies were particularly successful in those parts of the country – the Northeast, and in particular Veneto, in the case of the DC, the central regions, and in particular Emilia-Romagna, Umbria and Tuscany in the case of the PCI – where there already existed favourable political traditions. This led to the emergence of two territorially-based subcultures, the Catholic and the Marxist, with their distinctive features: a feeling of community and solidarity which, sustained by the socializing capacity of the family and reinforced by channels of communication specific to each sub-culture, served to maintain sets of values and beliefs that amounted to entire and opposed world–views.

It became common among social scientists to distinguish, in addition to the so-called 'white belt' of the Northeast and the so-called 'red belt' of the central regions, two further areas displaying rather distinct patterns of political behaviour: first, the Northwest where, in a relatively industrialized and urbanized environment, the forces of the left and of the right tended to be more or less evenly matched; and, second, the South. Until the 'economic miracle' of the 1950s and 1960s got underway, the South was largely populated by a peasantry that was desperately poor, brutally exploited and in constant competition within itself for those meagre resources that were available (Ginsborg, 1990). In such an environment fatalism, mistrust and what Edward Banfield (1958) famously described as 'amoral familism' were the most characteristic sociopolitical attitudes.⁴ Hardly surprisingly, the world of Catholic associationism was able to gain only a limited foothold and the DC (whose best performances outside the 'white belt' were traditionally registered in the South) managed to consolidate its position by gaining control over the distribution of public resources which thus allowed its politicians to establish clientelistic relations with their voters. Such clientelism frequently degenerated into out-and-out corruption.

With the development of the Cold War, the PCI was subject to the so-called *conventio ad excludendum* whereby the DC and the parties in its orbit agreed to exclude it from government because of its presumed 'anti-system' nature. On the one side stood the DC which, in addition to clientelism and the powerful backing of the Church, also benefited from an appeal that was essentially interclassist in nature, and hence from the backing of a national and international bourgeoisie that was not slow to see the advantages of such an appeal. On the other side stood the PCI which, though reformist in its practice (as was particularly evident from its activities in the sphere of local government), continued to perceive itself, and to be perceived, as a party that aimed not simply at providing the state with its leading personnel (or at modifying it in some way) but at its replacement with a qualitatively new kind of state. Certainly the party made a considerable contribution to the drawing up of the republican Constitution and consistently defended it as the heritage of the entire nation. It is also true that, in the post-war period, Communists were almost never to be found engaging in illegal acts. Furthermore, it is true that, like social democratic parties before them, the Italian Communists came to believe that the change they wanted would have to be achieved gradually through the winning of electoral majorities. However, until the end of the 1980s, the party continued to hold on to the idea that the sort of change it would introduce if and when it won office would be both *structural* and *permanent*. It is this that explains the seeming paradox whereby, although it was 'social democratic' in terms of its day-to-day actions in local government spheres, the trade unions and so forth, the party could continue to be perceived (by supporters and opponents alike) as millenarian, anti-system and revolutionary. And it was because of this that elections in Italy tended not to have the character of a collective judgement on the parties' policy proposals or performances (or to rest on the assumption that today's governing parties might lose office while keeping alive the hope of returning to office the day after tomorrow) but rather took on a 'special' character, resting on the assumption that to lose an election to the PCI would be to lose everything. In short, to prevent the PCI from taking office was, in the perception of a wide range of influential actors both within and beyond Italy, to avoid a political and historical catastrophe.

A further rule governing the construction of majorities in the legislature was the unavailability for coalition formation of the forces of the right, also perceived as being 'anti-system' and therefore illegitimate as government partners. Foremost among these was the neo-fascist, and violently anti-communist, Italian Social Movement (MSI), formed in 1946 by a group of young fascists who had been junior officers in Mussolini's *Repubblica di Salò* and whose vote averaged 5.5 per cent between 1946 and 1992. Its unacceptability was dramatically, if briefly, put to the test in 1960 when, between March and July of that year, a DC minority government held office with the external backing of the MSI. This gave rise to social disturbances of such severity that it served merely to confirm the centrality of anti-fascism to the dominant ideology and thus the rule of Italian politics that the road to DC reliance on the MSI to help sustain it in office was permanently closed (Ginsborg, 1990: 257–8).

The unavailability of both the PCI and MSI as coalition partners meant that, as the party of relative majority, the DC was destined to remain in office permanently in alliance with the smaller parties of the centre and (from 1963) with the Socialist Party (PSI).[5] This in turn meant that Italian politics would have three further consequential and characteristic features. First, since the governing parties were aware that the unavailability of the PCI and the MSI assured them power whatever their policy failures, squabbling over minor issues became both their preferred means of maintaining distinct identities and an effective substitute for fighting over government programmes (which would have risked undermining that minimum degree of coalition solidarity necessary to keep the *conventio* alive in the first place).[6] Second, governing-party rivalry meant unstable governments (there were over 50 between 1948 and 1992) and thus 'immobilism' in key policy areas (such as health, welfare, education, development of the South and reform of the state), together with a politicization of vast areas of the state and society as the parties engaged in a 'sharing out' (*lottizzazione*), on the basis of relative bargaining power, of ministerial and administrative posts, to be exploited for patronage purposes – a system which led to the Italian polity being dubbed a *partitocrazia* (literally, 'partyocracy'). *Partitocrazia* was the basic foundation for the practice of clientele politics and the spread of corruption which, as we shall see in Chapter 3, had become routine and systemic by the 1980s. Finally, all of the above helped sustain the Italian citizenry's traditional feelings of alienation from, and mistrust of, the state. Not surprisingly, surveys carried out by the *Eurobarometer* consistently find Italians to be far less satisfied with 'the way democracy works' in their country than the citizens of any other country in the European Union (Morlino and Tarchi, 1996).

## Electoral Discontent

The governing parties, and especially the Christian Democrats, were long protected from the adverse electoral consequences of such voter dissatisfaction by the strength of Catholicism, clientele politics and the strength of the subcultures – 'red' as well as 'white' – for, as Mastropaolo (1994a: 72) rightly observes, the great 'secret' of Italian democracy was that, with two ideologies as radically opposed as the Catholic and the communist, the strength of the one was a condition for the strength of the other. At the same time, the subcultures helped ensure a certain level of party unity and a degree of electoral stability. From the mid-1970s, however, this started to change as, with intergenerational turnover, the electorate began increasingly to consist of those cohorts whose political outlooks had been most affected by the dramatic social changes of the 1950s and 1960s – growing secularization, higher levels of geographical and social mobility, an expansion of education and of the mass media of communications, rising standards of living – all consequent upon rapid rates of economic growth. Between the early 1950s and the mid-1980s, real per capita gross domestic product rose from under 4 million lire to approximately 13 million; church attendance declined from 69 per cent to 34 per cent, illiteracy from 12.9 per cent to 3.1 per cent and so on.[7] The effect was a decline in the hold of the subcultures and growing electoral instability as fewer and fewer voters cast what Parisi and Pasquino (1977) had come to call a *'voto di appartenenza'* and more and more cast a *'voto d'opinione'*.[8] Voter dissatisfaction with the parties' performances was now reflected in changed electoral behaviour which could be seen in terms of declining turnout, growing fragmentation and increasing aggregate volatility.

Between 1976 and 1979, voter *turnout* fell from 93.4 per cent to 90.6 per cent, and it has declined at every election since then to reach 82.7 per cent at the 1996 election. If those who cast either blank or spoiled ballot papers are added to these figures, it reveals a rising trend in support for the so-called 'non-vote party' (NVP) which, by 1996, had reached 23.2 per cent of the electorate – a larger percentage than that given to any other party. Of course, the level of NVP support does not necessarily measure dissatisfaction: some abstentions will be involuntary as will some spoiled ballot papers, and intentional abstentions and spoiled ballot papers may be the expression of any one of a number of different possible motivations. Only from blank ballot papers does it seem reasonable to infer a desire to protest. However, because support for the NVP has risen at almost every election over the 1980s and 1990s and we have no reason to believe that the most common causes of involuntary abstention or spoiled ballot papers (failure to consign electoral certificates, sickness and intellectual incapacity) have risen concomitantly, and because the spread of this voting behaviour took place in concomitance with the growth of new formations – Radicals, Proletarian Democracy (DP), and from the late 1980s, the Greens and the Northern League – whose aims clearly *did* have a protest character, a desire to express dissatisfaction seems to be the most reasonable inference to draw.[9] With respect to *fragmentation*, between 1968 and 1987, the number of separate party lists presented at elections rose from 229 to 442, and, at the same time, the number of parties in the Chamber of Deputies rose from nine to 14. In 1992 the number grew to 16 and in 1994 to 20. The proportion of the electorate voting for the three largest parties (DC, PCI, PSI) declined from three-quarters in 1976 to under a half in 1992. *Aggregate volatility*, as measured by Pedersen's index,[10] rose from an average of 5.8 between the election-pairs of 1953–58 and 1972–76 to an average of 9.1 between 1976–79 and 1987–92.

In short, the period subsequent to 1976 gradually began to reveal an electorate that was, in aggregate, more volatile, more fragmented and more inclined to protest by abstaining or casting blank or spoiled ballot papers than the electorate of the previous two decades. Whatever weight should be given to changing proclivities on the part of voters (as opposed to changes in the nature of the political supply) in explaining the altered party configurations of the early 1990s, in so far as a willingness to abandon established parties is a necessary condition for the emergence and growth of new ones, the electoral changes thereby formed an essential 'backdrop' to developments in the period following the 1987 general election. For it was this period that witnessed an acceleration in the pace of party-system change which was a precursor to the rapid collapse of the longstanding party configurations after 1992.

### 1987–92: The Traditional Parties Shaken

The acceleration of change in the traditional parties came about as the result of two separate, but not unconnected, developments: the end of the 'communist question' and the emergence of new 'party movements'. The collapse of the Berlin Wall in the autumn of 1989 brought to a head the growing conflict between the 'internal' and 'external' pressures acting on the PCI – the internal pressures being the party's need to maintain its identity, or Leninist heritage, as the basis of party unity and a spur to the mobilization of party activists, the external pressures being the need to attack this identity in order to make it possible for the party to acquire legitimacy and overcome its isolation (Bull, 1991a; 1991b). This led Occhetto, the PCI leader, to propose a transformation of the party into a non-communist party with a new name, the Democratic Party of the Left (PDS). This significantly entailed a final renunciation of the desire to achieve any change, however mild, of a structural or irreversible kind as well as a removal of any ambiguity surrounding the 'anti-system' orientation of the main party of the Left. In effect, the party leadership made it clear that from then on, the party's policy goals would be determined, as they are for any other liberal democratic party, almost entirely by electoral expediency and by what the party activists could be forced to tolerate rather than by beliefs about the nature of the 'good society'. However, the proposal unleashed an unprecedented degree of internal conflict and provoked a major party split leading to the formation of Communist Refoundation (RC) which would not accept the change.

Although the instigators of the RC breakaway came from the pro-Soviet wing of the PCI, the party was, in fact, composed of a far more heterogeneous band of forces, as a result of the DP's decision to dissolve and merge with the new party. This brought in individuals whose concerns were wide-ranging (and which included libertarians, ecologists and feminists) but who nonetheless shared the view that the PDS would devote itself more to institutional manoeuvring than to aggressive social struggles (Foot, 1996: 174). In effect, the collapse of communism (and the sudden irrelevance of differing interpretations of the nature of the Soviet Union, which had once been the source of implacable hostility between DP and parts of the PCI) brought *rapprochement* on the left; and this, as well as its status as a small opposition party, meant that the RC found that its eclecticism was not damaging to it. Hence, the first consequence of the PCI's transformation was to leave Italy with two significantly sized left-of-centre parties in place of the previous one.

A second consequence of the end of the 'communist question' was to create significant difficulties for the DC and, to a lesser extent, all the governing parties, because the claim that the main opposition party was an 'anti-system party' could hardly any longer be sustained, and this, in turn, undermined the effectiveness of the perennial appeal to anti-communist sentiments. Since by far the larger of the PCI's two heirs was manifestly no longer a communist party, the governing parties' capacity to prevent significant proportions of their voters now choosing 'exit' as their response to a longstanding disgust with a lack of policy achievements and corruption was definitively destroyed.

However, the governing parties' plight was compounded by their belief that, since resolution of the communist question was accompanied by a major crisis of the Communist Party itself, far from losing, they might actually gain. The PSI leader, Bettino Craxi, in particular appears to have been convinced that the final outcome of the PCI's crisis would be a reorganization of the left under his own leadership – a belief in which he was encouraged by the results of the regional elections of 1990 which saw the PSI's vote advance to 15.2 per cent while the PCI lost 6 per cent. In the meantime, ever since the failure of the attempt at *rapprochement* between the DC and the PCI in the late 1970s, it had been clear that the PSI was indispensable to the formation of any coalition led by the DC. Hence the Craxian Socialists felt free to concentrate on an extortion of spoils in the present, comfortable in the belief that their position was secure in the future: this would be marked by bipolar competition between the DC on one side and themselves on the other as the leaders of a reconstructed left. The DC for its part – or at least for the most powerful factions within it – were content to conclude, with the PSI, a long-term power-sharing arrangement which, while acknowledging the DC's dependence on the Socialists, would at least bring predictability to, and contain conflict between, the two parties.[11] Thus, instead of reacting to the end of the communist issue by engaging in political renewal, the two principal parties of government preferred to try to maintain their stranglehold on change at a time when growing recession together with further moves towards European integration (especially the terms of the Maastricht Treaty) were exacerbating economic and social tensions. On the one hand, both the recession and Maastricht placed pressure on the ruling parties to tackle the large and growing budget deficits by means of cuts in public expenditure which nevertheless threatened to undermine the clientelistic base of their support, especially in the South. On the other hand, the corrosive effects of clientelism on social solidarity had begun to manifest themselves in growing levels of violent crime based on the activities of the *Mafia* (Sicily), *'Ndrangheta* (Calabria) and *Camorra* (Naples). Since, naturally enough, such social conditions tended to undermine the already weak incentives to industrial development in this area, there was a confirmation in the public mind that the South's problems (and the state's failure to resolve them) were inextricably intertwined with the governing parties' hold on power in the first place. This directly enhanced the fortunes of two hitherto insignificant 'movement parties' – the Northern League whose vote at the 1992 election rose from 0.5 to 8.7 per cent, and the 'Network' (*Rete*), which won 1.9 per cent of the vote in 1992 despite fielding candidates in only two-thirds of the constituencies (Foot, 1996: 181).

Taking advantage of the 'tax backlash' that had developed as the costs of the welfare state became harder to sustain through the recession, the League argued that a corrupt, party-dominated bureaucracy in faraway Rome sought to appropriate the resources of the North in order to maintain its own power in the underdeveloped South. Therefore, it argued that a set of federalist arrangements were needed as these – by limiting the functions of the state to external defence, internal security, the administration of justice and the provision of only the most indispensable of public goods – would remove from the central authorities all those functions which allowed them to tax the North without giving anything in return. Apparently wasteful public expenditure on the southern regions, combined with the fact that most of the total tax revenue needed to finance it necessarily came from the richer North, allowed Bossi and other leaders of the League to argue that the tax and spending activities of the *partitocrazia* were regionally biased against the North. In this way the League managed to use the taxation issue to focus discontent on a single and (as it saw it) inescapable conclusion: the need for regional autonomy.

If the League was a reaction against some of the effects of corruption in politics, the *Rete* was a reaction against the influence of organized crime in politics. Emerging from within Christian Democracy itself, its leaders regarded it not as a party, but as a 'movement for democracy' whose principal purpose was to expose, and to campaign against, the influence of organized crime in public life. Reflecting an eclectic mixture of Catholic, leftist and libertarian values, its programme called for an end to parliamentary immunity, a reduction in the number of parliamentarians and greater powers for the judiciary in the fight against the *Mafia*, *'Ndrangheta* and *Camorra* (Foot, 1996: 180).

The 1992 general election was the first compelling confirmation that the League, and to a lesser extent the *Rete*, were forces to be reckoned with. Increasing its share of the northern vote from 2.6 to 17.3 per cent, the League scored its most striking successes in traditional DC strongholds (Newell, 1994) while the *Rete* averaged 2.3 per cent of the vote in those constituencies in which it fielded candidates. In Sicily, where it was especially strong, it seemed to win votes mainly at the expense of the PDS – as might have been expected of an organization more closely identified with the left than the right. Dubbed by the Italian media as an 'earthquake', this election produced the most significant change in the configuration of parties since the war. The traditional parties of government and the opposition parties of the left suffered a combined net loss of votes that amounted to 10.8 per cent of the total, while the new parties of protest saw their combined share of the vote rise by 9 per cent (see Table 2.1). The DC and the PDS experienced striking falls, while the PSI – having clearly underestimated the potential of the Northern League – significantly failed to make any gains from the collapse of the ex-communist vote, which thus undermined the central plank of its long-term political strategy. The share of the vote of the three largest parties (DC, PDS, PSI) tumbled from 75.2 per cent in 1987 to 59.4 per cent. Finally, the four parties of government (the DC, PSDI, PLI and PSI) lost the overall majority of votes (though not of seats) that they had enjoyed in 1987 – an occurrence that was interpreted by many as a vote of no-confidence in the outgoing coalition.

In the absence of any politically viable alternative, however, the election's immediate aftermath saw the temporary resurrection of the

**Table 2.1   The Chamber of Deputies elections of 1987 and 1992**

| | 1987 Votes % | Seats | 1992 Votes % | Seats | Diff. 1987–92 Votes % | Seats |
|---|---|---|---|---|---|---|
| DC | 34.3 | 232 | 29.7 | 206 | −4.6 | −26 |
| PSI | 14.3 | 94 | 13.6 | 92 | −0.7 | −2 |
| PRI | 3.7 | 21 | 4.4 | 27 | +0.7 | +6 |
| PSDI | .3.0 | 17 | 2.7 | 16 | −0.3 | −1 |
| PLI | 2.1 | 11 | 2.8 | 17 | +0.7 | +6 |
| MSI | 5.9 | 35 | 5.4 | 34 | −0.5 | −1 |
| PCI | 26.6 | 177 | PDS 16.1 | 107 | −10.5 | −70 |
| DP | 1.7 | 8 | RC 5.6 | 35 | +3.9 | +27 |
| Greens | 2.5 | 13 | 2.8 | 16 | +0.3 | +3 |
| *Pannella* | 2.6 | 13 | 1.2 | 7 | −1.4 | −6 |
| *Rete* | – | – | 1.9 | 12 | +1.9 | +12 |
| League | 0.5 | 1 | 8.7 | 55 | +8.2 | +54 |
| Others | 2.8 | 8 | 5.1 | 6 | +2.3 | −2 |
| **Total** | 100 | 630 | 100 | 630 | | |

*Key*:
DC (Christian Democrats), PSI (Socialists), PRI (Republicans), PSDI (Social Democrats), PLI (Liberals) = the traditional governing parties.
MSI (Italian Social Movement) = opposition party of the right.
PCI (Communists), DP (Proletarian Democracy), PDS (Democratic Party of the Left), RC (Communist Refoundation) = opposition parties of the left.
Greens, *Pannella* (formerly, the Radical Party), *Rete* (the 'Network'), League (Northern League) = new parties of protest.

outgoing four-party coalition, this time under the Socialist Giuliano Amato as Prime Minister. Yet the fear of many (and the hope of some) that this marked a reassertion of the control of the traditional governing class over public life was not borne out by events. On the contrary, in the period up to the next election in March 1994, members of this class were all but swept away and the party system itself completely collapsed. Two factors above all others were responsible for this: the continuation of an anti-corruption drive initiated by prosecuting magistrates in February 1992 and a referendum on the electoral system held in April 1993.

## From the Election of 1992 to the Election of 1994

In one sense, the fact that the anti-corruption drive developed when it did was a matter of chance; in a more profound sense it was intimately linked to the collapse of communism and the already noted effects which this had on Italian politics. The date of its beginning is usually set at 17 February 1992, when the first defendant, Mario Chiesa, the head of a Milanese old people's home, was arrested – and as it quickly brought to light a massive network of 'mutually beneficial linkages' (Waters, 1994: 170) between the political parties and powerful economic groups in Milan, the investigation immediately took on the name *Tangentopoli* (meaning 'Bribe City') in order to highlight the irony that investigations centred on precisely that city which prided itself on a reputation for hard work and honesty. Later, the investigations would spread to other cities. The chance aspect lay in the fact that corruption scandals were, of course, not new so that, while the essence of *Tangentopoli* was the exposure of extensive illegal payments to the political parties in exchange for public works contracts, it was Chiesa's decision to confess which set the investigations in motion, this by implicating subsequent defendants, whose confessions in their turn implicated still others. At a deeper level it was not a chance affair because it depended on the actions of judicial investigators who, unusually among constitutional democracies, carry out much investigative work that elsewhere is carried out by the police and who can initiate penal proceedings not only at outside request but also at their own discretion. Prior to February 1992 there had been a number of celebrated instances of judges using their authority to pursue the powerful in corruption cases, but now that resolution of the communist question had subverted whatever ideological justifications there had once been for being lenient towards the more dubious clientele practices of the governing class, so the judges, supported by public opinion in the aftermath of the election, had apparently become even keener to use their powers as the champions of a campaign to moralize public life. Likewise, it has been argued that the end of communism made entrepreneurs more willing to cooperate in judicial investigations than they might otherwise have been in that big business, faced with the increasing costs of corruption (Della Porta, 1993), concluded, for the first time in 45 years, that it 'could foster a major crisis of the political system without risking its own survival' (Calise, 1993: 556).

*Tangentopoli* thoroughly undermined the traditional governing parties – directly, as well as indirectly through its effect on public opinion. Its direct impact was not only the subversion of the parties' financial resources by the elimination, at a stroke, of major sources of funding – the PSDI, for instance, effectively went bankrupt at the end of March 1993 – but also the subversion of their organizational resources in several respects. First, because the acceptance of bribes for public works contracts had become a central element of the politics of clientelism and of the 'partitocratic system' as a whole, *Tangentopoli* gravely weakened the membership base of several parties by destroying the incentives to be a member in the first place. For instance, if it had become an established practice that appointments to many of Italy's numerous public agencies would be made on a party basis, and if an appointee then used their position to collect bribes, the money so gathered could then be used to control packets of votes in the party's internal organs. This meant that the primary motives for joining the party tended to be highly self-regarding, which in turn meant that the rank-and-file tended to be highly passive. Therefore, to the extent that a party lacked a membership with a sufficient degree of the ideological commitment necessary for maintaining its effectiveness on the ground, its very existence as a free-standing organization was inherently fragile and, once the flow of resources from above dried up, it was vulnerable to complete collapse. Second, even if some members *were* mobilized by shared values rather than material concerns, they were likely to resign as a result of the alienation caused by the revelation of matters which had been concealed from them. Third, *Tangentopoli* created tensions and splits at leadership level between those who had been directly compromised by the investigations and were thus on the defensive and those who, though uninvolved, still had to bear the political costs of the crisis. In this way, divisions opened up between 'conservatives' and 'reformers', leading to eleventh-hour attempts at renewal and to acrimonious splits.

The immediate electoral consequences of *Tangentopoli* (which rumbled on through 1993) can be seen from Table 2.2 which shows the results of the regional, provincial and communal elections which took place between the general elections of 1992 and 1994. The figures are not, of course, comparable because of the differing electorates in each case, but they do serve to document the sheer scale of the electoral disaster provoked for the governing parties by *Tangentopoli*. By the time of the series of elections, which took place on 6 June 1993, all the traditional governing parties had begun to experience breakaways on the part of local federations which felt that the only way to save themselves was to field, in defiance of the national leadership, their own lists of candidates under different names or joint lists with other parties. Hence the very low, and non-existent, figures for governing-party candidates in columns 4, 5 and 6 reflect not only voter dis-enchantment, but also the fact that the disintegration of these parties as organizations had already become irreversible.

Meanwhile, the referendum movement had scored a decisive victory in the vote to change the electoral system held on 18 April. The movement itself consisted of a variety of cross-party organizations

Table 2.2   National, regional, provincial and communal elections,
April 1992–November 1993 (votes %)

|          | (1)  | (2)  | (3)  | (4)  | (5)  | (6)  | (7)  | (8)  |
|----------|------|------|------|------|------|------|------|------|
| DC       | 29.7 | 14.0 | 24.3 | 22.3 | 18.7 | 12.1 | 14.3 | 10.7 |
| PSI      | 13.6 | 7.2  | 9.9  | 4.7  | 2.5  | 0.6  | 0.6  | 1.2  |
| PRI      | 4.4  | 1.5  | 3.6  | 1.7  | 0.7  | 0.2  | 0.5  | 0.2  |
| PSDI     | 2.7  | 0.8  | 4.9  | 1.6  | 0.8  | 0.4  | 0.9  | 0.9  |
| PLI      | 2.8  | 1.2  | 2.9  | 1.3  | 0.2  | –    | –    | 0.1  |
| MSI      | 5.4  | 3.2  | 7.2  | 8.3  | 4.0  | 5.3  | 7.4  | 12.0 |
| PDS      | 16.1 | 17.8 | 11.4 | 9.9  | 7.7  | 19.8 | 4.6  | 12.1 |
| RC       | 5.6  | 6.7  | 6.3  | 5.5  | 5.1  | 8.0  | 1.3  | 5.3  |
| Greens   | 2.8  | 2.4  | 1.6  | 5.4  | 1.0  | 3.4  | 3.4  | 3.5  |
| *Pannella* | 1.2 | –   | 0.8  | –    | –    | –    | –    | 0.9  |
| Rete     | 1.9  | 2.7  | 4.0  | 1.8  | 2.0  | 1.8  | 5.2  | 3.1  |
| League   | 8.7  | 33.9 | 13.7 | 26.7 | 11.7 | 30.5 | 9.6  | 6.2  |
| Others   | 5.1  | 8.6  | 9.4  | 10.8 | 45.6 | 17.9 | 52.2 | 43.8 |
| **Total** | 100 | 100  | 100  | 100  | 100  | 100  | 100  | 100  |

*Key*:
(1) General Election, 5 and 6 April 1992
(2) Provincial elections, Mantova, 28 September 1992
(3) Communal elections, 55 communes, 14 December 1992
(4) Regional elections, Friuli Venezia Giulia, 6 June 1993
(5) Partial communal elections (1,192 communes), 6 June 1993
(6) Provincial elections (Gorizia, Ravenna, Viterbo, Mantova, Pavia, Trieste, Varese, Genova, La Spezia), 6 June 1993
(7) Regional elections, Trentino Alto Adige, 21 November 1993
(8) Partial communal elections (424 communes), 21 November 1993

(spearheaded by the dissident Christian Democrat, Mario Segni) which sought to adopt the tactic first experimented with by the Radicals in the late 1970s of seeking to influence the course of political change by strategically using the referendum device. The Radicals were an 'eclectic combination of environmental and civil rights causes' (Hine, 1993: 87) whose charismatic leader, Marco Pannella, had developed the theory that the referendum instrument could be used to bring together – especially around civil rights issues – coalitions of forces opposed to the Christian Democrats and, in this way, create pressure for a change in the party system mechanics in a bipolar, left–right, direction (Uleri, 1994). Since 1970 Italian law has provided for referenda to be held when requested by half a million citizens. Although referenda can only be used to strike down existing laws, or parts of laws, and not to make new ones, it was soon realized that they could be used in this way *de facto* – either because of the broader political significance which politicians and opinion-leaders tended to attribute to referenda outcomes or because the repeal of a given clause would create legal anomalies. Both would result in pressure on legislators to carry through change of the kind desired. The referendum movement, then, represented a fourth source of opposition to the governing class, alongside the League, the *Rete* and reform-minded judges – one which sought to dislodge it from its positions of power by using the referendum to promote institutional reform. The outstanding success of the referendum (held on 9 June 1991) which reduced the number of preference votes which could be expressed in elections from four to one, confirmed the presence of a groundswell of opinion for change. Encouraged by this, referendum campaigners were able to gather the number of signatures required to request several further referenda, eight of which were eventually held on 18 April 1993.

Of these, the most important was that which sought to abolish the so-called 'sixty-five percent clause' in elections for the upper house of Italy's bicameral parliament, the Senate (Bull and Newell, 1993). The effect of this would be to introduce the single-member, simple plurality system for three-quarters of the Senate seats. In essence, the reformers believed that a changed electoral system, more closely approximating 'first past the post' (FPTP), would strike at the heart of the hated *partitocrazia*. FPTP, by reducing voters' realistic choices to two 'front-running' candidates, one left-wing and one right-wing, would make it more likely that elections would produce a 'clear winner'. This would open up, for the first time in Italian politics, the possibility of alternation in government, and the greater competitivity that would result therefrom would make it far less easy for the parties to indulge in clientelistic and corrupt practices without paying a heavy electoral penalty. As anticipated, the positive outcome of this referendum placed parliament under immediate pressure to amend the law governing elections to the lower house of Parliament, the Chamber of Deputies, because the two houses have co-equal legislative powers and the members of each are elected on the same occasions. Not to have done so would have been to run the risk of single general elections throwing up different majorities in each house and thus producing legislative paralysis. Consequently, a new electoral law was introduced in August 1993, replacing the old party-list system of proportional representation with a hybrid system whereby three-quarters of the members of both houses are elected by the single-member, simple plurality method, with the remaining quarter of the seats being distributed proportionally (D'Alimonte and Chiaramonte, 1993; Agosta, 1994; Bull and Newell, 1996; Katz, 1996).

Electoral systems influence the characteristics of party systems not only *directly* – by determining the manner in which votes are translated into seats – but also *indirectly* by creating a structure of opportunities and constraints for parties in the pre-election period. Hence, while the party system was subject to the *de*composing effects of *Tangentopoli*, it was subject to the *re*composing effects of the new electoral system which placed intense pressure on the parties to find allies (through stand-down arrangements in the new single-member constituencies) in the elections for the new parliament which everybody knew would be held within a matter of months: in the aftermath of the referendum Giuliano Amato, announcing the 'death of a regime', had resigned saying that he was making way for a 'transitional government' which would pave the way for fresh elections on the basis of a new electoral law. Amato's place was accordingly taken by Carlo Azeglio Ciampi, former governor of the Bank of Italy, at the head of a government of technocrats – an event which represented the effective suspension of party government until a new electoral law could be passed and fresh elections organized. Given the timing and circumstances of Amato's resignation – the four parties which formally sustained his government were by then in full retreat from their positions of power in the state machine as *Tangentopoli* rumbled on catching ever larger numbers of ever more senior party figures in its net – the inevitability of fresh elections was a matter of common consent. The changes in the party landscape which took place in the months leading up to these elections can be described as follows.

*New Party Organizations*

On 12 October 1992 the DC appointed a new secretary, Mino Martinazzoli, who, it was hoped, would engineer a party reform that was sufficiently thorough to save it from the electoral oblivion towards which it was apparently heading. But Martinazzoli immediately found himself at the mercy of the party's powerful factions which were unwilling or unable to make the sacrifices entailed in effective adaptation and, by the beginning of 1994, the party had split into four groups: Segni's Pact for National Renewal; the left-leaning Social Christians (C-S) under Ermanno Gorrieri; the Christian Democratic Centre (CCD), a more conservative grouping under Clemente Mastella and Pierferdinando Casini; and the largest component, the Italian Popular Party (PPI), under Martinazzoli himself.

The PSI underwent a similar experience. Craxi's leadership was made untenable when he himself fell under the suspicion of the *Tangentopoli* magistrates at the beginning of 1993. Unable to reach any agreement on how to confront its difficulties, the party broke up into three groups: Giorgio Benvenuto's Socialist Renewal (RS), Del Turco's PSI (with the same name as the old party but with a new symbol), and finally, the *Craxiani*. The first two groupings eventually surfaced in the Progressive Alliance while the third entered the right-wing Freedom Alliance (see below).[12]

In the meantime, as the smaller parties suffered similar problems, new umbrella-type organizations emerged – organizations created to catch the fallout from the implosion of the older formations and which appeared to herald the end of the 'party apparatus'. The most important of these were the Democratic Alliance (AD), the National Alliance (AN), and *Forza Italia* (FI). The Democratic Alliance was launched in spring 1993 and was designed to bring together all the progressive forces of the centre-left, while refusing entry to parties as 'apparatuses' in their existing form. The National Alliance, on the other hand, was formed (in January 1994) with the decisive backing of the MSI which sought, by giving life to an organization with a broader base of support than its own, to overcome its pariah status. Finally, FI, a completely new formation, offered a further contrast in as much as it presented a 'party model' that was totally original: the *partito azienda* or 'business party'. Formed by the media magnate Silvio Berlusconi as a means of bringing together the forces of the right, it deliberately eschewed – in an endeavour to project itself as a modern organization in which voters could have confidence as a force for political renewal – the mass-party format, for it was these, with their bureaucracies and large memberships in need of servicing, which had occupied and pillaged the state's resources and, according to the analyses of Berlusconi's advisers, in a world of declining ideologies and growing disaggregation, they were destined to disappear (McCarthy, 1995). Hence FI was a large and sophisticated marketing organization designed to promote, above all else, the image and policies of its leader, rather than a political party in any hitherto commonly understood sense.

## New Party Alliances

Berlusconi began organizing in the spring of 1993. However, the decisive events in bringing together the forces of the right were the mayoral elections held on 21 November and 5 December 1993. The left swept several major cities and, largely owing to the collapse of the DC, the MSI emerged as the dominant party in the South entering, among others, two high-profile run-off ballots in Naples and Rome.

Meanwhile, the Northern League did less well than hoped, failing to capture two of its targeted cities (Venice and Genoa). The elections therefore did three things: first, they raised the spectre of a victory of the left; second, they suggested that the MSI would have to be part of any coalition strong enough to defeat the left; third, they revealed that the League needed an ally. However, an alliance between the AN and the League was never likely as an axis on which to build a right-wing alliance – the AN represented centralization, the South and voters who supported the welfare state; Bossi represented decentralization, the North and the goal of effectively ending welfare to the South, while the other forces available for coalition on the right – the CCD and the surviving Liberals in the *Unione di Centro* (UdC) – were too small to act as the basis for a winning coalition. On the other hand, Berlusconi could act as a link between AN and the League, by virtue of the fact that if these latter were split on two fundamental issues vital to their own identities – the unity and integrity of the nation state, and levels of state intervention – he could agree with the AN on the first issue and with the League on the second. Thus Berlusconi was able to conclude stand-down arrangements with the AN in the South, where the alliance became known as the 'Alliance for Good Government', and with the League in the North (the AN fielding its own candidates), where the alliance became known as the 'Freedom Alliance'. The CCD and the UdC joined the alliance because they needed a protector (McCarthy, 1996b: 142).

In the centre, the 'Pact for Italy' which opposed both coalitions to left and right, was made up of Segni's Pact for National Renewal and the PPI which, as an organization containing a variety of conflicting centre-left and centre-right tendencies, could only remain viable as long as it refused the choice of left or right.

Finally, on the left, it was clear that the PDS was the essential pivot around which any alliance had to be built, and its own proposal represented an attempt to avoid the choice between a genuinely left-wing alliance (which would exclude forces deemed to be too centrist, as the RC wanted) or an alliance of the centre-left (which would exclude the RC, as the AD wanted). Essentially, the PDS was faced with a dilemma which it tried to escape by embracing the widest alliance possible: on the one hand, it did not want to lose votes to its left by excluding the RC; on the other hand, its leaders were aware that if it wanted to win more centrally placed voters it would have to include groups such as the AD and the Social Christians. In the end, therefore, what became the Progressive Alliance was an unwieldy and conflict-ridden coalition consisting of eight partners: the PDS, PSI, RS, AD, RC, C-S, the *Rete*, and the Greens (Rhodes, 1994; Bull, 1996b) (see Figure 2.1).

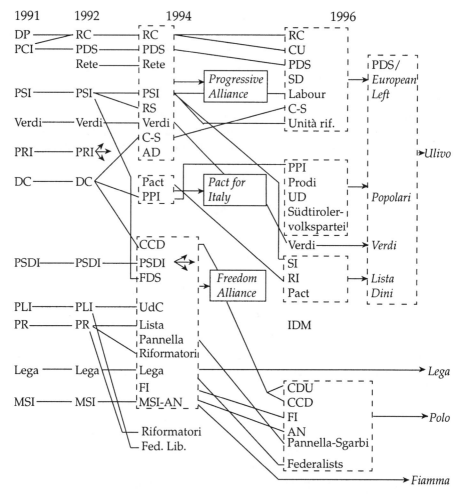

*Key*: DP = Proletarian Democracy; PCI = Italian Communist Party; PSI = Italian Socialist Party; Verdi = Greens; PRI = Italian Republican Party; DC = Christian Democrats; PSDI = Italian Social Democratic Party; PLI = Italian Liberal Party; PR = Radical Party; Lega = Northern League; MSI = Italian Social Movement; RC = Communist Refoundation; PDS = Democratic Party of the Left; Rete = Network; C-S = Social Christians; AD = Democratic Alliance; Pact = Pact for National Renewal; PPI = Italian Popular Party; CCD = Christian Democratic Centre; FDS = 'federation of socialists'; UdC = Union of the Centre; Lista Pannella = Pannella List; FI = Forza Italia!; AN = National Alliance; Riformatori = Reformists; Fed. Lib. = Liberal Federation; CU = United Communists; SD = Social Democrats; Unità rif.= Reformist unity; UD = Democratic Union; Südtirolervolkspartei = South Tyrolese People's Party; SI = Italian Socialists; RI = Italian Renewal; MID = Italian Democratic Movement; CDU = Christian Democratic Union; Fiamma = Tricoloured Flame.

*Source*: Newell and Bull 1997: 94.

**Figure 2.1   Evolution of the main party organizations and alliances 1991–96**

**1994 to the Election of 1996: The Final Achievement of Alternation?**

The nature of the victory of the Freedom Alliance in the March 1994 elections (see Table 2.3) had four consequences vital to the further shifts in the party landscape that would take place in the following months.[13] First, by bringing about a dramatic growth in support for the AN, they confirmed that the legitimacy which the alliance with Berlusconi had conferred on this organization had been successful in allowing it to emerge from the political ghetto to which it had hitherto been confined. Second, the election confirmed for the League that its alliance with Berlusconi was a double-edged sword. On the one hand, the League had needed Berlusconi because of the overlap in the nature of the two parties' electoral appeals and core support; on the other hand, this same similarity meant that an alliance might threaten the League's separate identity leading to just that slippage of votes to FI which the alliance had been designed to avoid. In the event, although the League more or less held its position in aggregate, exit polls revealed that, at the individual level, there had indeed been a considerable movement of support from the League to FI. This and the fact that so many of the newly elected League deputies (whose number rose from 55 to 117) so obviously owed their seats to FI votes (given the electoral system) meant that conflict between the two parties in the election's aftermath was hardly surprising. Third, the results confirmed that the attempt to field candidates lying in between powerful opponents to the left and to the right was, in a single-member, simple plurality context, likely to be an unproductive exercise. Of the 46 seats won by the Pact for Italy, only four came to it via the plurality formula, confirming the tendency for voters' effective choices to be reduced, constituency by constituency, to two front-runners, one of the left and one of the right.[14] Fourth, however, in bringing about, against expectations, a further increase in the number of parties represented in parliament, the elections confirmed that the process of forming electoral alliances had led to what one writer called the 'proportionalization of the plurality system' (Di Virgilio, 1994b), allowing the party system to continue in a state of extreme flux.

*Fragmentation of the Right*

The deep differences between the Northern League, on the one hand, and FI and the AN on the other came to the fore as soon as Berlusconi became Prime Minister at the head of a new centre-right government. The tensions between the League and FI were exacerbated not only by the government's failure to deliver on several of its promises (for example, institutional reform, privatization, jobs and the economy), but also by deep controversies surrounding Berlusconi as Prime

## Table 2.3   The Chamber of Deputies elections of 1994 (630 seats)

| Parties and alliances | List votes N (millions) | % | Proportional seats N | % | Plurality seats N | % | Total seats N | % |
|---|---|---|---|---|---|---|---|---|
| PDS | 7.86 | 20.4 | 37 | 23.9 | 72 | 25.2 | 109 | 17.3 |
| RC | 2.33 | 6.0 | 12 | 7.7 | 27 | 5.7 | 39 | 6.2 |
| Greens | 1.04 | 2.7 | 0 | 0.0 | 11 | 2.3 | 11 | 1.7 |
| PSI | 0.84 | 2.2 | 0 | 0.0 | 14 | 2.9 | 14 | 2.2 |
| *Rete* | 0.72 | 1.9 | 0 | 0.0 | 6 | 1.3 | 6 | 1.0 |
| AD | 0.45 | 1.2 | 0 | 0.0 | 18 | 3.8 | 18 | 2.9 |
| C-S | | | | | 5 | 1.1 | 5 | 0.8 |
| RS | | | | | 1 | 0.2 | 1 | 0.2 |
| Ind. left | | | | | 10 | 2.1 | 10 | 1.6 |
| Total Progressive Alliance | 13.24 | 34.3 | 49 | 31.6 | 164 | 34.5 | 213 | 33.8 |
| PPI | 4.27 | 11.1 | 29 | 18.7 | 4 | 0.8 | 33 | 5.2 |
| *Patto Segni* | 1.79 | 4.7 | 13 | 8.4 | 0 | 0.0 | 13 | 2.1 |
| Total Pact for Italy | 6.06 | 15.7 | 42 | 27.1 | 4 | 0.8 | 46 | 7.3 |
| FI | 8.12 | 21.0 | | | | | | |
| FI | | | 25 | 16.1 | 74 | 15.6 | 99 | 15.7 |
| CCD | | | 7 | 4.5 | 22 | 4.6 | 29 | 4.6 |
| UdC | | | | | 4 | 0.8 | 4 | 0.6 |
| Pld | | | | | 2 | 0.4 | 2 | 0.3 |
| *Riformatori* | | | | | 6 | 1.3 | 6 | 1.0 |
| AN | 5.20 | 13.5 | 22 | 14.2 | 87 | 18.3 | 109 | 17.3 |
| Northern League | 3.24 | 8.4 | 10 | 6.5 | 107 | 22.5 | 117 | 18.6 |
| Lp | 1.36 | 3.5 | 0 | 0.0 | 0 | 0.0 | 0 | 0.0 |
| Total Freedom Alliance | 17.92 | 46.4 | 64 | 41.3 | 302 | 63.6 | 366 | 58.1 |
| SVP | 0.23 | 0.6 | 0 | 0.0 | 3 | 0.6 | 3 | 0.5 |
| *Lista Valle d'Aosta* | | | | | 1 | 0.2 | 1 | 0.2 |
| *Lega d'Azione Meridionale* | 0.06 | 0.2 | 0 | 0.0 | 1 | 0.2 | 1 | 0.2 |
| *Social-democrazia* | 0.18 | 0.5 | 0 | 0.0 | 0 | 0.0 | 0 | 0.0 |
| *Lega Alpina Lumbarda* | 0.14 | 0.4 | 0 | 0.0 | 0 | 0.0 | 0 | 0.0 |
| *Verdi-Verdi* | 0.03 | 0.1 | 0 | 0.0 | 0 | 0.0 | 0 | 0.0 |
| Other leagues | 0.13 | 0.3 | 0 | 0.0 | 0 | 0.0 | 0 | 0.0 |
| Autonomist lists | 0.03 | 0.1 | 0 | 0.0 | 0 | 0.0 | 0 | 0.0 |
| Other lists | 0.57 | 1.5 | 0 | 0.0 | 0 | 0.0 | 0 | 0.0 |
| Total others | 1.37 | 3.6 | 0 | 0.0 | 5 | 1.1 | 5 | 0.8 |
| Total | 38.59 | 100.0 | 155 | 100.0 | 475 | 100.0 | 630 | 100.0 |

*Abbreviations*: PDS: *Partito Democratico della Sinistra* (Democratic Party of the Left); RC *Rifondazione Comunista* (Communist Refoundation); PSI: Italian Socialist Party; AD: *Alleanza Democratica* (Democratic Alliance); C-S: *Cristiano Sociali* (Social Christians); RS: *Rinascita Socialista* (Socialist Renewal); PPI: *Partito Popolare Italiano* (Italian Popular Party); FI: *Forza Italia*; CCD: *Centro Cristiano Democratico* (Christian Democratic Centre); UdC: *Unione di Centro* (Union of the Centre); Pld: *Polo Liberal-Democratico* (Liberal Democratic Alliance); Lp: *Lista Pannella* (the Pannella List); SVP: *Südtirolervolkspartei* (South Tyrolese People's Party).

Notes:
1  The list votes won by CCD (which presented a separate list only in Molise) have been included under 'Other lists'; the seven proportional seats obtained have been attributed to CCD candidates on the lists presented by FI.
2  Of the total 302 plurality seats attributed to the Freedom Alliance, 164 were won by the Freedom Alliance (of which Northern League 107, FI 38, CCD 8, *Riformatori* 6, UdC 3, Pld 2); 129 by the Alliance for Good Government (of which AN 79, FI 36, CCD 13, UdC 1); 1 by FI-CCD; and 8 by AN running alone.

*Source*: Stefano Bartolini and Roberto D'Alimonte, 'La competizione maggioritaria: le origini elettorali del parlamento diviso', *Rivista Italiana di Scienza Politica*, XXIV, No. 3, Dec. 1994, Table 2.

Minister. He continually procrastinated on the critical issue of how to resolve the conflict of interests between his role as Prime Minister and that of leader of Fininvest and controller of three television channels which accounted for more than 90 per cent of commercial television audiences. Furthermore, he clashed with several important institutions, including the presidency, the RAI (state television network), the Bank of Italy and the magistrates. Judicial–political conflict, in particular, ensured that the League kept its distance from the government.

The tensions between the League and the AN stemmed from their different philosophies (noted earlier), the AN's fascist heritage (which had yet to be unambiguously repudiated), and the AN's electoral success which could only be due to the legitimization it had received through its presence in the Freedom Alliance, and which could only be reinforced the longer it remained in office. Unsurprisingly, therefore, the League was instrumental in bringing down the government after only eight months (in December 1994), and this event spelled the end of the unity forged for the 1994 elections.

For the AN, the Berlusconi government (even though shortlived) constituted a significant step on the road to gaining full legitimacy. The AN had originally been created as an umbrella grouping to attract new members of the right and present the MSI with a softer image (hence the official name, MSI–AN). Therefore, after the fall of the government, Fini argued that it was time to 'put out the flame' (the MSI's symbol), formally replacing it with the AN. The MSI hardliners, however, were vehemently opposed to this idea, and, when the party congress of January 1995 approved Fini's line, they left the party to form a new neo-fascist party, the *Fiamma Tricolore* (Tricoloured Flame) led by Pino Rauti, which stood alone to the right of the Freedom Alliance.

Besides the addition to the alliance of the small and maverick Pannella-Sgarbi list, the other gain for the right was the Christian Democratic Union (CDU) which formed a federation with the CCD (which had been part of the Freedom Alliance in 1994) for the 1996 elections (see Figure 2.1). The CDU was the product of a significant split in the PPI, marking the collapse of the old centre which, in 1994, had refused to recognize the bipolar logic of the new electoral system.

*The Old Centre Crumbles*

As already noted, the results of the 1994 elections seemed to confirm that the centre was a redundant place in the party system. Nevertheless, divisions over whether to opt for the left or the right made a split in the centre inevitable. Segni was still convinced that there was sufficient political space for a centre party and attempted, in vain, to relaunch his Pact in late 1994. The PPI was ready to abandon the centre but was divided over whether, in doing so, to join the left or the right. Party leader Rocco Buttiglioni believed that the PPI's future lay in an alliance on the centre-right. Indeed he argued that there was no alternative since any coalition on the left meant allying with an ex-communist party which was big enough to dominate the PPI. He had, with the League, engineered the downfall of the Berlusconi government, expecting FI, once in opposition, to collapse, leaving a centre-right-oriented PPI to inherit the floating votes. He also felt that this move would reinforce the centrist weight of the alliance, thus constraining the AN either to democratize further or become isolated.

The left of the party, however, was fiercely opposed to any alliance with the AN, whose fascist roots remained all too apparent, and they were reluctant to renounce links forged with the PDS at the local and regional levels, even though they recognized the dilemmas of entering a national alliance with a larger party to the left of the PPI. Their solution was to persuade a progressive ex-Christian Democrat, Romano Prodi, to launch a new centre-left coalition, the Olive Tree (*Ulivo*) within which the PDS and centre parties could form an alliance. The birth of the *Ulivo* in early 1995 made a split in the PPI inevitable. Buttiglione broke away and formed the Christian Democratic Union (CDU) which, as already noted, formed a federation with the CCD in the Freedom Alliance. Gerardo Bianco, meanwhile, led the PPI into the *Ulivo*, followed, somewhat reluctantly, by Segni and his pact (see Figure 2.1).

### The Ulivo: Alliance for Government

The electoral defeat of 1994, combined with similarly poor results in the June 1994 European elections, was shattering for the Progressives. The leaders of the PDS, PSI and AD all resigned, leading the alliance to begin to shed its component parts and form a single, four-party grouping (called the Progressive Federation) in parliament, made up of the PDS, C-S, the Greens and the *Rete*.

D'Alema (who replaced Occhetto as PDS leader in the summer of 1994) argued that the principal cause of the Progressives' defeat was the failure to extend the alliance to the centre. The Progressives had based their appeal on the assumption that centrist voters would change their allegiance – something which they proved unwilling to do. He argued that the PDS should continue to renovate its identity with a view to eventually freeing itself from RC's influence, and be available to form a permanent federation with other parties of the left and centre (something he dubbed a 'liberal revolution'). This federation would be led by a single leader, who could be chosen by a primary election and should probably come from a party other than the PDS.

Three factors hastened the realization of a variant of D'Alema's 'coalition of democrats', the Olive Tree Alliance, which successfully brought together the more progressive elements of the centre and left in one coalition. The first was the fall of the Berlusconi government. Since no alternative coalition could be found, it ensured another suspension of party government, and Berlusconi's Treasury Minister, Lamberto Dini, formed (like Ciampi in 1993) a government of technocrats. The nature of the majority which, over time, came to support this government was significant. The Dini government was subjected to seven votes of no confidence in all of which both FI and the AN, anxious for immediate elections, voted against the government. Dini came to depend on the PDS, the PPI and the Northern League, and, once, was even dependent for survival on the abstention of the RC. This experience of centre and left working together was important for the development of the *Ulivo*, and proved to be crucial when, in early 1996, Dini decided to form his own political force and, against his natural instincts, to locate it in the *Ulivo* in recognition of the parties which had kept him in office during the previous year.

The second factor was the role of Prodi and the nature of the *Ulivo*. Prodi's reputation (as former president of the state holding group, IRI) was one of honesty, efficiency and popularity with businesspeople and the markets. He appeared to be the epitome of reasonableness and modesty and refused to use the election campaign techniques typical of Berlusconi. More importantly, in launching the *Ulivo*, he was not asking any of the parties to sacrifice anything in organizational terms beyond supporting him, as leader of the alliance and candidate for Prime Minister, and a moderate programme whose main characteristic was continuity with Dini. The *Ulivo*'s objective was simply to forge an alliance between the more progressive elements of the centre and left. In this it succeeded. The third factor which encouraged the formation of the *Ulivo* was the results of the regional elections of April 1995 which showed promising gains for the centre-left and the likely potential of its vote at the national level.[15]

In its final shape, the *Ulivo* comprised four component parts, three of which contained within them several separate elements (see Figure 2.1). The largest component was the PDS–European left, whose size was such that it provided approximately half the *Ulivo*'s candidates in the 1996 elections. It consisted of the PDS and the so-called 'shrubs' (*cespugli*), six tiny parties which were close to the PDS but unwilling to be completely absorbed by it: the *Laburisti* (Labour, led by Valdo Spini), the United Communists (the product of a split in the RC, and led by Sergio Garavini), C-S (led by Piero Carniti) the Social Democrats (led by Schietroma) *Unità riformista* (Reformist Unity) and (although some would question its position as a 'shrub') the anti-*Mafia Rete*.

The second component was based around the PPI and was known as the *Popolari*. In addition to the PPI (led by Bianco), there was the Prodi Group, the Democratic Union (UD), led by Antonio Maccanico, and the South Tyrolese People's Party (SVP). The UD, moreover, was an alliance in itself, bringing together members of the old PLI, PSI and PRI, including well known names such as Valerio Zanone, Giorgio Benvenuto and Giorgio La Malfa.

The third component was the Dini List (*Lista Dini*), which was made up of a small group based around Lamberto Dini (*Rinnovamento Italiano*, Italian Renewal), the Italian Socialists (SI), official heirs of the PSI, and led by Enrico Boselli, the *Patto Segni*, and the Italian Democratic Movement (led by Sergio Berlinguer). The final component consisted of the Greens.

The RC was not included in the coalition, but stand-down arrangements were reached for the 1996 elections which gave it a clear run at 27 seats in the Chamber and 17 in the Senate in return for not putting up candidates against the *Ulivo* in other constituencies, thereby preventing the left's vote being split in key areas. A formal inclusion of the RC in the *Ulivo* was not wanted by any of the latter's constituent parts: for the PDS leadership, the RC's inclusion in the Progressive Alliance had been a primary factor in the Alliance's defeat in 1994; for the centre parties, the RC's adherence to Marxism ruled it out, and they would not enter the *Ulivo* if the RC were to be included. The RC, for its part, regarded the *Ulivo* as too centrist a construction, and disagreed with key parts of its programme – for example, privatization, European Monetary Union and the refusal to reinstate Italy's former wage indexation system. There was no attempt, therefore, to paper over the differences as had happened in 1994, and the agreement with the RC was frankly acknowledged as being almost wholly motivated by electoral expediency.

### The Victory of the Ulivo

Dini had taken office with a limited mandate and resigned in December 1995 after he had succeeded in passing a budget which, like those of Amato and Ciampi in 1993 and 1994, sought to improve the position of Italy's public finances in view of the convergence criteria established by the Maastricht Treaty. An attempt was then made to form another non-party government (under Antonio Maccanico) in order to ensure that Italy would not be left without a Prime Minister during the period of its presidency of the European Union (during the first half of 1996) and in order to try to put together a package of institutional reforms – something which both Berlusconi and D'Alema agreed was necessary

– before fresh elections. Fini, however, wanted elections at all costs and Maccanico's attempt to form a government foundered on this intransigence. As a result, parliament was dissolved and elections were set for 21 April.

At these elections, the *Ulivo* emerged with an overall majority in the Senate and as the largest single formation in the Chamber where it was able to achieve majority backing with the support of the RC's 35 votes (see Table 2.4). Superficially at least, this result appeared to herald the final transformation of Italian party politics: after years of 'blocked democracy' in which the centre had been 'condemned to office' by the illegitimacy of the left and the right poles, a new electoral system seemed to have ushered in (with what degree of truth we shall see in more detail in Chapter 6) an era of centripetal competition within a bipolar logic, and alternation in office appeared at last to have taken place. The left and the right poles of the 'First Republic', the PCI–PDS and the MSI–AN, had been allowed to emerge from the ghettos to which they had been confined, and Italy appeared to be well on the way to achieving – if it had not already achieved – the elusive status of being what journalists called '*una democrazia moderna*'.

Much of this success seemed attributable to the incoming Prime Minister, Romano Prodi, himself. It was noticeable, for instance, that in the single-member district ballot for the Chamber, the centre-left won approximately half a million more votes than its combined list-vote totals for each of the parties making up the alliance, while the Freedom Alliance won 1.5 million votes less than the combined list-vote totals – suggesting that the centre-left had a capacity to mobilize support beyond the ranks of its target electorate. If this capacity was partly caused by the single-member ballot – which in effect invited voters to make a straight choice between alternative governing coalitions, so that one whose preferred *party* belonged outside the centre-left could nevertheless have preferred the centre-left as a potential *governing coalition* – this was in turn a consequence of the voters' tendency to perceive the centre-left as something more than simply the sum of its parts. This was immeasurably helped by Prodi's skill in portraying himself as a leader who simultaneously stood above the centre-left's parties while also being the essential element of their cohesion.

In the immediate aftermath of the election Prodi's image contributed to the feeling that something of great significance had happened and to the hope and expectation that there would be an end to the dubious methods and political corruption that had destroyed the old political class. The impression was that, until Prodi, most executives had been led either by politicians who were themselves under judicial investigation (for example, Berlusconi and, before him, Andreotti) or

## Table 2.4    Chamber of Deputies and Senate elections, 1996

### Chamber

| | Votes Majoritarian segment No | % | Votes Proportional segment No | % | Seats Majoritarian segment No | % | Seats Proportional segment No | % | Total No | % |
|---|---|---|---|---|---|---|---|---|---|---|
| PDS–*Sin. Eur.* | | | 7 897 044 | 21.1 | | | | | | |
| PDS | | | | | 124 | 26.1 | 24 | 15.5 | 148 | 23.5 |
| *Com. Unitari* | | | | | 6 | 1.3 | 2 | 1.3 | 8 | 1.3 |
| *Cristiani Soc.* | | | | | 4 | 0.8 | 0 | 0.0 | 4 | 0.6 |
| *Laburisti* | | | | | 6 | 1.3 | 0 | 0.0 | 6 | 1.0 |
| *La Rete* | | | | | 5 | 1.1 | | | 5 | 0.8 |
| *P. Sardo d'Az.* | | | 37 974 | 0.1 | 0 | 0.0 | 0 | 0.0 | 0 | 0.0 |
| *Verdi* | | | 937 684 | 2.5 | 15 | 3.2 | 0 | 0.0 | 15 | 2.4 |
| Pop. SVP–PRI–UD–Prodi | | | 2 555 082 | 6.8 | | | | | | |
| PPI | | | | | 58 | 12.2 | 3 | 1.9 | 61 | 9.7 |
| UD | | | | | 5 | 1.1 | 1 | 0.6 | 6 | 1.0 |
| PRI | | | | | 2 | 0.4 | 0 | 0.0 | 2 | 0.3 |
| *L. Dini-Rinnov. Ital.* | | | 1 627 191 | 4.3 | | | | | | |
| *Lista Dini* | | | | | 8 | 1.7 | 2 | 1.3 | 10 | 1.6 |
| *Patto Segni* | | | | | 6 | 1.3 | 2 | 1.3 | 8 | 1.3 |
| *Socialisti Ital.* | | | | | 3 | 0.6 | 4 | 2.6 | 7 | 1.1 |
| MID | | | | | 1 | 0.2 | 0 | 0.0 | 1 | 0.2 |
| *Ulivo* Indep. | | | | | 4 | 0.8 | 0 | 0.0 | 4 | 0.6 |
| *Ulivo* Total | 15 762 460 | 42.3 | 13 054 975 | 34.8 | 247 | 52.0 | 38 | 24.5 | 285 | 45.2 |
| *Progressisti 1996* | 982 248 | 2.6 | 3 215 960 | 8.6 | 15 | 3.2 | 20 | 12.9 | 35 | 5.6 |
| *Rif. Com.* | 17 996 | 0.0 | | | 0 | 0.0 | | | 0 | 0.0 |
| *Ulivo* + *Rif.* Com. Total | 16 762 704 | 44.9 | 16 270 935 | 43.4 | 262 | 55.2 | 58 | 37.4 | 320 | 50.8 |
| CCD–CDU | | | 2 190 019 | 5.8 | | | | | | |
| CCD | | | | | 13 | 2.7 | 6 | 3.9 | 19 | 3.0 |
| CDU | | | | | 5 | 1.1 | 6 | 3.9 | 11 | 1.7 |
| *Forza Italia* | | | 7 715 342 | 20.6 | | | | | | |
| *Forza Italia* | | | | | 81 | 17.1 | 37 | 23.9 | 118 | 18.7 |
| *Fed. Liberali* | | | | | 4 | 0.8 | 0 | 0.0 | 4 | 0.6 |
| *Part. Fed.* | | | | | 1 | 0.2 | 0 | 0.0 | 1 | 0.2 |
| *All. Nazionale* | | | 5 875 391 | 15.7 | 65 | 13.7 | 28 | 18.1 | 93 | 14.8 |
| Polo per le Libertà Total | 15 027 275 | 40.3 | 15 780 752 | 42.1 | 169 | 35.6 | 77 | 49.7 | 246 | 39.0 |
| L. Pannella-Sgarbi (LP) | 74 314 | 0.2 | 701 033 | 1.9 | 0 | 0.0 | 0 | 0.0 | 0 | 0.0 |
| *Polo* + LP Total | 15 101 589 | 40.5 | 16 481 785 | 44.0 | 169 | 35.6 | 77 | 49.7 | 246 | 39.0 |
| *Lega Nord* | 4 038 511 | 10.8 | 3 777 786 | 10.1 | 39 | 8.2 | 20 | 12.9 | 59 | 9.4 |
| SVP | 156 973 | 0.4 | | | 3 | 0.6 | 0 | 0.0 | 3 | 0.5 |
| *Lega d'Az Mer.* | 82 279 | 0.2 | 72 152 | 0.1 | 1 | 0.2 | 0 | 0.0 | 1 | 0.2 |
| PVA | 37 428 | 0.1 | | | 1 | 0.2 | | | 1 | 0.2 |
| MSFT | 633 385 | 1.7 | 338 721 | 0.9 | 0 | 0.0 | 0 | 0.0 | 0 | 0.0 |
| Others | 491 264 | 1.3 | 553 586 | 1.5 | 0 | 0.0 | 0 | 0.0 | 0 | 0.0 |
| Total | 37 304 133 | 100 | 37 494 965 | 100 | 475 | 100 | 155 | 100 | 630 | 100 |

| Senate | Votes | | Seats | | | | | |
|---|---|---|---|---|---|---|---|---|
| | | | Uninominal | | Proportional | | Total | |
| | No | % | No | % | No | % | No | % |
| PDS | | | 77 | 33.2 | 11 | 13.3 | 88 | 27.9 |
| *Comunisti Unitari* | | | 0 | 0.0 | 0 | 0.0 | 0 | 0.0 |
| *Cristiani Sociali* | | | 3 | 1.3 | 0 | 0.0 | 3 | 1.0 |
| *Laburisti* | | | 2 | 0.9 | 1 | 1.2 | 3 | 1.0 |
| *La Rete* | | | 1 | 0.4 | 0 | 0.0 | 1 | 0.3 |
| *Lega Autonomista Veneta* | | | 1 | 0.4 | 0 | 0.0 | 1 | 0.3 |
| *Partito Sardo d'Azione* | | | 1 | 0.4 | 0 | 0.0 | 1 | 0.3 |
| *Verdi* | | | 14 | 6.0 | 0 | 0.0 | 14 | 4.4 |
| PPI | | | 22 | 9.5 | 5 | 6.0 | 27 | 8.6 |
| *Unione Democratica* | | | 1 | 0.4 | 0 | 0.0 | 1 | 0.3 |
| PRI | | | 0 | 0.0 | 2 | 2.4 | 2 | 0.6 |
| *Lista Dini* | | | 3 | 1.3 | 1 | 1.2 | 4 | 1.3 |
| *Socialisti Italiani* | | | 4 | 1.7 | 1 | 1.2 | 5 | 1.6 |
| *Patto Segni* | | | 1 | 0.4 | 0 | 0.0 | 1 | 0.3 |
| MID | | | 1 | 0.4 | 0 | 0.0 | 1 | 0.3 |
| *Ulivo* Independents | | | 2 | 0.9 | 2 | 2.4 | 4 | 1.3 |
| *Ulivo* Total | 13 448 392 | 41.2 | 133 | 57.3 | 23 | 27.7 | 156 | 49.5 |
| *Progressisti 1996* | 940 980 | 2.9 | 11 | 4.7 | 0 | 0.0 | 11 | 3.5 |
| *Rif. Comunista* | 5 682 | 0.0 | 0 | 0.0 | – | – | 0 | 0.0 |
| *Ulivo* + *Rif. Com.* Total | 14 395 054 | 44.1 | 144 | 62.1 | 23 | 27.7 | 167 | 53.0 |
| CCD | | | 8 | 3.4 | 7 | 8.4 | 15 | 4.8 |
| CDU | | | 7 | 3.0 | 3 | 3.6 | 10 | 3.2 |
| *Forza Italia* | | | 23 | 9.9 | 24 | 28.9 | 47 | 14.9 |
| *Federalisti Liberali* | | | 0 | 0.0 | 0 | 0.0 | 0 | 0.0 |
| *Partito Federalista* | | | 1 | 0.0 | 0 | 0.0 | 1 | 0.3 |
| *Alleanza Nazionale* | | | 28 | 12.1 | 15 | 18.1 | 43 | 13.7 |
| *Polo per le Libertà* Total | 12 187 498 | 37.3 | 67 | 28.9 | 49 | 59.0 | 116 | 36.8 |
| *Lista Pannella-Sgarbi* (LP) | 511 689 | 1.6 | 0 | 0.0 | 1 | 1.2 | 1 | 0.3 |
| *Polo* + LP Total | 12 699 187 | 38.9 | 67 | 28.9 | 50 | 60.2 | 117 | 37.1 |
| *Lega Nord* | 3 394 527 | 10.4 | 18 | 7.8 | 9 | 10.8 | 27 | 8.6 |
| *L'Abete-SVP-PATT* | 178 415 | 0.5 | 2 | 0.9 | 0 | 0.0 | 2 | 0.6 |
| *Pour Vallée d'Aoste* | 29 536 | 0.1 | 1 | 0.4 | – | – | 1 | 0.3 |
| MSFT | 748 759 | 2.3 | 0 | 0.0 | 1 | 1.2 | 1 | 0.3 |
| Others | 1 191 117 | 3.6 | 0 | 0.0 | 0 | 0.0 | 0 | 0.0 |
| Total | 32 636 595 | 100 | 232 | 100 | 83 | 100 | 315 | 100 |

*Source*: Chiaramonte (1997: 40–1, Tables 2.4 and 2.5).

by non-elected technocrats (such as Ciampi and Dini). With the advent of Prodi, it was widely felt, things would be different (D'Alimonte and Nelken, 1997). Prodi himself would not have been unaware of this or of how his administration's success in projecting an image of propriety was likely to be essential to counterbalance its weaknesses. These weaknesses were, first, its dependence on the RC at a time when the demands of Economic and Monetary Union required further budgetary restraint, and second an inability to compensate for this dependence by acting as a minority government, relying on varying majorities for different issues (something that was effectively ruled out by the bipolar mechanic of the party system). And if the establishment of the Bicameral Commission for Constitutional Reform (the *Bicamerale*) at the beginning of 1997 gave the government something of an 'insurance policy' (since its downfall was likely to have the unpopular consequence of sinking the *Bicamerale* along with it) the suspicion gained ground during 1997 that the cooperation of opposition forces within the Commission (whose proposals would require support from across the political spectrum if they were to pass) was being bought at the expense of a less-than-helpful stance among at least some of the forces of the majority towards the work of the *Tangentopoli* magistrates.[16] So *Tangentopoli* and corruption were issues that, by early 1998, were still very high on the Italian political agenda. But how had political corruption come to be such a salient feature of Italian politics in the first place? How did it operate? And how and why had it contributed to the downfall of the old political class? It is to these questions that the following chapter is dedicated.

## Notes

1   Parts of this chapter rely heavily on an article I wrote with Martin Bull and which now appears as Newell and Bull (1997).
2   Patrick McCarthy argues the interesting thesis that anti-communism in Italy owed more to the strength of the Church than to the pressure of outside forces and that, indeed, Italy was reasonably free of international constraints with 'more decisions [being] taken in Rome (including the Vatican) than in Moscow, Washington or Brussels' (1996a: 4).
3   Some of the most prominent examples of these were: the DC's *Coldiretti* for small farmers, and the Italian Association of Christian Workers (ACLI) for workers, and the Communists' National Association of Ex-partisans (ANPI), the Union of Italian Women (UDI) and the *Case del popolo* (literally, 'houses of the people'). The significance of these latter is immediately apparent from Ginsborg's description of them:

> Especially in central Italy and in the smaller towns and the countryside, the Case del Popolo, which traced their origins back to the mutual-aid societies of the late nineteenth century, became focal points of community life. Here meetings and debates were arranged, films shown, children's and sports

activities organised. In some of the Case medical centres were set up; in the larger ones, like that of the Due Strade in Florence, there were public baths as well. (Ginsborg, 1990: 195–6)

4    Banfield achieved some notoriety with his concept of 'amoral familism' which he defined as the attempt to maximize the material, short-run advantage of the nuclear family, assuming that all others will do likewise. Among the consequences of this behaviour is an inability to act together for the common good, 'or indeed, for any end transcending the immediate, material interest of the nuclear family' (Banfield, 1958: 10).

5    The smaller centre parties which, in addition to the PSI from 1963 on, were periodic coalition partners for the DC were the Republicans (PRI), the Liberals (PLI) and the Social Democrats (PSDI). Together, their vote never exceeded the 14.5 per cent which they won at the 1963 election before their virtual disappearance in the early 1990s. The PRI 'was founded as an organised party as early as 1895, as a small radical force which was both anti-clerical and anti-monarchy (as its name emphasised), and from the later 1920s it emerged as uncompromisingly anti-fascist' (Pridham, 1988: 33). The PLI was more inclined to the right than the Republicans and presented itself after the Second World War as a vehicle 'for the conservative classes who feared radical change and political purges' (ibid.: 34). Both parties remained small as a result of the DC's success in monopolizing the broad centre-right. The PSDI dated back to 1947 when its founder, Giuseppe Saragat, left the PSI because of his disagreement with the party's then policy of 'Unity of Action' with the PCI.

6    As Cotta puts it: 'Electoral line-ups and governing alliances, dictated principally by choices regarding the level of metapolicies, necessarily required adherents to play down divergences in their programmatic outlooks' (Cotta, 1996: 31–2).

7    Figures taken from the Statistical Appendix to Ginsborg (1990), diagrams 13, 22 and 32.

8    Parisi and Pasquino define the *voto d'opinione* as 'above all the expression of a choice that accepts as a framework of options, the programmatic aims espoused by the contending parties' (1977: 221), while those who cast a *voto di appartenenza* (literally, 'vote of belonging') are voters who 'give relatively little importance to a dispassionate consideration of a series of programmatic alternatives. Rather, they see their vote above all as the affirmation of a subjective identification with a political party that they regard as being organically linked to the social group they belong to (rather than seeing the party as simply the institutional representative of that group)' (ibid.: 224). Advanced by Parisi and Pasquino in the late 1970s, the threefold distinction between *voto di appartenenza*, *voto d'opinione* and *voto di scambio* (an 'exchange vote' given in return for a favour) became, for Italian political scientists, a standard conceptual framework for understanding the social–psychological bases of voting.

9    See Gusso (1990), Baccetti (1990), Biorcio (1990), Nuvoli and Spreafico (1990). The combined vote for the Radicals (essentially a 'new politics' party which found its origins in a split on the left of the Liberal Party in 1955) and Proletarian Democracy (a party which lay to the left of the PCI and found its origin in the late 1960s protest movements) rose from 2.6 per cent in 1976 to 4.3 per cent in 1987. In 1987 the combined vote for the Radicals, Proletarian Democracy, the Greens and the Northern League was 7.3 per cent.

10   This is measured as half the absolute sum of the differences in the percentage of the vote received by each individual party between successive pairs of elections. See Pedersen (1979: 1–26).

11   This power-sharing agreement was known as the CAF axis, so-called after the names of the parties' leading spokespersons, Craxi, Andreotti, Forlani.

12   On the PSI meltdown, see Rhodes (1994).
13   On the election results see Bull and Newell (1995) and Bartolini and D'Alimonte (1996).
14   On the general collapse of the centre pole see Morlino (1996).
15   On the results of the regional elections see D'Alimonte (1995).
16   Things came to a head towards the end of February 1998 when one of the *Tangentopoli* magistrates, Gherardo Colombo, published, in the influential daily *Corriere della Sera* on 22 February, an interview in which he argued that it was necessary 'to uncover all the illegalities and to indicate the responsibilities of all involved'. Only in this way, he said, would the new Constitution not be founded on blackmail. As a result of this, the Minister of Justice, Giovanni Flick announced that he was initiating disciplinary proceedings against the magistrate.

# 3 Clientelism, Corruption and *Tangentopoli*

As noted in the last chapter, one of the major pillars of support for the traditional governing parties during the post-war period, especially in the South, was clientelism which in turn rested on the parties' penetration of vast areas of the state and society – a state of affairs which came to be popularly dubbed *partitocrazia* (literally, 'partyocracy'). *Partitocrazia* and the clientelistic management of power relations provided one of the basic presuppositions for the spread of political corruption, which by the end of the 1980s had become systemic and routine, until its exposure as a result of the so-called *Tangentopoli* ('Bribe City') investigations beginning in 1992. *Tangentopoli* destroyed the parties not only through its impact on their electoral following, by cutting off a major source of funding, or by leading to splits between those directly compromised by the investigations and those who, though uninvolved, still had to bear the political costs of the crisis, but also because – with venality having almost entirely displaced policy as the main motive for membership – corruption had fatally undermined the parties' organizational structures.

Since political corruption was one of the principal structural causes of the transformation of the Italian party system, and *Tangentopoli* was one of the major factors precipitating the traditional parties' collapse, this chapter explores the impact of these two phenomena in some detail. As the root cause underlying the routinization of political corruption, the structure and operation of *partitocrazia* is discussed first. Then we examine the logic and dynamic of the clientelistic relationships which *partitocrazia* sustained and analyse how these, in their turn, facilitated the spread of corruption. Fourth, we discuss why the *Tangentopoli* investigations took place when they did and, finally, we consider their party and electoral effects.

## Partitocrazia

*Partitocrazia* owed its origins to factors whose deepest roots extended

as far back as the birth of the Italian state itself. The Italy which came
to be created in 1861 was economically and culturally highly diverse.
Not only was there an awesome economic gap between an
industrializing North and an agrarian, largely feudal, South (Allum,
1973a: 20), but the new state also had to confront an enormous diversity
of legal systems, land tenures and dialects (Hine, 1993: 12). The
deepseatedness of cultural diversity is apparent from the startling
reminder that, even today, 62 per cent of the population habitually
speak a dialect rather than Italian and that 13 per cent of the population
are unable to speak Italian at all (De Mauro, 1994: 66). For the great
mass of the peasantry, the main effect of unification was to add the
oppression of the Piedmontese tax collector to that of the landlord and,
when anger and frustration spilled over into violence and banditry, a
virtual civil war was fought in the South (Hine, 1993: 12–13).
Meanwhile, the Church, which lost significant chunks of territory as a
result of unification and, in any event, had a vested interest in a
continuation of the political division of the peninsula, refused to
recognize the new state and forbade Catholics to participate in political
life. So economic and cultural diversity, along with the opposition of
the Catholic Church, meant that, from the outset, the Italian state
suffered from low levels of legitimacy – something that was
compounded by the suffrage restrictions which, although a common
feature of European states at this time, closed off channels for the
legitimate expression of grievances.

Under these circumstances, unification failed to produce a national,
integrative, ideology and the state had difficulty in asserting its
authority against alternative, unofficial, power centres organized on a
clientelistic basis around local élites (and in extreme cases, around
organizations such as the *Mafia*). This, as well as limited suffrage,
allowed local notables to manipulate state institutions in their own
interest, structuring the system around networks of personal
relationships based on exchanges of favours. For example, the fact that
no more than 2 per cent of the population could vote undermined the
possibilities for developing organized political parties, and
parliamentary politics were consequently organized around constantly
shifting coalitions. This meant that, in the absence of clearly defined
governing and opposition forces, prime ministers kept themselves
continuously in office by means of *trasformismo* – that is, by the
unscrupulous winning over of individuals and groups within
parliament in such a way as to prevent the emergence of a coherent
opposition capable of competing for power. Clientelism was perfectly
adapted to *trasformismo*, relying, as it did, on maintaining the ill-defined
parliamentary cliques and the mass of non-aligned deputies in a state
of permanent atomization. Manipulation was easy: as Allum (1973b:
69) notes, all the government had to do was to offer access to patronage,

in exchange for which large numbers of deputies were happy to give their votes without asking questions:

> You should see the pandemonium at Montecitorio when the moment approaches for an important division. The agents of the government run through the rooms and corridors, to gather votes. Subsidies, decorations, canals, bridges, roads everything is promised; and sometimes an act of justice, long denied, is the price of a parliamentary vote. (Crispi, 1890: 575, quoted by Allum, 1973b: 69)

Yet these practices – serving, as they did, as a constant reminder that conceptions of the public good came a poor second to individual ambition in the determination of public decisions – could only undermine the legitimacy of the state still further. If this revealed that low levels of legitimacy were self-reinforcing, its weakening of the state's authority meant that, once the fascist interlude had come to an end, 'colonization' by the parties of numerous sectors of the state would be particularly easy.

This 'colonization' was encouraged by the particular circumstances which came to be created upon fascism's fall. First, the growth of political participation which arose from the Resistance gave particular *after* legitimacy to the two largest parties, the Christian Democrats (DC) *fascism* and the Communists (PCI), and also ensured that mass loyalties to the new state institutions, unmediated by the parties, would be slow to develop; for neither the PCI, nor the DC (bearing in mind the Church's original hostility to unification) considered themselves as heirs to the liberal tradition of the *Risorgimento*, the nineteenth-century movement by which Italy acquired independence and unity, which had given the Italian state, up until the advent of fascism, what legitimacy it had had (Bourricaud, 1974: 90). Second, the power vacuum created by the fall of fascism allowed the parties to capture interest groups and, once they had consolidated their position, to become the principal channels of access to the bureaucracy and the principal transmission belts in the allocation of resources from centre to periphery. For, if government instability meant that the system found it very difficult to make major programmatic decisions, under these circumstances, demands for change became 'transformed into appeals for the distribution of resources through existing mechanisms and procedures' (Tarrow, 1977: 194). In this way, 'the clientele chains that had sprung up during the pre-Fascist period and stayed alive under Fascism were re-created after World War II with a partisan overlay' (ibid.: 69).[1] Finally, the Christian Democrats were encouraged to colonize the non-civil service public administration for patronage purposes by the electoral imperatives of the Cold War. A wide range of influential actors both within and beyond Italy looked to the Christian Democrats to act as the main bulwark

DC main bulwark against Communism

against communism, yet in order to play this role successfully the party had to broaden its appeal far beyond the ranks of the Catholic faithful – which in turn meant that it somehow had to escape from the Church dominance to which its early reliance on groups such as Catholic Action had tended to subject it. By occupying a wide range of public sector institutions, the DC was able to tap a rich seam of public resources whose exploitation through a continuous flow of clientelistic exchanges not only gave it autonomy but also – in ways described below – a powerful claim on the support of activists and voters, especially in areas such as the *Mezzogiorno* where the absence of associational energy meant that attempts at ideological mobilization through the expansion of party organization could meet with only limited success. Access to public institutions could then be extended to other governing parties – most significantly to the Socialists (PSI) from 1963 onwards – as and when coalition negotiations might require (a fact which makes immediately apparent how much the habits and practices of the post-war governing parties owed to the 'transformist' traditions handed down from the parliamentary politics of the pre-fascist era). *Partitocrazia*, then, constituted a complete system of power relations. Based on a weak state allowing for considerable overlap between the personnel of the parties on the one hand, and interest groups and administrative positions on the other, it made it difficult to draw clear boundaries between these entities and to know, in any given case, in what capacity individuals were acting.[2]

## Clientelism

*Partitocrazia* encouraged an informal and particularistic – that is, clientelistic – mode of managing power relations which was also encouraged by the specific economic and political circumstances of the immediate post-war years. First, significant parts of the country, notably the *Mezzogiorno*, were poor. Unemployment was (and still is) high. Traditionally, much private economic activity has been beholden to the state for its implantation and development (Allum 1973b: 166). Suspicion and mistrust frequently made collective action difficult. The elected politician thus found, on the one hand, that he controlled access to the principal source of wealth and, on the other hand, that he was faced with a mass of isolated individuals (electors) each in search of a protector.

Second, the new institutions of representative democracy themselves stimulated clientelism for, owing to the presence of competitior politicans, electors were not *totally* dependent on the single politician in their search for protection, and hence the latter was able to retain electors' support only for so long as he was able to supply the kinds of protection (favour) they sought. As those who have studied clientelism comparatively have pointed out, if a certain power disjunction is necessary for clientelism to arise at all, so is 'the existence of a real rivalry, such that no single actor could have a monopolistic control over political power' (Dogan and Pelassy, 1990: 89) – a situation which, were it to exist, would destroy any incentive of the powerful to patronize clients in the first place.

Third, the governing parties' mutual need to sustain the agreement that governing alliances with the left- and right-wing extremes were to be excluded at all times, prevented them from engaging in policy competition – something which would have posed a serious threat to governing-party solidarity. This then left the clientelistic distribution of resources as the only remaining means of voter mobilization available (Leonardi and Anderlini, 1991; Bull and Newell, 1993: 205; Cotta, 1996). Moreover, clientelism was self-reinforcing since, by creating networks of vested interests each of which had effective powers of veto it prevented the parties from developing clear policy programmes. Hence, parties were induced to rely even more heavily on distribution through such networks.

Finally, the imperative to maintain a constant supply of favours was considerably enhanced by the system of preference voting – that is, the option made available to each elector, once having selected a party, to express three or four preferences among the names making up the party's list of candidates for the given area. Giving voters the power to discriminate between candidates belonging to the same party significantly increased the competition among politicians as the suppliers of favours, as candidates from the same party were just as close, if not closer, rivals for the coveted parliamentary or local council seats as candidates from other parties.

Clientelism was practised in a variety of ways. Sometimes, it was of a repressive, bureaucratic kind. For example, LaPalombara (1964) describes how the small landowners' association, *Coldiretti*, managed to get a number of its officials elected as Christian Democratic deputies. Once elected, such deputies could secure the passage of *leggine* (literally, 'little laws') of interest to the association by taking advantage of the power of parliamentary committees to act in *sede deliberante* – that is, to enact laws on behalf of the legislature as a whole in relative isolation from public gaze. The election of *Coldiretti* officials was normally secured by making use of the preference vote. *Coldiretti* members in each area would be told what combination of preference-vote numbers to cast – a method which, while not completely destroying the secrecy of the ballot, did allow the leadership to gauge how closely each district adhered to the line established by the leaders. Where deviation was too pronounced, retaliatory measures could be taken, for:

> . . . [w]hen an association such as the Coltivatori Diretti establishes close ties with the government and is directly involved in the administration of certain social welfare activities though control of the *mutue* (social welfare agencies) and close ties with agencies of social insurance, the individual farmer refuses to join the organisation at his great peril. (LaPalombara, 1964: 149)

In other cases, the exchanges involved could be of a more personalistic kind as is apparent from Graziano's description of the southern party boss who:

> . . . almost literally lived in the streets, ready to help out the poor worker who had an ill daughter, the unemployed with huge families, and needy people in general, for whom he used to organise impressive Christmas banquets to which the Bishop was invited. (Graziano, 1973: 22)

*favors for votes*

He would typically act as an intermediary, using his connections on behalf of local people to obtain the intervention of powerful political figures in Rome to resolve their problems (ibid.: 22). The resources provided in exchange for these favours were, of course, votes.

In his analysis of *Politics and Society in Post-war Naples*, Percy Allum (1973b) vividly recounts how clientelism operated in connection with the parties' control of local government. Elected local councils have the right to appoint representatives to local banks and to municipally owned public utilities. Local politicians also control 'the fixing of local taxes, the awarding of public contracts, the enforcement of health and security regulations, the granting or withholding of licences to do certain types of business'. Clearly, then, the scope for patronage is enormous and, especially in areas like post-war Naples where private economic activity was limited and public funds thus more important than elsewhere, one could be sure that, in the management of this largesse, local politicians would 'stipulate conditions which enhance their power' (ibid.: 163). A common condition seems to have been the provision of employment for party workers. In a context such as Naples, where unemployment was (and still is) rife, the ability to influence hirings in this way was a source of considerable power. First it '[ensured] a supply of party workers whose loyalty to the party cause [could] be controlled to some extent because of their fear of losing their jobs if they [ratted]'. More importantly, however:

> . . . the positions are strategic because they bring their holders into contact with groups outside the direct influence of the party. Party activists can, thus, influence others of their group as the DC worker revealed: 'I can speak freely, someone else belonging to another party cannot make propaganda . . . nobody prohibits me from doing so.' (ibid.: 162)

In the final analysis, all of this happens because politicians seek to manage public resources specifically as an effective means of maintaining their own power – and it *is* effective because it is, by definition, individualistic and thus undermines the possibilities of collective action among those to whom it is directed. However, before any of it can happen, of course, the aspiring politician has to acquire a position that will give him access to resources in the first place. This, Allum's analysis continues, is done by acquiring a following or *clientela* – in other words, people who can be counted upon to vote either for the politician himself or for another person whom the politician is known to support. In the first place building a *clientela* gives influence over the votes of one's relatives (a number that can become quite large once relatives of relatives are taken into account). Then it means acquiring a position as a local party official, thereby bringing the politician into direct contact with higher-level elected politicians, such as mayors and local councillors, with resources under their immediate control. This allows the politician to expand his following even further using his contacts to do favours for supplicants and, in return, placing the votes of his following at the disposal of the higher-level politicians with whom he has connections. Thus the politician comes to find himself in an informal pyramidal structure of networks in which the level of his position depends essentially on his skill in the distribution of favours he is able to carry out.

## The Spread of Corruption

As thus practised, clientelism encouraged the emergence and spread of corruption, understood as:

> . . . a secret violation of a contract that, implicitly or explicitly, involves a delegation of responsibility and the exercise of some discretionary power . . . (2) by an *agent* who, against the interests or preferences of the *principal* . . . (3) acts in favour of a *third party*, from whom he receives a reward . . . Focusing on political and bureaucratic corruption in a democratic regime, we should add a fourth condition, (4) the principal is the state, or, better, the citizens. (Della Porta and Vannucci, 1997: 231–2)

Clientelism encouraged corruption because it had few 'incentives to remain within the confines of what is lawful and [was] at the same time subject to continuous pressures to cross the threshold of legality (Calise, 1994, quoted by Cazzola and Morisi, 1996: 20). That is, since clientelism involves particularistic exchanges, it by definition involves the supply of goods or services not sanctioned by the rules otherwise applied to members of the category to which the person receiving such goods and services belongs. It therefore embodies an arbitrary exercise of power in the sense that it is not limited by the enforcement of commonly accepted, universalistic, rules. Since its exercise is not rule-bound, where clientelism is the predominant form of the management of power relations the emergence of competitors creates an incentive for established politicians to do whatever is necessary to weaken such competitors (on pain of being weakened themselves) including having recourse to corruption.[3]

If these factors ensured the *supply* of corrupt acts, a *demand* for corruption was created by the same suspicion and mistrust that facilitated clientelism. Since suspicion and mistrust are self-reinforcing, they result in a great proliferation of state-sanctioned rules and regulations designed to compensate for the society's inability to regulate interaction on the basis of *in*formal norms of reciprocity. The administrative inefficiency created by the proliferation of rules and regulations stimulates a demand for the application of special 'fast-track' procedures which officials are then able to 'sell' in return for back-handers.

Once corruption has emerged, it tends to spread in a self-generating way, because of the needs politicians have to fulfil if corrupt exchanges are to be concluded successfully. These needs are of three kinds: the need to gain access to positions which will allow the politician to influence public decisions in the first place; the need to ensure that the third parties for whom he acts respect their side of any agreements; and the need to secure the silence of those who might otherwise report him to the authorities.

The first need was normally met by building up a *clientela* – whose size was measurable in terms of the number of party cards and preference votes the politician was able to control – within the party of which he was a member. Such a following could then be traded with faction leaders for appointment to public positions which could be exploited by exchanging bribes for public works contracts and other abuses of responsibility and discretion. Part of the illicit proceeds could then be invested in the acquisition of even larger clientele followings (for example, by paying the subscription fees of party members) which in turn could be traded for still further positions. Thus the power of the corrupt politician was self-reinforcing.

The second need arises from the illegality of the corrupt exchange, a circumstance which makes it impossible for the politician to use the authorities to force his client to pay, should the latter decide to cheat. Although the coercive power of the state is unavailable, the coercion offered by organized crime may be, however. This was a significant feature of corruption in southern Italy. In a context characterized by low levels of trust and where the state's protection either is, or is perceived to be weak, organized crime was able to produce and sell private protection as a black-market good used to underpin transactions by discouraging cheating and to provide a means of settling disputes. In such circumstances, the corrupt politician would receive, from organized crime, the services of the threat of physical violence in exchange for which he would give protection from the threat of intervention by the judicial authorities.[4]

The need to obtain the silence of outsiders to the corrupt transaction may be met either by the exchange of silence for the provision of a legal or illegal benefit (such as a share of the bribe itself), or else through the outsider's fear of the consequences of failing to keep silent – a fear which might, for example, be induced by using organized crime connections to establish a semi-public reputation for being 'dangerous'. Once corruption has spread to a certain point, little specific may need to be done to induce such fear: either a general climate of intimidation will be sufficient or else corruption will have become so routine that it is impossible to get anything done without it. For example, Della Porta and Vannucci (1994: 224–8) cite business managers who, in explaining their attitudes towards corrupt behaviour sought to justify the payment of bribes by saying that since everyone did it, they had to too if they were to meet their obligations to their workers and shareholders. In this way, the managers were able to preserve their self-images as moral individuals, saying, in effect, that reporting requests for bribes to the authorities was all very well, but that legal procedures in Italy were lengthy, and, in addition to a duty to uphold the law, they also had a duty towards their enterprises.

*Corruption commonplace*

Thus, corruption is self-generating. The further it spreads, the less willing people are to report it to the authorities. The less willing people are to report it, the fewer are the risks it involves; and the fewer the risks it involves the less likely it is that the anticipated costs will outweigh the anticipated benefits for other individuals contemplating corrupt exchanges. As these individuals too are drawn into networks of corrupt exchange, so it becomes more difficult to eliminate the phenomenon because the resources available to investigate it have to be deployed more thinly. This in turn lowers the moral and material costs of corruption even more, and so the phenomenon spreads still further. Not surprisingly then, by the time the *Tangentopoli* scandals first exploded in February 1992 (and as the investigations appeared subsequently to confirm), political corruption seemed to have spread to the point where it had become routine in certain areas of public life and to the point where Ginsborg (1995: 3) could express the view that Italy was 'one of the most corrupt democracies in Europe'.

Reflecting this spread was the dramatic growth in the numbers of *reported* instances of political corruption that has been documented by Cazzola (1988). From the mid-1970s reported crimes of corruption and embezzlement involving the public administration rose from 412 in

1975 to 1065 in 1985. Meanwhile annual averages rose from 514 for 1963–75 to 681 for 1976–78 to 808 for 1979–86. As regards press reports of corruption, the influential national daily, *la Repubblica*, carried reports of 117 separate cases of political corruption between 1976 and 1979; 110 between 1979 and 1983; and 208 between 1983 and 1986 (ibid.: 67). Of the 272 cases of parliamentarians accused of political corruption and against whom the judicial authorities moved requests for the lifting of parliamentary immunity between 1945 and 1987, there were 101 cases involving a total of 619 billion lire at 1986 values. If this left 171 cases for which the relevant figures were unavailable, then this probably suggests, as Cazzola himself notes, that the foregoing sum constituted not even the visible part of the corruption iceberg but only a very small portion of that part (ibid.: 138).

## The *Tangentopoli* Investigations

On 17 February 1992 Mario Chiesa, the Socialist head of a Milanese old people's home, the Pio Albergo Trivulzio, was arrested 'in the act of taking a 7m lire ($4000) bribe from the owner of a cleaning company' (Gilbert, 1995: 126). A high-living individual, Chiesa was almost a caricature of the 'business politicians' who had come to dominate the internal life of the governing parties during the 1980s: that is, a person with little or no sense of civic morality, with an almost exclusively instrumental attitude to politics, with virtually no ideological or programmatic commitments to speak of, and having a semi-public reputation for arrogance as well as a special ability to operate 'in the shadows' (Della Porta, 1996). As a business politician, Chiesa had built his career through the skilful combination of corruption and the clientele practices described earlier. As head of the Pio Albergo Trivulzio, he was also in charge of the large number of properties owned by this institution, a circumstance that had allowed him to establish stable, but corrupt, relations with the firms with which he did business and thus to further his career by collecting bribes and building command of a personal packet of votes among the firms' employees. His ambition was to consolidate and extend his position such that he might one day lay claim to the position of Mayor of Milan. This required him to ingratiate himself with Bettino Craxi, the PSI leader. Unfortunately for Chiesa, Craxi did not appear to have as high a regard for the health manager as the latter, outwardly at least, had for him and when Craxi refused to help Chiesa, publicly dismissing him as a *mariuolo* ('little rascal') – which he had an incentive to do in order to create the impression that the whole affair was merely an isolated incident (Della Porta, 1993: 221) – Chiesa decided to empty the sack. His confession set off a domino effect as his naming of names led others to confess and they in their turn to do likewise. In this way it quickly brought to light a massive network of 'mutually beneficial linkages' (Waters, 1994: 170) between the political parties and powerful economic groups in the city.

The investigations really began to take off in May once the general election was over and investigating magistrates knew that they would be less exposed to the risk of being accused of political interference. On 3 May the Milanese public prosecutor's office issued requests for the lifting of the parliamentary immunity of the ex-Mayors of Milan, Carlo Tognoli and Paolo Pilittieri, and by the middle of the month the notorious *avvisi di garanzia* advising them that they were under judicial investigation had been received by the DC's administrative secretary, Severino Citaristi, and by the leader of the Republican group in the Chamber of Deputies, Antonio Del Pennino. Meanwhile, in Milan, the investigations quickly spread from the Pio Albergo Trivulzio to the municipal transport company, to the *Ente Comunale di Assistenza*, to the Sacco and Fatebenefratelli hospitals, to the airport authority, to the *Piccolo Teatro*, and revealed bribes ranging from those in connection with the 2000 billion lire contract for the realization of the airport project, Malpensa 2000, to the 100 000 lire back-handers paid by the undertakers working for the Pio Albergo Trivulzio (Della Porta, 1993: 220). One of the most singular features of the *tangenti* system to be revealed by the investigations was the way in which otherwise opposed parties would collude in the share-out of bribe money – a practice which helped the politicians of each party obtain the silence and complicity of representatives of each of the others. Thus, when the PDS politician, Sergio Soave was arrested in May, he explained to the investigating magistrates that the division of bribe money resulting from the award of contracts by the municipal transport company took place according to the relative 'weight' of each party on the governing board (Della Porta, 1993: 230; Colaprico, 1996: 21–2).

By mid-July arrest warrants had been issued in Florence and the Veneto and, with the issue of an *avviso* to ex-Foreign Secretary, Gianni De Michelis, and the arrest of the builder, Salvatore Ligresti, the investigations had begun to involve politicians and businessmen of the very highest rank. In the history of *Tangentopoli* 15 December 1992 was to become an unforgettable date. It saw an officer of the *carabinieri* deliver to the luxury suite of the hotel Raphael in Rome an *avviso di garanzia* addressed to the Socialist leader, Bettino Craxi, himself. Among the charges were that he had conspired with the PSI's administrative secretary, Vincenzo Balzamo, to receive bribes in connection with contracts issued for the building of the third line of the Milanese underground system. Craxi's defence was to argue that he was being made to account for matters that were the responsibility of the administrative branch of the party – a defence whose plausibility was weakened by the tightness of the control which the Socialist leader notoriously exercised over his party. When, in January, it was claimed by magistrates that a large part of the money raised by the PSI in Milan had in fact been paid over not to Balzamo but to Craxi's personal friend, Silvano Larini, the former's position began to look very precarious indeed. Finally, in February, Larini confessed that he had acted as an intermediary between Craxi's Milan office and the business community of the city for the payment of bribes and the Socialist leader was forced to resign (Gilbert, 1995: 136–7).

In March it was the turn of the ranking politicians of the DC and the other governing parties. Towards the end of the month an *avviso di garanzia* was served on no less a figure than the Health Minister, the PLI's Francesco De Lorenzo. Keeping him company were: former Interior Minister Antonio Gava; Enzo Scotti, who had resigned as Foreign Secretary the previous July; Paolo Cirino Pomicino, one-time Minister of the Budget; Giulio Di Donato, one-time Vice-Secretary of the PSI. Finally, on 27 March, with the accusation of *Mafia* involvement, it was the turn of the 'boss of bosses', the former DC Prime Minister, Giulio Andreotti, himself. By the end of 1993 no fewer than 251 members of parliament were under judicial investigation, including four former prime ministers, five ex-party leaders, and seven members of the Amato cabinet. Ten suspects had killed themselves (Bull and Newell, 1995: 74; Nelken, 1996: 109). As each day brought news of increasingly well known names having been caught up in the tidal wave of scandal, a single event on 29 April symbolized the effect of *Tangentopoli* in delegitimizing the entire 1992 legislature. On that day, parliament refused to grant the magistrates' request to lift Bettino Craxi's parliamentary immunity in connection with four of the six charges he then faced. As Craxi himself continued to insist that he was a scapegoat and the victim of a plot since all parties had taken illicit contributions to finance their activities, a flood of street protests and letters, telephone calls and faxes to national newspapers demonstrated popular derision and disgust at parliament's decision. As Craxi left his Rome residence to attend a television interview he was greeted by a hostile crowd throwing small coins and chanting '*Buffone!, Buffone!*'[5] – an incident which stood as a metaphor for the fate of an entire political class.

How was the *Tangentopoli* phenomenon to be explained? Part of the answer rests on the nature of the institution to which the investigating magistrates belonged, for it is an institution whose mode of functioning provides scope for considerable judicial activism. First, the judiciary enjoys considerable external and internal independence. External independence from other branches of government is guaranteed by the *Consiglio Superiore della Magistratura* (the Higher Council of the Judiciary) which is the body responsible for all matters to do with the recruitment, promotion and discipline of members of the judiciary, and 20 of whose 33 members are elected from among members of the judiciary themselves. Internal independence is ensured by the fact that each public prosecutor's office is autonomous of every other office. Second, the three phases of criminal procedure in Italy arguably provide for an imperfect separation of the functions of judge and prosecutor – a feature which, it is often argued, allows investigating magistrates to use their powers for political purposes.

The first phase of Italian criminal procedure, known as the pre-instruction phase, consists of preliminary investigations carried out by the *pubblico ministero* ('public prosecutor'), to ascertain whether the facts of which he has been notified disclose the elements of a crime and therefore whether it is necessary to proceed to the instruction phase. This phase (carried out either by the *pubblico ministero* or by an examining judge) involves the collection and analysis of evidence designed to ascertain whether there are sufficient grounds to warrant proceeding to the third, or trial, phase and results either in a decision to acquit the accused or to send him or her to trial. A number of features characterize the trial. First, there is no jury – inadmissible in the Italian legal system 'because the unreasoned verdict of the traditional jury would fail to comply with the Constitutional requirement that all judicial decisions must be reasoned' (Certoma, 1985: 225–6); second, proceedings tend to be dominated by the results of the instruction phase (since the main body of evidence on which the court bases its decision is the written evidence emerging from the instruction phase and it may not be in a position to know what weight to give to the interpretative and filtering processes of the author of that evidence); third, witnesses are examined by the judge and there is no cross-examination. Hence, the claim that there is an imperfect separation between judge and prosecutor. During the instruction phase, judge and prosecutor are materially joined in the person of the examining judge and it is the latter who must decide whether to acquit the accused or to proceed to the third phase. In this phase, although judge and prosecutor are not literally joined (for the examining judge may not also form part of the bench at the trial) they are arguably one and the same for all practical purposes: on the one hand, the proceedings are so overshadowed by the results of the previous phase that they represent little more than its 'formal confirmation' (Certoma, 1985: 243); on the other hand, examining judges and trial judges 'still belong to the same body and usually work in neighbouring offices' (di Federico, 1989, 31). This, it is argued, allows members of the judiciary to use their offices for political purposes by virtue of the risk that the convictions as to guilt or innocence held by the judicial officer in his role as prosecutor so influence the view of the case that he takes in his role as judge, that the proceedings are heavily influenced from the outset.

Such broad judicial powers make it natural to ask why *Tangentopoli* unfolded when it did and not before; after all, the exposure of corruption was nothing new in Italy, nor were attempts by the judiciary to use its powers to combat it. Indeed, largely owing to the influx of a new generation of younger magistrates from the early 1970s, a novel interpretation of the judge's role had gained ground within the judiciary: from being a passive *bouche de la loi* (Guarnieri, 1997: 158) the judge was to adopt a far more active stance and – through penal initiatives in the areas of workplace safety, environmental pollution, tax evasion, fraud, corruption and so forth – to act as a 'problem-solver', attempting to tackle the great social issues of the day (di Federico, 1989: 33).

A significant factor in explaining the timing of *Tangentopoli* seems to be the outcome of the 1992 general election which made it clear to investigating magistrates that they were likely to have the solid backing of public opinion. It must be remembered that, in the city where the investigations started, the DC and PSI vote fell from 24.4 and 18.6 to 16.3 and 13.2 per cent respectively while the League, whose own perceived *raison d'être* was the struggle against the clientelism and corruption of the Rome-based *partitocrazia*, exploded from 0.7 to 18.1 per cent to become the largest party in the city (Colaprico, 1996: 16). Results such as these were unheard of in post-war Italy and it is difficult to believe that they did not have an effect. The overall context in which they took place – especially the fact they immediately followed the end of the all-important 'communist issue', the striking advance of the League in the 1990 regional elections and the crushing defeat of preference voting in the 1991 referendum despite Bettino Craxi's explicit invitation to Italians to spend the day of the referendum vote by the seaside[6] – must have decisively influenced editorialists and journalists in keeping the progress of the investigations at the forefront of public attention day after day after day.

> The constant stream of revelations kept public interest high and the party leaderships on the defensive. Craxi, especially, was not accustomed to being in the humiliating position of having constantly to reply to charges, and to having the political agenda set by others. (Gilbert, 1995: 135)

The support of public opinion was crucial, for it ensured that, as the investigations gathered momentum, the threat that the politicians would be able to defend themselves using their powers of *insabbiamento* diminished. *Insabbiamento* is a term meaning, literally, 'covering with sand', and it is used to refer to informal processes whereby, despite the legal powers available to the judiciary, politicians had in the past been able to manipulate proceedings in politically sensitive cases so as to avoid personally undesirable outcomes. Much of the power of *insabbiamento* derived from the informal relations of connivance which politicians had been able to establish with individual members of the judiciary whereby judicial favours could be exchanged for political favours.[7] Given such relations, the hierarchical organization of the judiciary could be used – via marginalization, transferral or pressure by superiors more sensitive to 'political needs' (Della Porta, 1998: 11) – to curb the activities of excessively zealous junior magistrates:[8]

> Those, such as Judge Carlo Palermo, who initiated investigations which brought them too close to centrally organised plots involving networks of politicians, masons and organised criminals met fierce resistance; the case would be taken from their hands to be given to a colleague or taken over by another court. Just as in the fight against 'Organised Crime', troublesome judges could find themselves moved by disciplinary proceedings to other parts of Italy and the policemen working with them could be transferred even more easily at the will of their respective Ministries; they became targets for defamation or even assassination. (Nelken, 1996: 98, quoted by Della Porta, 1998: 11)

A second factor helping one to understand why *Tangentopoli* unfolded when it did rather than earlier is the simple fact that, in 1992, the corruption to be exposed was more extensive than it had been in previous decades. The suicide note written by the Socialist deputy Sergio Moroni, who killed himself on 2 September 1992 having been accused of receiving numerous bribes for public works contracts, provides a vivid impression of the sheer pervasiveness of the corrupt system at work.

> An enormous veil of hypocrisy (shared by all) has for many years shrouded the mode of functioning of the parties and the means whereby they have been financed. The establishment of regulations and laws that one knows cannot be respected is a typically Italian way of doing things – one that is inspired by the tacit assumption that at the same time it will be possible to agree upon the establishment of procedures and behaviours which, however, violate the very same regulations ...
> I began my political activity in the PSI when I was very young, only 17 years of age. I still remember passionately many political and ideological battles, *but I made a mistake in accepting the 'system', believing that accepting contributions and help for the party was justified in a context in which this was the normal practice.* .... (Colaprico, 1996: 31–2; author's translation and emphasis)

By their very nature, corrupt transactions require the development of a degree of trust which is very difficult to establish and yet very easy to break. Hence, as Nelken points out, once the silent collusion, or *omertà*, between bribe-takers and bribe-givers had been broken, the entire system was almost bound to unravel 'as politicians, administrators and, more often, businessmen scrambled to explain or to "confess" their account of the part they had played' (Nelken, 1996: 104).

A third explanatory factor is the end of the Cold War and the crisis of the PCI. This meant that investigating magistrates could now attack the governing class without the risk that, in so doing, they would thereby enhance the likelihood of the Communists coming to power. In the Cold War climate of the initial post-war years, the judiciary gave every indication of sympathizing with conservative political views and therefore of supporting the governing parties' interests. At least until the 1960s, most highest-ranking judges had been socialized under fascism (Della Porta, 1998: 5). From the early 1970s things began to change: while remaining predominantly 'moderate' in its political outlooks – *Magistratura Democratica*[9] could still only count on 24 per cent of the votes in elections to the *Consiglio Superiore della Magistratura* as late as 1994 (Guarnieri, 1997: 163) – the judiciary became willing to take a more activist stance on social problems whose inevitable political implications did not always work in the governing parties' favour (Cazzola and Morisi, 1996: 31). Meanwhile, the PCI under Berlinguer, a man noted for the highest personal integrity, had made the so-called 'moral question' one of its own great battle cries. If this suggested that judicial anti-corruption crusades were likely to play directly into the PCI's hands, it was by the same token a reasonable supposition that legal initiatives in the area might increase once the communist 'threat' had gone.[10] Thus Della Porta refers to 'a weakening in the attitude of complicity of some judges with political forces' in the late 1980s and the 1990s as a new generation of '*giudici ragazzini*' ('child judges') 'began a series of investigations into administrative and political misconduct' (Della Porta, 1998: 8).

The final factor was an increased willingness of entrepreneurs to collaborate in the investigations – again, partly due to the collapse of communism. Thus, Calise refers to a willingness of several of the largest national private corporations 'to co-operate in disclosing their bribes', something that was due to an awareness that for the first time in 45 years they 'could foster a crisis of the political system without risking [their] own survival' (1993: 556). Another apparently significant factor in conditioning entrepreneurs' attitudes, however, was the rising cost of corruption, which, by the early 1990s had, for many, ceased to be sustainable. Della Porta (1993) describes what seems to have been an impossible situation for some of the businesses involved in corrupt networks. On the one hand, the system was so well developed that the entrepreneur could not afford not to accede to it: to refuse to pay bribes was to risk being cut out of the charmed circle of the enterprises which until then had survived and prospered as a result of their privileged relationships with the controllers of public funds. On the other hand, the need for greater competitiveness, especially as a result of the continuing process of European integration, meant that politicians began to have fewer favours to dispense. As one entrepreneur put it:

> The enterprises would pay but the politicians were no longer able to help them. All of them, whether large or small, ended up in the same boat and so one would pay more in order to undermine the others: it was an infernal mechanism. It was pointless . . . . Public funds gradually diminished and the number of aspiring firms increased. (Della Porta, 1993: 236)

## The Effects of *Tangentopoli*

With variable timing, the *Tangentopoli* investigations virtually destroyed all five of the traditional governing parties which were able to survive only in much reduced form (as was the case with the PRI, for example) or else as new parties under different names having in the meantime suffered a number of acrimonious splits (as was the case with the DC and the PSI). The damage inflicted by *Tangentopoli* was financial, organizational and electoral. Financially, the investigations eliminated major sources of funding by disrupting the illegal system of party financing associated with corruption. Organizationally, the investigations fatally undermined the membership bases of the parties while creating divisions and splits among party leaders who sought desperately to find a way out of the crisis. Electorally, the investigations led to unprecedented losses of voting support.

The financial impact of the investigations was straightforward. During the 1970s and 1980s the parties had become increasingly dependent on corrupt forms of funding (despite the passage of measures such as Law 195/74 designed to eliminate them) while at the same time facing mounting accumulated debts.[11] Therefore, by reducing the amounts available from illegal sources of financing to just a trickle, the investigations pushed all the traditional parties fairly quickly towards bankruptcy. In the spring of 1993, PSI indebtedness was placed by resigning party secretary Benvenuto at 160 billion lire. Other official sources placed the total debt at about 130 billion lire, while unofficial estimates placed it at 300 billion lire. The historical Via del Corso headquarters in Rome were put up for sale, as were most PSI real estate possessions. By May that year, when the leadership of the collapsing party was passed on to Ottaviano Del Turco, the day-to-day functioning of the party ground to a halt when, due to unpaid bills, the party's telephones and electricity were cut off. This state of affairs was paralleled in the Social Democratic Party (PSDI) where the resignation of its secretary, Carlo Vizzini, in March was provoked in part by the party's bankruptcy. Vizzini – who soon became caught up himself in the burgeoning investigations – had discovered that the rent on the party's headquarters had not been paid for years and that, with debts amounting to 20 billion lire, public finance had been going straight to the Banco di Napoli, the party's principal creditor (Rhodes, 1997).

The second effect of *Tangentopoli* was to wreak havoc on the parties' organizations thus bringing about their virtual disintegration. The spread of corruption itself had considerably weakened the parties' organizational structures by raising the relative value of given characteristics and abilities and downgrading others. In particular it favoured the recruitment of individuals with all those personal skills necessary in order to create and consolidate networks of relationships based on mutual obligations – discretion, tact, pragmatism, affability – while leading to correspondingly less emphasis on the technical and intellectual abilities required for administration and the elaboration of policy programmes, and penalizing ideological commitment (which might have threatened the spread of corruption itself). If ideology and policy programmes had therefore become less salient features of the internal life of parties, this then affected the motives for joining them in the first place, creating a vicious circle whereby a gradual decline in the numbers of ideologically committed members tended to reduce the attractiveness of membership for those with similar ideological beliefs. Equally, the growth in the number of members whose motives were venal tended to make membership more attractive for those of like mind. Furthermore, the growth in the extent to which the internal life of parties was based on relationships of an instrumental kind weakened them organizationally by virtue of the concomitant decline in the reserves of loyalty and commitment. Hence, when *Tangentopoli* destroyed the basis for such instrumental relationships by effectively cutting off the flow of resources that sustained them, it left the parties vulnerable to complete collapse. In addition, even those members who were motivated by shared values rather than material concerns were likely to resign as a result of the alienation caused by the revelation of matters of which they had been kept ignorant. Emblematic in this regard was the reception given to Gianni De Michelis, Deputy General Secretary of the PSI, at a party meeting in Venice in September 1992:

> Outside, the 'Venetian socialists for renewal' distributing leaflets 'to restore honour to a party dishonoured by a minority in the pursuit of their personal interests'. Inside, other socialists protesting in the way the radicals protest: in silence and by raising placards: 'Let's suspend the suspects from the PSI: no to De Michelis as deputy general secretary'. And in the middle, him: Gianni De Michelis. On the contrary, the De Michelis affair. That is, the extraordinary event of the Socialist 'doge' challenged by the socialists of his own Venice; the unforseeable difficulty of this lord-protector forced to defend and justify himself; the unexpected vitality of a 'socialist rank-

and-file' taking advantage of a party meeting to shake off fear and subjection and rebel against the old leaders. (Geremicca, 1992: 3)

The sudden collapse of the parties is reflected in the dramatic decline in membership levels which, according to one estimate, went down from 3 804 000 in 1991 to 1 330 000 in 1993 when *Tangentopoli* was at its height (Follini, 1997a: 250).

Meanwhile, *Tangentopoli* created tensions and splits at leadership level. Once again, the PSI furnishes the best illustration. After Bettino Craxi had become caught up in the *Tangentopoli* investigations and was forced to resign as PSI general secretary in February 1993, the machinations of his followers were such as to prevent his successor, Giorgio Benvenuto, from establishing effective control over the party:

> Benvenuto had harshly criticised the decision by the Chamber of Deputies (backed by the crucial votes of many PSI deputies) to deny the judiciary the authority to try Bettino Craxi; a few weeks later PSI deputies openly defied Benvenuto's leadership when they voted against the choice of a single-member constituency two-ballot electoral system. (Bardi and Morlino, 1994: 274)

This led to Benvenuto's resignation. Meanwhile, disagreements over the party's basic strategy and how it would confront its growing difficulties had led to the emergence of three factions. One, called 'Socialist Renewal' and organized around Craxi's one-time dauphin, Claudio Martelli, sought to associate the party with the growing movement to reform the electoral system and theorized a new alliance strategy that would include, besides the PDS, the lay, centre parties,[12] as well as greens and radicals. Opposed to all this were those who remained faithful to Craxi and, thirdly, there was a smaller grouping which, while critical of Craxi, distanced itself from Martelli's proposed new alliance strategy. The turmoil thus created led to the first signs of the party's base breaking up as its regional organizations reacted to the confusion by beginning autonomously to implement their own electoral alliances in preparation for the regional elections of June 1993. From then on, the party simply entered a downward spiral from which it became impossible to recover. As almost every day seemed to bring fresh corruption allegations against senior party figures, party activists began resigning in their hundreds. Split down the middle over the electoral reform referendum in April, in the June local elections the party's vote-share declined to 2 per cent from the 17 per cent it had obtained in the local elections of 1990. The *coup de grâce* came at the beginning of August with passage of the new electoral law which meant that the party would finally have to decide where it would position itself within the system of electoral alliances that began to take shape for the general election which everyone knew would be held within a matter of months. Hopelessly divided, over the ensuing months the party broke up into Giorgio Benvenuto's *Rinascita Socialista* (Socialist Renewal), Del Turco's PSI and thirdly, the *Craxiani*.

The DC's experience was no less torrid. As the *Tangentopoli* investigations spread (bringing no less than 500 party functionaries and a quarter of the party's parliamentary representatives under investigation (Wertman, 1994: 121)), the DC's national council reacted by electing a new secretary, Mino Martinazzoli. However, obstructed by the powerful factions, Martinazzoli's attempts to exclude from the high-profile *direzione* some of the more compromised party figures failed to find the necessary majorities. He then attempted to reduce the power of the factions themselves by annulling all existing memberships and obliging members to rejoin by presenting themselves at local offices of the party in person – the idea being to thwart the attempts of factions to increase their voting strengths at congresses by enrolling inactive members on a clientelistic basis. But while large numbers of committed members – especially in the North – refused to rejoin as a gesture of protest against the party's degenerative condition, in areas with the highest proportions of 'clientele members', the reform was simply not implemented by the local officialdom (Wertman, 1994: 127). In January 1994 the party changed its name to *Partito Popolare Italiano* (PPI) (recalling the name of its pre-fascist predecessor) while a (smaller) conservative grouping which took the name *Centro Cristiano Democratico* (CCD) left the party altogether to become an ally of Silvio Berlusconi and the *Alleanza Nazionale* in the *Polo delle Libertà*. And, as befitted a party whose 'ideology' was essentially a 'patchwork', there were other breakaways. Thus, besides the CCD, there were the Social Christians (C-S), led by Ermanno Gorrieri and formed by the progressive left-wing of the party, who surfaced as part of the Progressive Alliance at the 1994 elections; and there was Mario Segni, the leader of the referenda movement, who, having left the DC in spring 1993 and after numerous changes of strategy, finally led his followers (in the 'Pact for National Renewal' more commonly known as the 'Segni Pact') into an alliance with the PPI – an alliance which presented itself at the 1994 election as the 'Pact for Italy'.

Finally, then, the *Tangentopoli* investigations led to a haemorrhage of electoral support for all the traditional parties of government. Having already in 1992 polled its lowest share of the vote at any general election in the post-war period, by November 1993 DC support, at 11 per cent, stood at less than a third of its post-war average. The PSI's collapse was such as to reduce it to the small change of electoral politics, but none of the traditional governing parties was spared. The dynamic of their downward spiral was illustrated in the previous chapter by the figures contained in Table 2.2 (page 27). Facing the breakaways of local federations and the desertion of members *en masse*, after June

1993, the five parties from which governments had continuously been drawn since 1945 had largely ceased to exist as credible political forces. An analysis of the emergence and growth of the political forces that were to replace them is a task which we undertake in Chapters 4 and 5.

## Notes

1   For an analysis of how the transition from clientelism of the notables to party-directed patronage took place, see Graziano (1973).
2   Cotta (1996: 16) is unhappy with the concept of *partitocrazia*, arguing that its derogatory connotations make it unsatisfactory for descriptive purposes. Although the attempt to describe using heavily evaluative terms *is* problematic, evidently this has not stopped political scientists using such equally loaded terms as 'democracy' and 'democratization' with gay abandon. It is also true, as Cotta's argument implies, that if one retains the term *partitocrazia*, one must be able to say how it differs from straightforward *party government*. In my view, the reality which the concept of *partitocrazia*, unlike 'party government', captures is: (a) the need for a party card to obtain certain administrative positions and the identification of each individual interest group with only one party, 'either as a structure conditioning what the party does or as a mere instrumentality and extension of the party itself' (LaPalombara, 1964: 97); this (b) as a means of distributing resources on a particularistic basis and as a result of which (c) parties lose their aggregative capacities becoming vehicles for the mere articulation of demands. That, in the long run, all this weakens and undermines parties (a fact which is obscured by uses of *partitocrazia* which emphasize the notion of *subordination* of sectors of state and society to party control) is something with which I entirely agree and which is the main thrust of my argument in this chapter.
3   As Graziano puts it: 'Whenever a new actor appears in the political market of the South and is provided with a sufficiently threatening bargaining power, the ruling party has the instinctive reaction of a monopolist: first it tries to intimidate the newcomer and if unsuccessful to corrupt him' (1973: 26).
4   By its very nature, the threat of violence supplied by organized crime can be made to serve a wide range of the corrupt politician's purposes including those whose connection with the corrupt exchange itself is only indirect – for example, the intimidation of political rivals. However, the ability of organized crime to wield violence has a variety of implications which, paradoxically, may serve to reduce the scale of corruption; for the threat of violence can in principle be used to coerce politicians themselves. For example, from around the early 1980s, the Sicilian *Mafia* turned its attention to the field of public works contracts – an area that was particularly lucrative since the state accounted for a very large proportion of the total demand in the building sector. By forming cartels, building firms were able to coordinate their bids and thus control the award of contracts, taking it in turns to obtain contracts and dividing earnings among themselves on a pre-agreed basis. In exchange for an appropriate share of such earnings the *Mafia* would underwrite the relevant agreements by using the threat of violence to discourage possible defectors and any new entrants who might refuse to join the cartel. In such circumstances politicians were in a weaker position to extract bribes since the collusion involved in the *Mafia*-organized cartel itself was sufficient to protect firms from the potentially destructive competition of rivals.
5   A word which conveys far more contempt than its English equivalent, 'buffoon'.

6   Referenda are declared null and void if less than 50 per cent of those having the right to vote participate – so Craxi's intention was obvious.

7   A typical example of the kind of relationship that could be struck up between politicians and members of the judiciary is given by the career of Claudio Vitalone:

> According to the boss of the Roman DC Vittorio Sbardella, the career of Claudio Vitalone, ex-magistrate, senator and DC minister closely associated with Andreotti, resulted from a transaction between the two men: 'Since Vitalone had no electoral or political support of his own he got Andreotti's support by performing miracles in order to get him politically advantageous results by judicial means. What I mean is you can do something which will gain the appreciation of a politician either by judicial favours for their friends and supporters or, on the other hand, damaging political personalities who might inconvenience your friend judicially' ... Claudio Martelli, justice minister in Andreotti's final government, stated: 'Claudio Vitalone was a man very close to Andreotti who had, at the same time, considerable influence in Roman judicial circles; not just in the Roman Public Prosecutor's office but also among judging magistrates and the Court of Cassation. You could say that Vitalone was the "long arm" of Andreotti in judicial circles.' (Della Porta, 1998: 10)

8   Collusion between politicians and judges was arguably also encouraged by the mode of operation of the *Consiglio Superiore della Magistratura*. The fact that 20 of its 33 members are elected by members of the judiciary as a whole *whatever their rank* has given rise to a tendency for it to take decisions according to political, rather than hierarchical, criteria – a tendency that has been further encouraged by the fact that ten of the 33 members are elected by parliament. Thus most members of the judiciary belong to one of four organized factions, each of which has a clearly identifiable location on the left–right spectrum: from *Magistratura Democratica* on the left through *Movimento per la Giustizia*, *Unità per la Costituzione* and *Magistratura Indipendente* on the right. As a consequence, though the factions were not formally linked to the parties, matters such as the distribution of resources, disciplinary sanctions and transfers from one judicial office to another became highly political issues on which individual members of the judiciary had an incentive to ally themselves with one party or the other.

9   See above, note 8.

10  In this connection it is significant that most of the corruption scandals of the early post-war years were the result, as Galli (1991) shows, not of judicial initiatives but of attempts by the members of one governing-party faction to gain advantage by blackmailing and implicating those of another.

11  The growing dependency of the parties on illegal financing during the 1970s and 1980s had a number of causes. First, Law No. 195 of 1974, which sought to regulate party finance in the wake of the previous year's oil scandal, outlawed donations to the parties from public companies, which, since the establishment of the Ministry of State Participation in 1956, had been significant sources of funds for the governing parties (Bardi and Morlino, 1994: 270). And, although the law provided for public funding, the available amounts could only be changed by means of legislation so that the law was insufficient to counteract pressures on the parties to gather ever higher sums of money deriving from other sources (Rhodes, 1977). These included rising costs associated with the 'media' and 'office revolutions' and changes in interparty relations. In particular, growth in the PSI's vote at a time when that of the DC was declining, increased the former's 'blackmail potential' in coalition formation, allowing it to exact a growing share of the public positions available through the system of *lottizzazione* and increasing the attractiveness of the party for a new type of politician, the 'business politician'

described earlier. As money increasingly became the key to success and to positions of power within the parties, competition between individuals and groups (encouraged by factionalism and the system of preference voting) soon gave rise to an inflationary dynamic whereby the pressure to obtain higher and higher amounts of illicit funding became, as a result, unremitting. Although accurate estimates of the sums involved are impossible to obtain for obvious reasons, it appears that by 1993, illegal financing of the parties was running at around 3400 billion lire per year (Rhodes, 1997).

12   That is, the smaller parties of the secular, democratic centre that had traditionally formed the DC's minor coalition allies: the PLI, the PRI and the PSDI.

# 4 Electoral Change and the Growth of the Northern League

The clientelism and corruption laid bare by the *Tangentopoli* investigations throw a spotlight on the role played by electoral change and the growth of the Northern League in bringing about the transformation of the Italian party system. First, if '[t]he development of a clientelist network in post-war Italy ... generated sustained electoral support' (Waters, 1994: 174), it also ensured that that support would be fragile: since clientele networks are based on instrumental relations, their maintenance is conditional on the continued supply of favours. Therefore, if the *other* bases of support for the traditional parties were to be undermined, then these parties would become especially vulnerable. The emergence and growth of the League was, as we shall see, directly related to this vulnerability. Second, the growth of the League played a crucial role in the unfolding of *Tangentopoli* itself: as Calise notes,

> ... it is difficult to imagine that Milan would have become the headquarters of judicial investigations of political corruption had not the once all-socialist capital of the old establishment been transformed into the very core of the Lombardy League's electoral and social power. (Calise, 1993: 556)

And once the investigations were under way, the League played a significant role in the electoral disintegration of the parties by providing a rallying cry and focal point for the remainder of the traditional parties' supporters who were now prepared to abandon their loyalties in the light of what the investigations had revealed.

The aim of this chapter is to explain the emergence and growth of the League. To do this, we begin by describing the principal factors conditioning Italian voting behaviour in the period after 1945 and then how these began to lose their strength from the mid-1970s onwards. This provided the essential precondition for the growth of the League – namely, a willingness of voters to stop voting for the established parties.

## Electoral Behaviour until the Mid-1970s

Prior to the dramatic events of the early 1990s observers were apt to comment on the apparent puzzle involved in the coexistence, within the Italian electorate, of numerous signs of political dissatisfaction with high, and stable, levels of support for the established parties. On the one hand, the Italian electorate was said to suffer from mistrust and resentment: 'alienation' (Almond and Verba, 1963), 'detachment' (Morlino and Tarchi, 1996), and low levels of 'civic awareness' (Ginsborg, 1994) were common expressions used to characterize the electorate. On the other hand, between 1948 and 1976, turnout at elections never fell below 92 per cent, while the party that might have been expected to be the principal victim of voters' dissatisfaction, the Christian Democrats, showed rock-like stability: if one excludes the 1948 election when it reached 48.5 per cent, support for the party varied between a high of 42.3 per cent (in 1958) and a low of 38.3 per cent (in 1963). Meanwhile, the PCI – the party seemingly most likely to benefit from any anti-government protest – was almost equally stable: it managed to increase its vote by only 4.5 per cent over the two decades between 1953 and 1972. In fact, this puzzle is easily explained.

Despite their dissatisfaction, Italian voters had stronger reasons to support the established parties than not to support them. One such reason was clientelism. If practised on a large scale, clientelism will by its nature tend to result in high levels of party *support* while at the same time sustaining discontent with *the way parties and institutions work*: from the individual citizen's point of view, support for a given party is worthwhile as long as resources continue to be forthcoming. However, because the resources are distributed in an arbitrary fashion and because it creates policy paralysis (in that it creates a whole series of vested interests each with a power of veto), the clientelistic management of power relations can only undermine confidence in political agents (parties and institutions) collectively. As Morlino and Tarchi put it:

> Italians have been accustomed to the dominance of the parties which they despise and regard as responsible for the malfunctioning of public life, but at the same time they seek their patronage whenever their personal interests are involved. (Morlino and Tarchi, 1996: 56)

Estimating the actual extent of clientelistic voting is extremely difficult. On the basis of the results of a 1985 survey Mannheimer and Sani (1987: 58) suggested that approximately 20 per cent of respondents' expressed motives for choice of party could be taken as indicative of 'exchange voting'.[1] However, in surveys people tend to find it much easier to claim that they vote in order to resolve the country's problems than to admit that their vote is given in order to receive a favour. Thus, it may be, as Cartocci (1990: 115) suggests, that the rate of preference voting (where 'rate of preference voting' refers to the number of preference votes cast as a percentage of the number of preference votes possible) constitutes the best available indicator of the presence of clientele ties between candidates and voters.[2] On this basis, it would appear that as many as 35.5 per cent of votes cast for the DC in 1979 – and, indeed, as many as 44.9 per cent and 52.8 per cent of such votes in the central and southern regions – could be traced to clientelistic motives (Cartocci, 1990: 116). These are impressive figures by any standards.

A second factor which long constrained the overt manifestation of dissatisfaction was the Cold War-induced, 'Christ or communism', ideological conflict. Since it concerns the fundamental characteristics of the polity, ideological conflict presents the voter with a choice not of alternative *programmes*, but of alternative *systems*, and thus tends to be non-negotiable. Indeed, when fundamental ideological questions are the basis of the alternatives presented, the voter tends to feel that he or she does not really have a 'choice' at all, so vast is the change in his system of assumptions and beliefs that a switch to 'the other side' would require him to make. Any political choice is a choice made in opposition to the alternative not chosen and, if this alternative is seen as being sufficiently negative, the characteristics of the alternative that *is* chosen may be of little relevance. So again we have another situation in which dissatisfaction could coexist with high levels of support for parties perceived as responsible for that dissatisfaction. It was a situation aptly captured in 1976 by Indro Montanelli, editor of the conservative newspaper, *Il Giornale*, when, in the face of the PCI's predicted advance, he famously exhorted his readers to hold their noses and vote Christian Democrat.

One estimate of the extent of this kind of voting is given by the proportion of voters who said that they would refuse to consider voting for one or more parties 'under any circumstances'. Mannheimer and Sani's research mentioned above suggested that 96 per cent of voters fell into this category. Moreover, 57 per cent of those responding to the question, 'Which parties would you never vote for?' indicated not a small, extremist party, but the second-largest party, the PCI, while 45 per cent indicated the DC (Mannheimer and Sani, 1987: 109). This latter figure is a rather significant piece of evidence of ideologically motivated voting since the DC's central location on the left–right spectrum would lead one to expect it, otherwise, to be the object of rather few *a priori* preclusions.

A third factor conditioning the voting behaviour of Italians in the post-1945 period was the territorially based 'red' and 'white' subcultures described in Chapter 2 and whose significance lay in the sheer proportion of the support for the two major parties which they each accounted for (especially so in the case of the Communists, a third of whose voting support regularly came from the 'red belt'). The subcultures owed their origins, like so much else in the country's politics, to the manner in which Italian unification itself came about:

> ... the White provinces are those where, under the Austrian Empire before unification, the local clergy led and defended Italian nationality against the foreign ruler. Conversely, the Red provinces formed part of the Papal States: the Church played the role of oppressive ruler and unification took the form of a virulent anti-clericalism which the nascent Socialist movement infused with an ideological and institutional backing at the turn of the century. After the war the Communists, through their leading role in the Resistance, acceded to the Socialist institutional inheritance. (Allum, 1973a: 42–3)

The principal characteristics of the subcultures, besides a high concentration of support for one or other of the two major parties, were the presence of 'a specific local political system' offering 'a high capacity for the aggregation and mediation of local-level interests' as a result of the existence of 'a dense network of institutions co-ordinated by the dominant party' (Trigilia, 1986: 47–8). Given such dominance, individual members of the subculture would be the carriers of a distinct world-view sustained by participation in a variety of political and recreational organizations and by exposure to flows of communication specific to the subculture itself. Such mechanisms of socialization served to reinforce – via intergenerational transmission through the family – the voting patterns that were also an integral part of the attitudes and patterns of behaviour characteristic of the subculture membership. Such a context thus provided an additional set of circumstances in which voting tended to lose its character as a 'choice': rather, it was 'merely one of a number of acts which reaffirms one's belonging' (Parisi and Pasquino, 1977: 224–5).

There were therefore at least three sets of reasons – clientelism, ideological conflict and political subcultures – for thinking that partisanship would be rather strongly anchored to the organized political forces which emerged at the end of the Second World War, despite widespread dissatisfaction with the performance of parties and institutions. With increasing visibility from the mid-1970s onwards these anchors gradually began to slip.

### Electoral Change from the Mid-1970s

First, economic and social change beginning in the 1950s led, particularly in the case of the DC, to a decline both in the size of the subcultures and in their capacity to condition the votes of those who remained influenced by them. In the 12 years between 1950 and 1962 Italy's gross national product doubled, while in the two decades between 1951 and 1971 the country's growth rate of 6 per cent per annum was exceeded only by that of Japan (Allum, 1973a: 25). The 'economic miracle', as it was called, was a quintessentially northern phenomenon offering the southern rural labourer who was prepared to move the certainty of at least doubling his wages. It thus led to massive internal migration, predominantly from the rural South to the urban North. It also, of course, brought about a dramatic growth of *per capita* income. These two factors thus stimulated a growing cultural homogenization and social fragmentation. If television, for instance, had conveyed to the southern rural labourer the lure of the North – bringing 'images of a consumer world, of Vespas, portable radios' and so forth (Ginsborg, 1990: 222) – it also isolated people for, as television ownership rapidly spread, 'the habit of watching television in bars or at neighbours' houses died out' (Ginsborg, 1990: 242) and each family was left to be exposed to the delights of consumerism in its own flat. Second, urban living brought greater privacy and new leisure opportunities. Third, the expansion of car ownership brought new mobility and a weakening of local attachments.

In the face of such changes, a weakening of the subcultures was hardly surprising and, in fact, the aforementioned developments 'were not much to the liking of either of the dominant ideologies in Italy at the time' (Ginsborg, 1990: 248–9). The Catholics were worried that urbanization and consumerism equalled secularization, while the Communists watched aghast as the new isolationist trends led to a decline in interest in the activities of the *Case del Popolo*, lower levels of participation in the party organizations and decline in attendance at section meetings. Three sets of figures serve as indicators of the shrinking of the 'white' subculture and of its capacity to mobilize support for the DC. In 1956, 69 per cent of the adult population claimed to have attended mass the previous week; by 1976 this had dropped to 37 per cent and in 1990 it was 30 per cent. In 1968, 77 per cent of practising Catholics voted for the Christian Democrats whereas in 1985 only 63 per cent did so (Mannheimer and Sani, 1987; Newell, 1995: 10). Finally, from Table 4.1 we can see that, while the DC suffered a fairly steep decline throughout Italy from 1976, this was most marked in its subcultural stronghold of the north-east where, in 1992, its share of the vote was 37 per cent smaller than it had been in 1976. This compares with the trend in the remaining three areas where the DC's vote-share fell by less than 20 per cent between 1976 and 1992. Meanwhile, the decline of the communist subculture was reflected in the decline of the PCI's vote-share from 34.4 per cent in 1976 to 26.6 per cent in 1987 – the last election fought by the party under its traditional name and symbol.

Table 4.1   Percentage of the total vote going to the DC within
geographical areas, 1972–87

| Area | Year 1976 | 1979 | 1983 | 1987 | 1992 |
|---|---|---|---|---|---|
| White belt | 47.1 | 44.9 | 39.0 | 39.2 | 29.5 |
| Industrial area | 38.4 | 36.6 | 30.9 | 31.2 | 22.8 |
| Red belt | 31.2 | 30.0 | 25.5 | 26.5 | 21.3 |
| South | 40.1 | 41.5 | 36.0 | 38.5 | 38.5 |

*Sources*: For the 1976–1987 elections, Corbetta *et al.* (1988, Tables b8–b11); for the 1992
elections, adapted from *Corriere della Sera*, 8 April 1992.

DC
anti
communism        Ideological motivations and anti-communism also became wasting
assets for the traditional parties. In 1987 – by which time Gorbachev
had come to power in the Soviet Union and the Cold War had clearly
lost much of its previous intensity – Mannheimer and Sani noted that
'the figures for the mid-eighties would seem to indicate a diminution
in the level of preclusion [against the PCI]' while other indicators
suggested a growing legitimation of this formation (1987: 110). Anti-
communism had always been one of the principal pillars on which
support for the DC had traditionally rested, but:

> ... [i]n 1985, the DC gained about half (48 per cent) the votes of those
> rating the PCI between 0 and 20 [on a 100-point 'feelings thermometer'],
> with the parties which are the DC's most direct competitors, the three small
> lay parties (16 per cent), the MSI (16 per cent), and the Socialists (12 per
> cent), also, not surprisingly, the major competitors for these votes; in 1968,
> 74 per cent of the most anti-Communist and in 1972 73 per cent said they
> supported the DC. (Leonardi and Wertman, 1989: 181)

After the collapse of the Berlin Wall led Occhetto, the PCI leader, to
propose transforming the party into a non-communist party with a
new name, many DC supporters no longer felt compelled to vote for
the party as the main bulwark against communism and instead felt
free to express their dissatisfaction with the system of clientelism and
corruption in which the DC had been involved by abandoning the party
altogether (Newell, 1994: 140). Yet the PCI was unable to benefit. In the
meantime, it had been making efforts, though the 'historic compromise'
and other initiatives, to increase its appeal by lowering the temperature
of ideological conflict,[3] but the decline in its vote-share after 1976
suggested that increasing moderation and liberalization were, just
possibly, leading to disillusionment and apathy. By making its political
product increasingly similar to others offered on the political market

the PCI was, perhaps, bound to disappoint consumers of *its* product while creating little incentive for the consumers of *other* parties' products to switch brands.[4]

Finally, clientelism eventually sowed the seeds of its own destruction, for it was a very expensive means of mobilizing electoral support and the costs involved were bound to become increasingly difficult to sustain as time went by. The process of inter- and intraparty competition ensured that clientelism was inherently inflationary and it became doubly so from the late 1970s as the PSI used its indispensability in coalition formation, and its 'pivotal' role in the party system, to turn up the heat on the Christian Democrats, extracting ever-increasing shares of spoils as the price of its cooperation. The consequences can be seen in the figures showing trends in the public debt which, as a percentage of gross domestic product, grew from 61.1 per cent in 1981 to 100.9 per cent in 1990 (Romano, 1992: 296). Then in December 1991, after a year of negotiations, Italy signed the Maastricht Treaty which provided for the Economic and Monetary Union (EMU) of the EU member states.

It was clear from the start that significant sectors of Italian industry were likely to benefit considerably from EMU which held out the prospect of a reduction in interest rates, lower inflation and healthier public finances (Daniels, 1993: 203). At the same time, if Italy *failed* to qualify for the single currency, she risked being marginalized within Europe and thus, given the interdependence of the European economies, placed in a situation of disadvantage in the single market. But clientelism and the politics of patronage placed a fundamental obstacle in the way of Italian participation in EMU: the Maastricht convergence criteria stipulated that each state's public sector deficit was not to exceed 3 per cent of its gross national product, its accumulated public debt, 60 per cent. In 1991 Italy's were 10.7 and 102.5 per cent respectively (ibid.: 205) – in other words, a gap so large as to require not just a change of policy but a fundamental restructuring of public finances. In the run-up to the 1992 election, the press gave ample space to the problem while the Northern League insisted repeatedly on the possible exclusion of Italy from EMU, condemning the Rome-based *partitocrazia* for wasteful expenditure in favour of the South (ibid.: 206, 218).

To sum up, then, the period from the late 1970s witnessed a gradual weakening of voters' attachments to the established parties and this could be seen clearly in the combined share of the vote received by the DC and the PCI at successive general elections: 73.1 per cent in 1976; 68.7 per cent in 1979; 62.8 per cent in 1983; 60.9 per cent in 1987; and 45.8 per cent in 1992. Social change and the decline of the subcultures led to a progressive opening up of previously 'closed' sectors of the 'electoral market' to potential capture by new forces (Newell, 1994:

138). Then, when the viability of ideological oppositions and clientelism finally became exhausted at the beginning of the 1990s, the way was opened for voters to express their longstanding dissatisfaction with the performance of parties and institutions. But why did the votes released by the established parties benefit an organization such as the Northern League in particuar? Clearly, to answer this question we have to consider, in addition to the 'push' factors causing voters to move away from the established parties, the 'pull' factors that would make the League a relatively attractive proposition in comparison with alternative parties such as the greens, radicals, or any one of a number of alternative formations which emerged from the mid-1970s.

## The Northern League's Appeal

The 'pull' factors were ultimately rooted in the League's capacity to take advantage of a range of social trends and political developments which accentuated the localism and the north–south economic disequilibria, as well as the latent hostility towards southerners, widespread throughout the North, that have been salient features of Italian society since unification itself.

Despite the economic and social heterogeneity of the areas involved, and despite the way in which it penalized the South economically, unification nevertheless brought together eight states on terms of *formal* equality. This led northerners quickly to assume 'that if the South did not make the same progress as the North it must be due to the racial inferiority of the southerners and hence was congenital' (Allum, 1973a: 41). Nevertheless, for 40 years after the Second World War, the North–South divide was not a significant source of conflict, since local and regional interests were successfully mediated by the two political subcultures and by the governing parties through clientelistic networks which connected centre to periphery through a variety of intermediary organizations which in turn were linked to the governing parties themselves (Woods, 1992a: 57). By using the resources deriving from their colonization of public institutions the governing parties were able to construct stable vertical relationships within themselves between national and local elites (ibid.: 62). The subcultures helped to attenuate the potential conflict arising from the economic disparities between North and South by virtue of the solidaristic and universalistic world-views which (being based on Catholicism and Marxism) they provided (Biorcio, 1997: 105).

Rapid economic growth then accentuated economic disparities between the North and South. On the one hand, infrastructural shortcomings and the spread of organized crime conspired to ensure that rates of growth would, by and large, be slower in the South than elsewhere, consequently widening the gap between the *Mezzogiorno* and the rest of the country over the years. On the other hand, rapid growth brought the emergence of the so-called 'Third Italy' in the central and north-eastern regions where the desire of large-scale industry to cut labour costs by subcontracting led to the spread of small-scale enterprises which were able to compete successfully in world markets through 'flexible specialization' and short production runs. Localism offered material and non-material resources that ensured that small-scale enterprise would be especially successful in the 'Third Italy'. Such resources included: reciprocal acquaintance, and in some cases, family ties (facilitating mutual trust, the rapid transfer of knowledge and information, advances of capital and loans) (Bagnasco, 1988: 55); low levels of class conflict (consequent upon the fact that the small-business owner would often be an ex-worker with a workforce that itself aspired to the position of entrepreneur); and the influence of the political subcultures (which facilitated a localistic mediation of interests through their influence on industrial relations and on the activities of local government) (Trigilia, 1986: 32).

At first, the Third Italy's dynamism helped shore up clientele politics and its attendant public mismanagement and inefficiency, by sustaining, through traditionally high levels of saving, the public sector deficits on which the former rested (Trigilia, 1994: 433). However, because clientele politics mainly tended to benefit the *Mezzogiorno* and the large-scale industries of the North, during the 1980s, as small firms came under increasing competitive pressure from abroad, they began to feel the effects of public mismanagement in terms of the inadequacy of policies for professional training, for research and innovation, and for collective services in general (Trigilia, 1994: 433). At the same time, the poor quality of public services helped to heighten the salience of the taxation by which they were partly funded – an issue to which small businesses have always been especially sensitive.[5] Consequently, the DC's original strategy of attempting to link centre to periphery through clientelistic networks began to unravel and to hasten its decline: hence its relatively rapid retreat in its traditional north-eastern stronghold (see Table 4.1).

As the DC retreated, revealing itself decreasingly capable of defending the small business interests that were now in conflict with its clientelistic support in the South, it left in its wake strong feelings of relative deprivation arising out of the limited influence that an area based on small businesses – however rich – can exercise over the state's resource allocation decisions. In these circumstances, the League was able to step in as a new 'spokesperson' for these interests and to exploit the taxation issue by cleverly linking it to the latent hostility towards southerners. By claiming that the larger proportion of the total tax take needed to finance public expenditure necessarily came from the richer

North, and by blaming the inefficiency of public services on the efforts of a corrupt, party-dominated bureaucracy in far-away Rome to maintain its clientele-based power in an underdeveloped South, the League was able to tie small-business discontents firmly to its own autonomist concerns. It did this by arguing that a set of federalist arrangements were needed as these – by limiting the functions of the state to external defence, internal security, the administration of justice, and the provision of only the most indispensable of additional public goods – would remove from the central authorities all those functions which allowed it to tax the North while giving little or nothing in return.

Meanwhile, the League was able to benefit from a variety of other concerns perceived as contributing to the same problem. One of these was the spread of organized crime. It had long been widely suspected that the *Mafia* and other criminal organizations such as the '*Ndrangheta* (Calabria) and the *Camorra* (Naples) had worked for the support of at least parts of some of the established parties in the South (Leonardi and Kovacs, 1993: 135). Such links between organized crime and politicians in parts of southern Italy became considerably more important in the 1980s. In Naples, for example, the previously casual relations between politicians and *camorristi* were replaced by routine and systematic ties as a result of the vast sums of money (50 000 billion lire) made available for reconstruction in the wake of the Irpinia earthquake disaster, which in November 1980 affected almost all the communes in the Campania region. Since these funds were made available through emergency procedures and hence subject to the minimum of financial control, directing them to *Camorra*-controlled firms was simply a matter of controlling the election of mayors and local councillors. In the meantime, the level of violence soared as rival *Camorra* gangs fought over control of the available public works contracts.

As Sabetti (1992: 194) explains, there were a number of reasons why voters were likely to be disturbed by the spread of violence: the tendency of acts of violence to take place in rapid succession; their brutality; and the fact that Italy has one of the lowest homicide rates in the world. At the same time, the state institutions seemed to face growing difficulties in tackling the problem.[6] Finally, the seriousness of the spread of organized crime and of the growth of its influence in politics was powerfully symbolized for voters in 1991 by the establishment of *la Rete* ('the Network'). This was an organization founded by Leoluca Orlando who, as Christian Democratic mayor of Palermo had led, in the mid-1980s, a struggle known as the 'Palermo Spring' against *Mafia* infiltration of the city council. Its aims 'were a heady mix of Christian values, anti-Mafia ideals, puritanical morality and libertarianism . . .' (Foot, 1996: 180). Although it later ran into difficulties, the extent of its initial influence was revealed at the 1992 elections when it won 12 seats in the Chamber of Deputies and 24.5 per cent of the vote in Palermo. All this meant that, although *la Rete* was a very different political animal to the League, the latter was, as a consequence strengthened in that a new movement of some influence was seconding the League's denunciations of the *partitocrazia* for its inability or unwillingness to deal with the politico-criminal crisis.

A second issue that the League was able to exploit was immigration, in part because of its novelty: prior to the 1980s Italy had been a nation of emigrants rather than a country that experienced any significant influx of foreigners, and the first piece of immigration-related legislation dated back only to 1986. Consequently, when, from the early 1980s, the number of immigrants began to rise, immigration became a political issue primarily because of its growing visibility and because of what, in a number of quarters, were perceived as inadequacies in the relevant legislation. Growing hostility towards immigrants was almost bound to push voters towards the League given the requirements of the latter's electoral strategy. If it was to be electorally successful, as a regional autonomy party the League had to raise voters' awareness of their identities as the members of a geographically defined category, and, since to define oneself as the member of a social category is simultaneously to define those who are not members, it was no accident that increasingly significant shifts in public opinion in favour of less liberal immigration policies should coincide with growing support for the League. Particularly significant was the public debate surrounding the so-called Martelli law (after its sponsor, the Socialist Claudio Martelli) passed in 1989. This aimed to increase the legal obstacles to entering the country while 'regularizing' the position of illegal immigrants already present, but was the subject of widespread criticism (spearheaded by the Republicans and the Italian Social Movement). Hence the law provided a ready-made issue which could be exploited by Bossi as further proof of the incompetence of a clientelistic *partitocrazia*.[7]

## The League's Electoral Growth

Following the suggestions of Ilvo Diamanti (1993; 1996), it has become conventional to divide the period of the League's emergence and growth into a number of clearly defined subperiods demarcating the different phases of its electoral expansion: 1983–1987; 1987–1990; 1990–1992; and the period after 1992. Each phase also corresponds to significant differences in the nature of the political supply on offer.[8] The first three phases are discussed here, while issues relevant to the period following 1992 are taken up in Chapter 5.

*Phase 1: 1983–1987*

During this first phase, which runs from 1983 to the general election of 1987, the Northern League – which was not formally constituted until 4 December 1989 – did not exist, and the embryonic autonomy leagues active in various regions of the North were entirely marginal phenomena, quite unnoticed by mainstream political commentators. Most histories of the League begin with Bruno Salvadori of the *Union Valdôtaine*, since it was largely as a result of his initiative in making contact with exponents of autonomy in other regions that the embryonic leagues were set up in the first place. Through splits and schisms and changes of name, these leagues all attempted to build a following behind the idea that the region they sought to represent, as the supposed repository of its own genuine linguistic and cultural traditions, was exploited economically and denied access to political power by outside, dominating, forces. The problem for the leagues was, of course, that the regions were politico-*administrative* divisions more than anything else and their cultural and linguistic distinctiveness was not very marked. For a while the leagues attempted to overcome this problem by emphasizing the importance of dialects, but their leaders soon realized that this was likely to encourage identification with the locality rather than the region and to make it easy for hostile critics to dismiss them as 'folkloristic cranks'.

These difficulties were, naturally, fully reflected in the leagues' electoral achievements, or rather lack of them (Table 4.2). The most successful of the early leagues was the *Liga Veneta* which had the advantage of operating in a part of the country where levels of regional identification were, as compared to other areas, relatively strong. But if the *Liga* gave voice to communities that had come to perceive

Table 4.2   **Percentage share of the vote in local and national elections for the Leagues in six Italian regions, 1983–94**

| Region | Year 1983 | 1984 | 1985 | 1987 | 1989 | 1990 | 1992 | 1994 |
|---|---|---|---|---|---|---|---|---|
| Veneto | 4.2 | 3.4 | 3.7 | 3.1 | 1.7 | 8.6 | 25.5 | 24.8 |
| Lombardy | 0 | 0 | 0.5 | 3.0 | 8.1 | 18.9 | 23.6 | 24.4 |
| Piedmont | 0 | 0 | 1.1 | 4.3 | 3.1 | 5.1 | 16.3 | 16.2 |
| Liguria | 0 | 0 | 0.9 | 1.3 | 1.4 | 6.1 | 14.3 | 11.4 |
| Emilia | 0 | 0 | 0.4 | 0.5 | 0.5 | 2.9 | 9.6 | 6.4 |
| Tuscany | 0 | 0 | 0.5 | 0.3 | 0.2 | 0.8 | 3.1 | 2.2 |

*Source*: Diamanti (1996: 115, Table 7.1).

themselves as economically central but politically marginal, this at once limited its scope for expansion, for what was demanded was precisely 'centrality' rather than 'autonomy'. 'It was no coincidence therefore that after its initial success the *Liga Veneta* went into a progressive decline, becoming almost marginal in the 1989 European elections (when it won less than 2 per cent of the regional vote)' (Diamanti, 1996: 118).

*Phase 2: 1987–1990*

If during the first period it was the *Liga Veneta* which had the highest profile, during the second period – between the 1987 general election and the regional elections of 1990 – it was the turn of the *Lega Lombarda*. And if during the first period the 'political offer' had been of an 'ethno-regionalist' kind, with autonomy being sought in the name of the 'Venetian nation', during the second it was the region as a 'community of interests' for which autonomy was demanded (Diamanti, 1993: 17). At the 1987 general election, then, Lombardy began to emerge as the centre of the league phenomenon, and, at the two subsequent elections – the European election of 1989 and the regional elections of 1990 – this tendency became very marked indeed: in 1989 the *Lega Lombarda* outperformed all the other leagues for the first time, winning 8.1 per cent of the Lombard vote. Then, in 1990, it experienced a real take-off; by taking 18.9 per cent of the vote in Lombardy, it considerably increased the distance between itself and other leagues despite their similarly improved previous performances too (see Table 4.2).

The *Lega Lombarda* is a rather different political animal as compared with the other leagues, and it is the difference in the nature of its appeals which largely account for its relatively greater success, as Diamanti (1993) explains. Cultural initiatives and 'ethno-regionalism' were always going to have an even more limited appeal in Lombardy than elsewhere given its even lower levels of cultural homogeneity, lower concentrations of dialect-speakers and so forth. In the absence of ready-made bases for the inculcation of a regional identity, the *Lega* was going to have to look for alternatives. At this point it, and especially its leader Bossi, was able to make a virtue of necessity by drawing on sentiments much more powerful than cultural or linguistic attachments for the creation of a 'Lombard' identity. Such sentiments were, of course, those of hostility to southerners, *partitocrazia*, an inefficient state, and other 'common enemies'. By casting these in the role of 'outsiders', counter-posing them to notions of a 'laborious Lombard people', of an industrious Lombardy 'colonized' by a *Roma ladrona*, Bossi was able to present regional autonomy in the much more appealing guise of a solution to concrete, *economic*, problems rather than, as the *Liga* tended to do, as the realization of some abstract, *cultural*, identity.

Meanwhile, all the leagues were helped in this period by the attitudes of the established parties which responded to the new phenomenon with unmitigated hostility. Instead of reacting in a positive way to the complaints which lay at the base of the leagues' support (the inefficiency of public services, corruption, the weight of taxation, and so forth) they concentrated their efforts on attacking the leagues, their language and values, with every means available – an approach which eventually revealed itself as wholly counterproductive in so far as it contributed to the further legitimation of the leagues as well as to a reinforcement of their own image as organizations incapable of any real reform.

Owing to the centrality of the *Lega Lombarda* to the league phenomenon, no one was very surprised when, in 1990, Bossi emerged as the leader of a new formation, born of an amalgamation of the leagues that was implemented in two stages: a confederation of the *Lega Lombarda* and five other leagues which fought the 1990 regional elections as *Alleanza Nord*, and then the formation of a single league, the *Lega Nord*. This development was a product of the realization that the leagues' success throughout the North implied that the region was no longer adequate as the basis of political organization. In other words, although the leagues presented themselves as implacable opponents of the centre, individual regions were likely to have little bargaining power *vis-à-vis* the state and, if regional interests continued to be the presupposition on which political activity was based, then the conflict with Rome would, sooner or later, inevitably be threatened by conflict between the regions themelves (Diamanti, 1993: 72). The emergence of the Northern League was therefore also accompanied by a shift of policy: no longer was the aim that of autonomy for the single region, but rather, the creation of three macro-regions – of the North, the Centre and the South – within the framework of an overall federal reform of the state. This posed a problem of identification, for 'the North' simply didn't exist as a single historical and cultural entity and was altogether too nebulous a territorial unit with which to expect people to be able to identify. Considerable efforts were therefore made to 'create' the North 'artificially' by means of collective rituals (such as the annual *giuramento di Pontida*)[9] and the continuous production of objects – from banknotes and flags to T-shirts and passports – designed to bring 'the North' to life through symbolism. On the other hand, extending the confines of the League's 'catchment area' to the whole of the North (a larger, and therefore more credible, entity than the region) made it easier to convince people that autonomy really was the solution to concrete, everyday needs.

*Phase 3: 1990–1992*

During the third period – from the regional elections of 1990 to the

1992 general election – the League's electoral performance was immeasurably helped by the concurrence of a number of the events and circumstances favourable to it. Thus, the upheaval provoked by the PCI leader responding to the collapse of the Berlin Wall in 1989 by announcing a change of the party's name continued through 1990 and well into 1991. Late 1991 had seen the signing of the Maastricht Treaty and thus the public realization that the governing parties' corruption and profligacy might cause Italy to miss the European train. The growth of immigration was high on the political agenda as was the governing parties' response to (southern) organized crime, as we have already seen. This synchrony allowed the League, as Diamanti (1993: 75) points out, to 'create the conditions for its own success', intervening in public debate by raising themes and issues that were at once favourable to itself and highly awkward for the governing parties.

The 1992 general election subsequently saw the League reach a pinnacle of its success. Nationally, it became the fourth largest party with 8.7 per cent of the vote and the election of 55 deputies, and did well not only in its strongholds but also in areas where it had previously been weak. Thus it won 23.6 per cent in Lombardy and 18 per cent in Veneto (25.5 per cent with other autonomist parties), but also managed to achieve 9.6 per cent and 3.1 per cent in the hitherto inhospitable 'red' regions of Emilia and Tuscany (see Table 4.2). This success was achieved at the expense of all the governing parties but particularly of the DC (Newell, 1994). It was an achievement all the more striking for the fact that it came at the end of a five-and-a-half year period during which the League had never once lost votes: never in the history of the post-war Italian republic had a new party emerged and managed to achieve success as striking or as longlasting. To the extent that the League saw itself as waging war on a whole range of external threats to the well-being of the ordinary Northerner, it was tempting to draw parallels between it and Giannini's *Fronte dell'Uomo Qualunque* of the late 1940s.[10] But Giannini's party had disappeared within two years whereas the League of the early 1990s appeared to go from strength to strength. This suggests that an especially important role in its success had to be attributed to the political resources that it itself was able to bring to bear on its situation.

## The League's Internal Resources

That the League's emergence and growth cannot be explained by reference to external factors alone is immediately obvious as soon as one asks why it was that, of all the regional autonomy parties operating in northern Italy in the late 1980s and early 1990s, only the organization led by Bossi was successful (while the others either disappeared or were absorbed by it). This means that the League must be understood as being as much the result of the nature of its own message and of the organizational and other resources it was able to bring to the social and economic context in which it operated as of this context itself. In fact, it is unlikely that the League can be understood without a full appreciation of the interaction between the two, for not only was the League able to respond effectively to its environment, but, through its responses, was also able to *modify* its environment so that it would, in subsequent phases, present altered conditions for the party's growth (Diamanti, 1993; Biorcio, 1997).

If we assume that the mobilization of political support relies essentially on the successful communication of a political message, then there are, in effect, three internal resources available to be exploited by the political entrepreneur: the substantive content of the message; the style in which it is communicated; and the organizational resources with which to communicate it.

Evidence of the success of the substantive content of the League's message is given by the party origins of those who voted for it – the wide spread of parties suggesting a particularly effective message, able to find an echo even among people whose political outlooks might otherwise radically conflict. In 1992 the League drew 6.4 per cent of its support from those who had voted for the MSI in 1987; 26.0 per cent from those who had voted for the DC; 9.8 per cent from those who had voted PRI, PLI or PSDI; 12.1 per cent from those who had voted PSI; 17.9 per cent from those who had voted for the PCI; and 27.8 per cent from those who had voted for other parties, had abstained or had been too young to vote.[11] In other words, it drew its support from across the political spectrum.

The features of the League's message which allowed it to appeal to such a wide range of political forces were several and interlinked. First, there was the demand for autonomy itself – which both established a non-negotiable objective helping fix the League's distinct identity, and offered a basis of political representation different from that offered by all the other parties (thus allowing the League to draw on widespread 'anti-partitocratic' sentiments). Second, its demand for autonomy and its corresponding appeal to voters as citizens of a *Repubblica del Nord* allowed it to draw on latent anti-southern sentiment to offer a new political identity at a time when the large-scale economic and social changes considered above were rapidly eroding traditional identities. This meant that it was able to offer a response to a widely felt lack of meaning and significance arising from such phenomena as growing secularization, attenuation of the ideologial conflict sustained by the Cold War and so forth. By denouncing things like the internal exile of *Mafia* bosses in the regions of the North, the 'excessive' concentration of southerners in the public administration of the North, the waste of resources on clientelism in the South and the like, the League was able to ensure that the voters' hostility towards southerners would raise their awareness of their identities as 'northerners'. Furthermore, this allowed the League to create a link between voters' *material* concerns and the demand for *autonomy* such that the one appeared to follow from the other. Third, its appeal to voters as citizens of a *Repubblica del Nord* gave its message a populism which placed it outside of the conventional left–right dimension – and thus an ability to circumvent the politico-ideological barriers that would prevent a formation such as the MSI (for example) from placing itself at the head of 'anti-partitocratic' protest. At the same time – fourthly – its populism would allow it to appeal successfully to left-wing voters. Indeed, some of its populist appeals even recalled the PCI's denunciations of monopoly capital during the early post-war period (and, of course, had the same intent – namely, that of unifying worker and small-business interests):

> The League hereby accuses – openly denouncing as an accomplice – the close interdependence between the partitocratic regime, the Establishment, the centralised State and large capital, co-ordinated, controlled, represented and defended by the Confindustria. (Bossi, 1991 quoted by Biorcio, 1997: 60)

The nature of the League's communicative style and of its organization followed from its populism. Its communicative style was an especially remarkable feature. As an 'ethno-regionalist' party, the League faced the problem that linguistic and other ethno-cultural differences between the North and the rest of Italy were too limited to assure a significant basis of support. As a populist party, however, the League presented itself as the defender of the common people of the North against the centralized state and the parties, and against political, economic and social oligarchies in general. This allowed it to create its own unifying language or, more precisely, *linguistic style* that deliberately broke with conventional and official styles of political communication. In place of the specialist terminology, rhetorical flourishes and the syntactically complex and in place of the euphemisms and abstruse language, opaque to the mass public, but typical of the established players of 'the Italian political game',[12] the League chose a language that was simple, understandable, sometimes crude and occasionally vulgar. This strategy allowed it to draw strength from the latent popular resentment at the expropriation of power inevitably involved in the use, by élites, of 'cultured' styles designed to give authority to those that use them. This in turn established its identity more firmly as an implacable opponent of the traditional parties and thus, through this juxtaposition, allowed it to create a sense, among supporters and sympathizers, of identity and belonging as ordinary Northerners:

> The importance of this popular style in the process of identifying with the League is emphasized by a number of the interviews with League activists: 'The arguments of the League are the ones that you hear in bars, on the commuter trains and in the workplace'; 'Bossi tells the politicians to their faces what we say among ourselves'; 'The League says and thinks what the Lombards say and think'; 'When Bossi speaks, it's as if I'm speaking'. (Biorcio, 1997: 195)

Even more importantly, and as the above quotations make clear, the League's language helped to increase voters' receptiveness to the substantive content of its message, for, by using the same linguistic codes in which the most widespread popular beliefs tended to be couched, the message could thereby be made to appear as the mere extension of 'common sense' (Biorcio, 1997: 196).

Finally, as a centralized organization, under strong, charismatic leadership, the League was effectively protected against the threats inherent in its rapid growth – that is, by taking on new members and supporters very quickly during the late 1980s and early 1990s, the risk of centrifugal forces developing and precipitating the movement's rapid demise. A strong organization under tight, central, control was therefore necessary to prevent this happening. In fact, in designing the organizational structure of the *Lega Lombarda*, and later of the *Lega Nord*, Bossi went out of his way to prevent too rapid an expansion of a difficult-to-control army of activists by stipulating that ordinary membership could be conferred only after application for this status had been approved by the relevant local body and endorsed by the national leadership and, in any event, only after a lengthy period of candidate membership during which the individual had no voting rights. Second, 'top-down' organizational steps were taken to protect the movement against the risk of outside infiltration. To this end, the party statutes stipulated that membership could be withdrawn from those who demonstrated insufficient levels of activism, and laid down increasingly lengthy periods of membership as prerequisites for accession to successive levels in the party hierarchy – all of this designed, of course, to ensure that positions of responsibility could only be given to those who had given certain minimum guarantees of fidelity to the movement. Third, Bossi's ability to exercise charismatic authority within the movement ensured the maintenance of internal unity, protecting it against the development of factions. Hence when internal disagreements did develop, they invariably led to expulsions since dissidents could only be perceived as traitors and wreckers. Charismatic leadership was arguably essential to the Northern League given that it was, formally speaking, born as a *federation* of leagues each of which retained its own leadership.

As a political entrepreneur, then, the League, and especially Bossi, could only be admired for their astuteness. As the years have gone by, it has become clear that alongside implacable hostility to an organization that now aims at outright secession of the regions of the North, there has grown up among the League's opponents a more-than-justified respect for its leader's political abilities. In essence, the League's growth could be explained in terms of its unique capacity to combine communication style and organizational resources in such a way as to translate favourable social and political – and thus electoral – conditions into growing electoral support for itself. At the height of the crisis of the so-called 'First Republic', the League was the *only* organization offering voters a political *project* or a convincing image of 'the good society' (as opposed to a promise of the better management of the extant). Hence it was by far the most successful of the organizations seeking to spearhead and to channel popular discontent with the established parties of government (Biorcio, 1997). Yet, if, in the overall struggle for power, the League was one of the principal challengers of the old party system, it has not so far been able to take the place of the vanquished (which has, instead, been taken by the AN and *Forza Italia* on the one hand and by the PDS on the other) and it retains its status as an 'external challenger' to the system (Cotta, 1998). This means that there is still something vital missing from our account of the transformation of Italian party politics – namely, certain *additional* factors that were involved in shaping the nature of the system which emerged. It is to the analysis of these that we turn in Chapter 5.

## Notes

1   For a definition of this term see Chapter 2.
2   The main drawback of this indicator is its ambiguity: by giving the voter a further choice, additional to that of party, its use could be argued to reflect the more sophisticated, opinion-based, choices rather than 'exchange voting' (Cartocci, 1990: 105).
3   The so-called 'historic compromise' strategy, elaborated by PCI leader Berlinguer in the early 1970s, found its origin in a crisis of the 'centre-left' governing coalition formula and in the appearance, at the end of the 1960s, of the workers' and students' protest movements – both of which 'seemed to mark the exhaustion of the social and political relations which had provided the bases for Communist exclusion' (Lange, 1980: 114) increasing the possibility of a governing role for the party – with the result that it was forced to clarify its position *vis-à-vis* the Catholic world in general and the DC in particular. The basic tenets of the 'historic compromise' were that 'a programme of democratic renewal', the first step on the road to transformation, would require the consent of a large majority of the population (well over 51 per cent) and hence the development of a wide-ranging set of social alliances in order 'to impede the development of a mass-based reactionary front around those sectors of the population which would be most damaged' by reform. Such alliances could not be achieved, however, without the building of political alliances to include the Christian Democrats, since failure to do so 'might well

result in an organic and stable alliance of the centre and right and a reactionary victory'. Success in building an alliance with the DC, on the other hand, might potentially shift that party to the left (Lange, 1980: 117–18).

4   During the second half of the 1970s the PCI supported a strong line against left-wing terrorism and advocated an austerity policy for dealing with economic difficulties. The year 1981 saw the famous *strappo* (break) with the Soviet Union following Jaruzelski's seizure of power in Poland that same year (Bull and Daniels, 1990: 24). The eighteenth party congress (March 1989) following Achille Occhetto's assumption of the party leadership (June 1988) saw the end of democratic centralism and official acceptance of the 'irreversibility' of capital accumulation and of the market economy (Bull, 1991a; 1991b). Yet the party's support at successive elections continued to decline.

5   Arguably, the sensitivity of small businesses and the self-employed to tax issues lies in a significance which such questions do not have for employees. For the latter, tax payments can be said to represent private consumption opportunities foregone. For the small business, tax payments represent not only these but also a reduction in investment opportunities (and therefore opportunities for future income) as well as a possible source of depression on the level of demand for the firm's goods.

6   Emblematic in this regard was the final outcome of the so-called 'maxi-trial' against the *Mafia* held between February 1986 and December 1987. In December 1990, Corrado Carnevale – a judge who became known as the 'sentence-killer' and who was later himself to be charged with *Mafia* involvement – reduced on appeal the number of life sentences handed down at the trial from 19 to 12. Then, in February 1991, in accordance with a new law which provided for the provisional release of prisoners whose appeal proceedings had not been held within one year, Carnevale released 40 convicted *Mafia* bosses. The government was forced to issue a decree law, to be applied retroactively, in order to bring the *mafiosi* back to prison – an act which gave rise to the accusation that it was substituting itself for the judicial authorities, signing what was, in effect, an arrest warrant (Catanzaro, 1993: 245), and which cost the life of the public prosecutor, Antonio Scopelliti, who dared to defend the constitutional legitimacy of the decree before the Court of Cassation.

7   As the mayor of Milan, the League's Marco Formentini, would put it some time later, 'Faced with a State that has raised the white flag, it will have to be Padania that assures Europe a block on illegal immigration that brings with it crime and degradation' (quoted by Biorcio, 1997: 164).

8   Alternative divisions into periods have been proposed. For example, Biorcio (1997) proposes a fourfold division into: 'prehistory of the movement', 1979–1989; 'emergence', 1989–1992; 'the League in the transition from the first to the second Republic', 1993–1994; and 'the League's "second wave"', 1995–1997. Still others have been proposed. (See Biorcio, 1997: 100, fn. 1.)

9   Pontida is the site where, in the twelfth century, 21 northern Italian city states, led by Alberto di Giussano, formed a coalition by taking an oath (*giuramento*) to join forces against the invading armies of Frederick Barbarossa.

10  Created immediately after the war, the *Fronte dell'Uomo Qualunque* (or 'Common Man's Front') waged an unceasing battle on everything that threatened the 'ordinary Italian' (Ginsborg, 1990: 99) and gained 5.3 per cent of the vote at the Constituent Assembly elections of 1946.

11  Proportions calculated from Figure 2.2 in Biorcio (1997: 65).

12  Use of the expression, 'the Italian political game' is deliberate; for it should be noted that the language in which Italian politics is typically carried on is in no sense incidental. Rather, as Marengo (1981) shows in his brilliant study entitled *Rules of the Italian Political Game*, it is an inherent feature of the behaviour of Italian political actors in taking, maintaining and surrendering power.

# 5 The Referendum Movement and the New Electoral System

If the first two agents responsible for the transformation of the post-war Italian party system were the judges and the Northern League, the third was the referendum movement. This consisted of a variety of cross-party organizations which, from the end of the 1980s onwards, had sought to use the referendum instrument as a means of forcing fundamental change on an unwilling political establishment. Its challenge culminated, on 18 April 1993, in the holding of eight referenda concerning issues regarded as fundamental to achieving long-needed change in the Italian political system and which included a proposal to change the law governing elections to the Senate. Since Italy's parliamentary system is one of 'perfect bicameralism' – that is, the Senate and the Chamber of Deputies have co-equal legislative powers – the objective of the referendum's sponsors was clear: namely, to force a change in the electoral law for the Chamber as well, and in this way to bring about a change in the way parliament as a whole was elected.

The supporters of reform anticipated that a change in the electoral system would catalyse a fundamental change in the political system as a whole. For those who championed the reform at this time, the aim was no less than to bring down an entire political class and, in line with a long tradition of admiration for an idealized version of the so-called 'Westminster model' of government,[1] it was hoped that a move towards something more nearly approximating 'first-past the post' (FPTP) of the kind which Italy actually made in 1993 would bring with it what was considered to be the cornerstone of that model: alternation in government. The *sine qua non* of a healthy democracy, alternation would be assured by an electoral system whose effect would be to reduce voters' realistic choices to the two front-runners in each constituency, thus minimizing the number of parties winning parliamentary representation and thereby maximizing the chances of the emergence of a single-party government. This, in turn, would raise the degree of popular influence over the partisan composition of government and thus the likelihood of a successful implantation of responsible government, which, in turn, might be expected to reduce the degree of clientelism and corruption characteristic of the political system. These were the *aims* of the reformers. The extent to which they were *realized* is considered in some detail in Chapter 6. In the meantime, the purpose of this chapter is to trace the sequence of events responsible for bringing about the electoral reform of 1993, and to consider its immediate consequences in the period leading up to the general election of 1994.

### The Emergence of the Referendum Movement

Institutional and constitutional reform had been on the agenda of Italian politics for a very long time before 1993 (Pasquino, 1997: 35). In 1983 a parliamentary commission was appointed under the chairmanship of the Liberal Senator Aldo Bozzi, with the task of formulating proposals for institutional reform, and this had also discussed electoral system reform. Although the interlocking vetos of the various political actors meant that nothing came of it, in subsequent years electoral reform became a central issue for all the major parties.

Within the Communist Party, thinking on the issue was coloured by the party's strategy for overcoming the *conventio ad excludendum*. Following the failure, in the late 1970s, of the 'historic compromise' strategy of attempting coalition with the Christian Democrats, the party espoused a policy which it called 'the democratic alternative' and which seemed to point towards a reform of the electoral system that would favour the emergence of two large groupings (McCarthy, 1992: 43). However, for a number of reasons the issue was a thorny one. Togliatti's vision (in a country with a minoritarian working class and where division between the democratic forces had allowed the triumph of fascism) had favoured collaboration with the Catholics and therefore support for the principle of proportionality. Second, previous reforms and attempts at reform of the electoral system – from the Acerbo law to the *legge truffa*[2] – had unfortunate connotations so that the defence of proportionality had come to be regarded as synonymous with the defence of Italian democracy itself (Pasquino, 1991a: 47). Finally, some feared that a reduction in proportionality might not actually favour the party but oblige it to pursue an alliance with the Socialists, no longer from a position of strength but of weakness, to avoid becoming completely marginalized. Therefore, it was only after Occhetto (for whom the issue was a priority) became General Secretary in June 1988 that the cause of electoral reform was able to make any real ground in the party.

Meanwhile, the PSI was pushing for a reform that was an integral part of the strategy it had begun to pursue in the light of the results of the 1983 elections. These had seen the DC suffer its worst defeat since 1948; they had provided the third successive confirmation that the DC was no longer in a position to choose between 'centrist' and 'centre-left' coalitions;[3] and they had allowed the PSI leader, Bettino Craxi, to gain the premiership. Proceeding to build on his reputation for decisiveness and attempting to construct a party iamge of being capable of delivering efficient and stable government,[4] Craxi hoped that, with the PCI's retreat after the failure of the 'historic compromise' and with the fortunes of the so-called 'lay' parties rising, the PSI might be able to place itself at the head of a so-called *polo laico* (literally, 'lay pole') capable of 'unblocking' the system by providing a non-communist alternative to the DC.[5] As an integral part of the strategy towards this end the Socialists proposed the introduction of a German-type 5 per cent threshold: in this way, government stability would be facilitated by the reduction in the number of parties achieving parliamentary representation, while the other 'lay' parties (whose support rarely reached 5 per cent) would be forced to accept an electoral alliance under Socialist leadership – or disappear (Merkel, 1987: 228–229).

For the DC, too, the issue of electoral reform was inextricably bound up with more general strategic considerations. Existing political and institutional arrangements had assured it continuous power since the Second World War, and this provided a strong argument for opposing reform. Until 1976, it had always been in a position, theoretically at least, to use the votes of the PLI, PRI and PSDI to govern *without* the Socialists had it wanted to, and even after its disastrous 1983 performance it was still only 22 seats short of being able to do so again. On the other hand, the party *was* in electoral difficulties – the slight improvement in its vote in 1987 being nowhere near sufficient to cancel out its record-breaking losses of 1983 – and some in the party, notably General Secretary, De Mita, looked to electoral reform as a means of confronting what they presumed to be the main causes of the party's difficulties. According to de Mita, the party's troubles were due to what he called a 'loss of moral authority' on account of its image as a party of clientelism and bad government. His vision was therefore of a 'modern conservative party, capable of sound economic management and attractive to the growing numbers of managers and technocrats' (Daniels, 1988: 269). Electoral reform could help create such a party by helping to create the conditions for bipolar competition and thus for alternation in office – a state of affairs which De Mita called an 'accomplished democracy' (Pasquino, 1989: 286). De Mita proposed that voters be given two votes: one for their preferred party and one for a preferred governing coalition. Then, if several parties joined together in a pact meant to last for an entire legislative term, and if this pact emerged as the winning coalition identified by the voters, a so-called *premio di maggioranza* (literally, 'majority prize') of 50 seats would be distributed among the minor parties of the coalition; otherwise, all seats would be distributed proportionally (Pasquino, 1989: 286).

It was the parties' inability to proceed with any of these plans that was ultimately responsible for the emergence of the referendum movement. Needless to say, the Socialists refused to entertain De Mita's ideas, for they were clearly designed to give the DC the option of governing without the PSI while forcing the latter to make a clear choice between an alliance with the DC or with the opposition PCI. In an effort to advance this strategy, De Mita launched a ferocious attack on the Socialists during the 1987 election campaign insisting that they would have to choose which of the major parties they wished to align with. Although he was confident that this would effectively force the PSI to accept its subordination to the DC – since Craxi had already made abundantly clear his unwillingness to align with the PCI – others in the DC, notably Andreotti and Forlani, were less sure. Indeed, especially after the 1987 election result revealed the failure of De Mita's strategy for freeing the party from the Socialists' influence (its advance to 14.3 per cent coupled with the 'lay' parties' decline gave the PSI even more power in coalition formation than ever) they preferred an alternative strategy for dealing with the problem:

> This [strategy] would seek to woo the Socialists into government, making concessions if necessary, with the aim of ensnaring the PSI in the web of governmental institutions to such an extent that the party would be unable to contemplate, or pose as a credible leader of, a 'reformist alternative' government. Such a strategy is consistent with the time-honoured Italian tradition of 'trasformismo', the process of turning political opponents into allies. (Daniels, 1988: 269)

After De Mita's position had been weakened by the 1987 election outcome (and by his subsequent disappointing term as Prime Minister), his replacement as party secretary by Forlani in February 1989 paved the way for the full implementation of the above strategy. This took the form of the so-called CAF axis: a long-term power-sharing arrangement between Craxi and the DC factions headed by Andreotti and Forlani, which would govern Italy until the next election. The CAF agreement represented a recognition that an impasse had been reached, symbolizing, as it did, the existence of precisely those mutual vetos which would ensure that no move away from the extant proportionality was possible. It also signified a further degeneration in the quality of Italian government itself, for it was a *power-sharing* arrangement –

meaning a tightening of party control over public institutions and an increasing share of resources to be made available for distribution through the mechanisms of clientelistic power-broking.

If the CAF agreement was the underlying factor responsible for the emergence of the referendum movement, the catalysts for its emergence were the government crisis which took place immediately following the PSI Congress in May 1989 and the government's refusal, in October of that year, to accept amendments to legislation regarding local government – amendments which would have had the effect of altering the electoral system for provincial and communal elections. Officially cited as the result of Socialist dissatisfaction with the apparent lack of direction in government policy, the crisis was widely thought to have been engineered by Forlani and Craxi in order to oust the Prime Minister, De Mita, and to make way for Andreotti after the European elections in June (Bellu and Bonsanti, 1993; Galli, 1991; Gilbert, 1995). The strange way in which the President of the Republic appeared to subordinate resolution of the crisis to the partisan interests of the DC and the Socialists when his constitutional duty was to try to resolve it as speedily as possible (Pasquino, 1991b), as well as the strange way in which all the earlier obstacles placed by the Socialists in the way of prime ministerial candidates were suddenly removed as soon as the post was conferred on Andreotti (McCarthy, 1992: 48), seemed emblematic of the sheer decline in the quality of government that the parties had managed to achieve. By October – when, on Socialist insistence, the government blocked reform of the electoral system for provinces and communes by making the issue the subject of a confidence motion – the post of Prime Minister was firmly in the hands of Andreotti: a man 'decisively dedicated to immobility, obsessive continuity and obstinate conservatism' (Pasquino, 1991b: 50).

The man who spearheaded the referendum movement, the Christian Democrat politician, Mario Segni, now announced that he was gathering the required number of signatures necessary to hold referenda on three issues: partial abrogation of the law governing elections to the Senate; a reduction in the number of preference votes available to each elector, in Chamber of Deputies elections, from three or four (depending on the size of the relevant district) to one only; and an extension of the majority voting system in force for communes of under 5000 inhabitants to all the communes of Italy. Events had made clear that change to the electoral system was a case of the reform paradox – that the actors from whom change is required are precisely the actors most likely to oppose change. Faced with this vicious circle, the referendum instrument offered the only possible way out.

## Run-up to a Revolution

Article 75 of the Italian Constitution makes it possible to hold referenda in order to decide on the partial or total abolition of laws when such referenda are requested either by 500 000 electors or five regional councils. Although Article 75 only allows for referenda aimed at striking down existing laws (that is, not ones designed to consider proposals that have not already been passed by parliament), following the first ever referendum – on divorce in 1974 – it soon became apparent that, depending on *how*, and on *what*, questions were framed, popular initiatives could take on a quasi-propositional character (Uleri, 1994: 2) and that, partly because of this, the accepted political significance of referenda might often be far greater than the referenda questions formally considered (Neppi Modona *et al.*, 1995: 243).[6]

Segni's initiative was no exception, and there were four factors which considerably heightened its political significance. First, two of the referenda questions were declared inadmissible by the Constitutional Court, for reasons which probably had more to do with political, than with purely legal, considerations (Pasquino, 1991a: 58).[7] Second, the organizations which undertook to collect the necessary half-million signatures for the question which remained (on preference voting) constituted a genuine cross-party alliance of political forces – from Christian Democrats, through Liberals, Republicans, Radicals and Communists – and associations of civil society – including the Italian Association of Christian Workers, the National Association of Women Electors, the Italian Catholic University Federation and many more – so that, together, they took on the strong connotations of a broad-based movement against the power of a small oligarchy.[8] Third, the movement's political significance was heightened even further by the implacable hostility of the political establishment. With the exception of Scalfari's *la Repubblica* and Montanelli's *il Giornale*, the media – including the state-run television network under its Socialist Director General, Enrico Manca – were silent on the referendum. The Christian Democrats' official line on it was one of neutrality (not calling on their supporters to vote either 'yes' or 'no') thus ensuring that, in the event of victory for the referendum's promoters, the resulting political damage would be borne entirely by Craxi. Craxi then duly obliged by famously inviting Italians to take a trip to the seaside on the day of the referendum – Sunday 9 June 1991. His intention had been to try to ensure that the referendum failed to reach a quorum (referenda outcomes are legally null and void, whatever the result, if the turnout fails to reach 50 per cent) but it was a fateful mistake: it broke the wall of silence erected by the mass media; left him open to the charge that he was behaving unconstitutionally (since exercise of the vote is considered a duty as well as a right in Italian constitutional law); and meant that he was, in effect, offering himself up as the personification of the hated *partitocrazia* (McCarthy, 1992: 47).

Finally, the unexpectednes of the referendum outcome itself – 95.6 per cent in favour of abolishing preference voting on a turnout of 62.5 per cent – heightened its political significance. The silence of the media, the hostility of established politicians, the difficulties that had been encountered in gathering the necessary number of signatures, the failure, for lack of the necessary quora, of three referenda the previous year, the relatively technical nature of the question had all indicated public apathy and therefore, if not a straight defeat, a failure to reach the magic 50 per cent turnout. Instead, to everyone's surprise, Italians in all parts of the country turned out massively and voted overwhelmingly in one direction. That the implications of this outcome went far beyond the change in voting procedures it resulted in was not lost on anyone.

Encouraged by these results, Segni announced three further referenda to replace the two declared inadmissible by the Constitutional Court and on 16 October 1991 his supporters began to gather the necessary signatures with the aim of maintaining pressure on a political establishment which would have to face elections when the tenth legislature came to the end of its natural life the following year (McCarthy, 1992: 54).[9] The echo which the movement had found among the electorate was reflected in the 1 300 000 signatures deposited with the Court of Cassation on 14 January: a figure that was well above the 608 000 collected for the 1991 referendum and which, in exceeding so massively the 500 000 required, had political value as a sign of strength (Corbetta and Parisi, 1994: 144; Pasquino, 1991a: 54).

A significant contribution to this strength was made by President Francesco Cossiga's *picconate* ('pick-axe blows') which reached their culmination in autumn 1991. These 'blows', or series of vehement criticisms of the deficiencies and inertia of a wide range of state institutions transformed Francesco Cossiga, in the last two years of his mandate, from 'a quiet and rather dull President into someone who embarked on a wholesale crusade against the Italian body politic' (Bull and Newell, 1993: 211). Cossiga 'called for constitutional reform and a "second republic" which would be strengthened through a greater role being given to the presidency' (Bull and Newell, 1993: 211–12). The *picconate* ensured that while the signatures for the new referenda were being gathered the irresponsibility of the political establishment would be kept at the forefront of the public mind. First, it was widely suspected that Cossiga's behaviour was an aggressive form of self-defence in the face of revelations about his involvement in the formation of *Gladio*, a secret, armed, anti-communist organization set up in 1956 by the CIA and the Italian government without the knowledge of parliament;[10] and *Gladio* itself served to remind the public yet again about the difficulties experienced by the Italian state in exercising democratic control over its institutional underworld (Bull and Newell, 1993: 211; Ferraresi, 1992: 90).[11] Second, Cossiga's verbal attacks and insitutional threats were widely denounced as unconstitutional, given that he was failing to remain above party politics (Balboni, 1992; Neppi Modona *et al.*, 1995) and was, in effect, attacking the very constitution whose values and integrity he was supposed to defend!

The *picconate* therefore supplied the context for reinforcing the referendum movement and in autumn 1991 the Committee for Electoral Reform, COREL, was joined by CORID, the Committee for Democratic Reform. Chaired by the austere constitutional lawyer Massimo Severo Giannini, CORID gathered signatures for proposals to: abolish the Ministry of State Participation (the ministry responsible for overseeing the state holding companies); abolish the laws providing for special financial aid for the South; and remove from government the power to nominate the boards of publicly owned banks. Meanwhile, the Radicals succeeded in gathering the necessary number of signatures for proposals to: abolish state funding for political parties, provided for by Law no. 195 of 1974; abolish the penal sanctions on drug users, which had been introduced by Law no. 162 of 1990; and abolish the role of local health boards in environmental protection matters. Finally, on 22 January, referenda were requested by a number of regional councils on proposals to abolish the Ministries of Health, of Industry, of Agriculture and of Tourism.

It really did seem as though the success of the 1991 referendum had 'sparked off a veritable surge of petitions' (Newell and Bull, 1993: 607) on a range of additional proposals designed to remove the sources of patronage, and undercut the power bases, of the established political parties. Of the 13 proposals, ten were eventually declared admissible by the Constitutional Court.[12] Of these ten, two – Giannini's proposal to abolish special financial aid for the South and Segni's on local-level electoral laws – became redundant when reform legislation was passed just before the date fixed for the referendum and therefore prevented the questions being put. In essence it meant that parliament had been forced into action and that two of the referendum movement's goals had been achieved.

This left eight referenda proposals. On 23 July 1992, parliament appointed a Bicameral Commission (the so-called 'De Mita–Iotti Commission') charged with devising electoral system and other institutional reform proposals. Given the context in which it was appointed – in the aftermath of the 1992 elections, with *Tangentopoli* fully underway and the League apparently spreading like a plague throughout the North – the Commission had all the appearances of a last-ditch attempt by the political establishment to head off the most important of the referenda – the proposal regarding the voting system for the Senate – in the way in which the local electoral system proposal had been headed off, by changing the law to make it redundant. However, the necessary agreement was not forthcoming and, in the end, the parties threw in the towel, each deciding to ride the tiger of popular protest as best it could: in what was clearly a damage limitation exercise all the traditional governing parties now invited Italians to vote 'yes' to the electoral law proposal (as they did of most of the other proposals as well).

Dramatic though they were, the results were of no great surprise to anyone. On a 77.1 per cent turnout, support for the electoral law proposal was overwhelming (82.7 per cent in favour) as it was for each of the other proposals[13] which benefited (as had been intended) from the 'bandwagon effect' exerted by the electoral law proposal on which media coverage of the campaign had almost exclusively focused. By the day of the vote itself, support for the proposal had come to encompass all but four small parties – the Greens, *la Rete*, Communist Refoundation and the MSI.[14] If these parties believed that they had the most to lose from any move away from proportionality, the other parties' support for a 'yes' vote was clearly dictated by their awareness that although the referendum outcome seemed inevitable, it still left open the question of what would *replace* the system about to be abolished. In short, the political and social breadth of support for the 'yes' campaign was such that the result never appeared to be in doubt. What was of most interest to people during the campaign was the likely margin of victory and what would be its immediate political consequences.

These were not long in making themselves felt. On 22 April the Prime Minister, Giuliano Amoto, announced his resignation saying that he was making way for a 'transitional government' which would lay the foundations for a 'Second Republic' through the reform of the electoral system that was now inescapable. Amato had been appointed following the 1992 elections after it had become clear that, with his closest lieutenants already engulfed by the *Tangentopoli* investigations, Craxi's pretensions to the position were no longer sustainable. Amato's government had been by no means ineffective as the rising tide of scandal had already forced the governing parties to retreat from their positions of power in the state apparatus by the time it had taken office: the Republicans had felt unable to join it and it drew strength from the decisive support of President Scalfaro and the inability of the parties in crisis to plot its downfall (Pasquino and Hellman, 1993). But Amato was the Socialist head of a government sustained in office by a legislature which, with no fewer than 300 of its members under judicial investigation by the time he resigned, had, by common consent, lost most of its legitimacy.[15] Already, by the end of 1992, the traditional governing parties were beginning to disintegrate and the expression

'Second Republic', referring to the need for a root-and-branch reform of the entire political system, had also become common currency. In view of the referendum outcome, a new electoral law would have to be passed as a matter of urgency and, once that had happened, fresh elections would have to take place in order to restore to parliament its lost legitimacy. Amato therefore preferred to resign in order to allow the installation of a government whose express purpose would be to reform the electoral law and then make way for fresh elections. The new government, headed for the first time in Italy's post-war history by a technocrat – ex-governor of the Bank of Italy, Carlo Azeglio Ciampi – took office on 7 May.

## The New Electoral Law

The question voters had been asked on the day of the referendum was whether they favoured deleting the last ten words of Article 17, Section 2, of Law 29/1948 as modified by Law 33/1992, which read:

> In accordance with the results as verified, the returning officer declares elected the candidate who has obtained the largest number of valid votes in the college, *provided these are not less than 65% of the total*. (Corbetta and Parisi, 1994: 142)

The effect of deleting these last ten words was to introduce the single-member simple plurality system for the distribution of 237 of the 315 Senate seats, since the law divided the 20 Italian regions into 237 single-seat 'colleges' in each of which the voter was expected to choose a single candidate. Each region also received a share of 78 further seats to bring the Senate total up to 315. Any candidate receiving at least 65 per cent of the vote was declared elected. In the almost invariable circumstance that this did not happen, the seat would be added to the others in the region to be distributed proportionally.[16]

If the Senate now had a largely FPTP electoral system, that for the Chamber remained highly proportional. The Chamber was elected by dividing the country into 32 multi-member constituencies of varying sizes, with voters being expected to choose between party lists. Having made this choice, voters could then select up to four (one after 1991) of their preferred party's candidates to whom to give preference votes. Once the votes had been cast, seats were then distributed according to the *'imperiali'* largest remainder formula.[17] The problem, in the immediate aftermath of the referendum was that, with a now largely FPTP system for the Senate and a still highly proportional system for the Chamber, a general election would almost certainly throw up different majorities in the two branches, which both have co-equal legislative powers.

Although almost everyone actively involved in the referendum campaign would have been aware that something would have to be done about this as soon as possible once the referendum had been held, campaigners for a 'yes' vote were in no sense united in their views of what this 'something' should be. The PDS wanted a system of *doppio turno*, similar to the French 'double ballot' system, which would effectively force voters to choose between a left and a right coalition of forces with the PDS as the dominant left force, thus undermining the DC's central fulcrum position and opening the way to alternation in government. All the other forces in the 'yes' camp were resolutely against such a possibility for a plethora of stated reasons. Perhaps the most significant explanation, however, was the DC's awareness that, if the Senate's new electoral law were subsequently to be introduced for the Chamber, the party's electoral position would be more secure than under a system of *doppio turno*. Psephological analyses suggested that, under a straight plurality, single-ballot system, Italy's geographical distribution of voting strengths would probably give the DC control of the South, the PDS the centre and the League the North – thus effectively leaving the DC as the fulcrum of the party system with the PDS to its left and the League to its right. Moreover, some members of the 'yes' camp began to suggest (to violent protestations from the PDS) that, if the majority in support of the senate's electoral law turned out to be large enough, then this could be interpreted as implicit public support for the introduction of a similar, if not identical, system for the Chamber of Deputies, and that no other kind of reform could therefore be countenanced (Newell and Bull, 1993: 611).

In the end, the latter view won the day. Since the referendum outcome had not thrown a question mark over the single-ballot system, it was a short step from there to arguing that the referendum tied parliament's hands in this respect, which in turn made it easy for Christian Democratic speakers to shift the burden of justification on to those who proposed changes (Pappalardo, 1994). On the other side, the PDS was unable to keep together the coalition of forces it had built around the double-ballot idea, its desire to provide leadership being compromised by its traditional habit of mediating and giving priority to consensus over content (Pappalardo, 1994: 299).

Once it had been decided that the new electoral law would embody a mixed plurality–proportional system based on a single ballot along the lines of the one that the referendum had created *de facto* for the Senate, the crucial issue of contention between the parliamentary parties was what was to be the number of proportional, as opposed to plurality, seats, and how such seats would be distributed. An initially restrictive text proposed by Matarella, the Christian Democratic deputy with the principal responsibility for drafting the legislation, was then amended to make it more 'permissive' in terms of proportionality. This was done at least partly to offer something to the smaller parties in exchange for opposing the double-ballot system (ibid. 304).

As finally approved, then, the new electoral law provides for 75 per cent of the members of each house to be elected according to the plurality formula, with the remaining 25 per cent to be elected proportionally. In the case of the Senate, the law essentially acknowledges the effect of the outcome of the referendum, thus introducing the single-member, simple-plurality system for 237 of the 315 seats. As for the remaining 78 seats, these continue to be distributed according to the d'Hondt formula, and voters are still required to make a single choice of candidate in the college where they are registered. Once the votes have been cast, each party's regional total is calculated and then discounted by the total of its votes that have already been used in electing candidates by means of the plurality formula. The d'Hondt formula is then applied and seats allotted to parties accordingly. Precisely which of a party's *candidates* gets elected is determined by their rank ordering in terms of the percentage of the vote they received in their individual colleges.

In the case of the Chamber of Deputies, the country is divided into 26 constituencies which are in turn divided into 474 single-member colleges (with the addition of a single-seat, single-college constituency in Valle d'Aosta). Voters are given two votes: one is for their most preferred candidate in the college in which they are registered, these candidates then being elected according to the straightforward plurality formula. The other vote is for the constituency's share of the remaining 155 Chamber seats. As under the old system, each party (or coalition of parties) presents a list of candidates for these seats, and voters are expected to use their votes to make a single choice between lists. There is no preference voting.

Although the calculations required by the electoral formula used to distribute these seats are rather complex, the distributive consequences of the formula itself are basically little different to those of the old one. As before, the procedure begins with the computation of a 'quota' representing the number of votes required by a party to obtain one seat. In essence, the quota is obtained by dividing the sum of each party's list votes by the number of seats to be distributed – the crucial differences, as compared to the old system, being that prior to making this calculation each party's list vote is discounted by an appropriate figure to take account of those of its candidates that may have already been elected in the single-seat colleges, and that the list votes of any party which, at national level, has less than 4 per cent of the valid list votes are excluded from the calculation and such parties are not entitled to any of the proportionally distributed seats at all. Small parties are thus heavily penalized if they fall below 4 per cent but favoured if they rise above it. Each party's list-vote total is then divided by the quota to obtain the number of seats due to it. Any seats remaining unallocated at the end of this procedure are then assigned to the parties with the highest remainders. Which of a party's candidates gets elected is determined by their rank ordering in the party list except that, where a party is allocated more seats than it has list-candidates available (which can happen because the number of candidates on each list can be no more than one-third of the number of list-seats available for distribution), its defeated single-seat candidates will also be elected – this according to their share of the vote in their individual colleges.

The outcome of the 1994 general election was, like any other election outcome, the product of supply and demand factors both of which, through the law of anticipated reactions, were influenced by the new electoral system. On the supply side, electoral systems will influence the nature of the party line-ups among which voters are expected to choose; on the demand side they will influence voters' choices by determining the most likely impact of a vote cast one way or another. Finally, once all the votes have been cast, the electoral system will determine the outcome directly by the formula it embodies for converting votes into seats (Newell and Bull, 1996: 632). The new electoral system which came into being as a consequence of 18 April therefore played a crucial role in the transformation of the party system that took place in the period before, during and after the 1994 elections.

**The Run-up to 1994 and the Emergence of *Forza Italia***

As the months following the electoral law's passage passed, the old parties entered a vortex. The loosening of their control of the state machine begun under Amato continued under Ciampi (whose government contained an even larger number of technocrats), and membership and votes continued to collapse. If the new electoral system made clear to the parties that they would have to find allies in the run-up to the elections that everyone knew would be sooner rather than later, splits were finally prompted by conflicting views as to the alliance strategies most desirable both from a substantive perspective and from the (more opportunistic) perspective of limiting the damage being inflicted on the parties (Di Virgilio, 1994a: 130–1; Vassallo, 1995: 68). By early 1994 the DC had split into four groupings – the PPI, Segni's Pact for National Renewal, the C-S and the CCD – and the Socialists into three – what remained of the PSI, the RS and the *Craxiani*. Meanwhile, three new (and not-so-new) formations had emerged: AD, AN and *Forza Italia*. Of these new formations, the most significant was *Forza Italia* – not only because it was the fulcrum around which the Freedom Alliance was built but also because of the novel form of party organization that it represented: the *partito azienda* (or 'business party').

The local elections held on 21 November and 5 December, according to the new local-level electoral law introduced in March, played a crucial role in the emergence of *Forza Italia*. The new law provided that, in mayoral elections in communes of over 15 000 inhabitants, where no candidate reached 50 per cent of the vote, a run-off ballot would be held with the top two candidates being admitted to the second round. Table 5.1 shows the results of the mayoral races held in the cities of Venice, Genoa, Rome, Naples and Palermo. As can be seen, the left won in all five cities. This set of victories was fully reflected elsewhere. When combined with the results of the June local elections, the left ended up with well over half the mayors of the councils where voting took place.[18] This was a result of its greater capacity to forge electoral alliances, and especially of the capacity of the significantly-sized PDS to construct electoral alliances around common candidates of the left. In this way, the left-wing vote was prevented from being split and this maximized the chances that the left-wing candidate would proceed to the run-off ballot which he or she did not win the first time round. In short, since the electoral system created a strategic situation fairly similar to the one that would be created by the single-ballot system to be used in the forthcoming parliamentary elections there was a tendency to take the results as a guide to what could be expected at these forthcoming elections. This was especially evident in the euphoria of the left once the outcome was known.

What the elections revealed, then, was that there was the need for a 'coagulator' capable of bringing together the forces of the right in a coalition strong enough to withstand the left. This required, first of all, that the MSI be brought out of its ghetto to have the mantle of legitimacy finally conferred upon it,[19] for it was clear, especially looking at the results for Rome and Naples, that the DC was definitively compromised as a force able to withstand the left on its own. The MSI, however, though performing far above its traditional levels, lacked the strength to tackle this task on its own. This meant that a coalition of parties was necessary, and the case for Berlusconi's *discesa in campo* as the entity most likely to bring together this coalition was strengthened by the difficulties which the already available forces seemed likely to encounter in coming together on their own. The DC was essentially split between leftward- and rightward-looking factions and, during the period leading up to the autumn local elections, Martinazzoli's reaction to this had been to locate the party firmly in the centre, refusing alliances with other forces. Even after the autumn elections had revealed that the future was likely to be bipolar and a centre location without allies unproductive, Martinazzoli insisted that his emerging PPI would work to establish a clear 'centre' identity for itself as a means of allowing the party to preserve, as a future resource, its relationship with its strongest supporters, seen as consisting largely of the Catholic faithful

(Vasallo, 1995: 74). Meanwhile, the need to preserve distinct electoral followings also dictated the thinking of Bossi and Fini: neither could contemplate an alliance with the ex-DC given the latter's past record, but nor could they contemplate an alliance with each other for *exclusion* of the other was too central a component of the thinking and identity of their respective electoral followings (Vassallo, 1995: 74–5).

Thus it was that Berlusconi made his debut as a politician announcing, on 26 January, his intention of entering the campaign with *Forza Italia* in order to forge an alliance capable of 'saving Italy from communism'. In fact what he forged was not one, but two, alliances: a set of stand-down arrangements with the AN in the central and southern regions, known as the 'Alliance for Good Government' and another set of stand-down arrangements, known as the 'Freedom Alliance', in the North (where the AN fielded its own candidates). Bossi was ultimately ready to conclude an agreement because the autumn elections had revealed, especially in Venice and Genoa (see Table 5.1), that he needed an ally and, second, because he recognized the dangers of *not* concluding an agreement given *Forza Italia*'s likely appeal (with its connotations of novelty and political renewal) to precisely those segments of the electoral market that the League was attempting to attract. The AN was more than ready to ally itself with Berlusconi given that doing so would allow it to overcome its political isolation and its traditional status as a pariah party for the first time since the Second World War. Indeed, it could expect to do very well since an alliance would probably result in Berlusconi's reassuring and moderate image being transferred to some degree on to the AN itself, thus making the party a realistic proposition for voters who might otherwise have been deterred by its connections with the fascist past. The expedient of the two alliances was, in fact, a shrewd device since it was thanks largely to this – and to the fact that, if the League was uncompetitive in the South, the AN would be uncompetitive against a League–*Forza Italia* alliance in the North – that Berlusconi was able to bring together under his leadership two parties so hostile to each other. As the final piece in the jigsaw, once Berlusconi's initiative had gathered momentum, it had no difficulty in drawing in the remaining forces available for coalition on the right – namely, the CCD; surviving Liberals in the *Unione di Centro*; the *Craxiani*; and followers of the Radical leader, Marco Pannella, all small parties aware that their very survival in a largely single-member, simple plurality, environment depended on their finding a dependable, larger, ally.

But Berlusconi's debut also largely shaped the contours of what would be the alliance of forces on the left (which became known as the 'Progressive Alliance'), since, with the emergence of a strong coalition on the right and the rapidly fading possibilities of building a centre-left coalition (given the attitudes of Martinazzoli and Segni), it was

**Table 5.1    Mayoral elections 1993: cities of Venice, Genoa, Rome, Naples and Palermo**

| First round: 21 November | | | Second round: 5 December | | |
|---|---|---|---|---|---|

### Venice

| Candidates | % | Parties supporting candidature | Candidates | % | Parties supporting candidature |
|---|---|---|---|---|---|
| Cacciari | 42.3 | Pds, Rif.com., Fed.dei verdi La Rete-Mov.dem., All. Venezia e Mestre, Progresso socialista | Cacciari | 55.4 | Pds, Rif. com., Fed. dei.verdi, La Rete-Mov.dem., All. Venezia e Mestre, Progresso socialista |
| Mariconda | 26.5 | Liga veneta-Lega nord | Mariconda | 44.6 | Liga veneta-Lega nord |
| Castellani | 23.4 | Lega aut. veneta, Patto Venezia Mestre, Progr. autonomia, Verso part.pop. | | | |
| Canella | 2.9 | Msi-Dn | | | |
| Salvadori | 2.6 | Unione dei cittadini | | | |
| Merlo | 1.2 | L. Ven autonomo | | | |
| Minchillo | 1.1 | Il gruppo | | | |

### Genoa

| Candidates | % | Parties supporting canditature | Candidates | % | Parties supporting candidature |
|---|---|---|---|---|---|
| Sansa | 42.9 | Pds, L. Pannella, Fed.dei verdi La Rete-Mov.dem., All. per Genova, Patto solidarietà | Sansa | 59.2 | Pds, Rif.com., Fed. dei.verdi, La Rete-Mov.dem., All. per Genova, Patto solidarietà |
| Serra | 26.5 | Lega nord | Serra | 40.8 | Lega nord |
| Signorini | 15.0 | Un. di centro, Rin soc., Popolari Genova | | | |
| Boffardi | 7.4 | Rifondazione comunista | | | |
| Plinio | 6.2 | Msi-Dn, Part. pens. | | | |
| Di Rella | 0.8 | Giovani per Genova | | | |
| Genta | 0.3 | Pens. U.V.-Lega ligure | | | |
| Romeo | 0.3 | Mov. lav. autonomi | | | |

### Rome

| Candidates | % | Parties supporting candidature | Candidates | % | Parties supporting candidature |
|---|---|---|---|---|---|
| Rutelli | 39.6 | Pds, L. Pannella, Fed. dei verdi, All. roma | Rutelli | 53.1 | Pds, L. Pannella, Fed. dei verdi, All. Roma |
| Fini | 35.8 | Msi-Dn, Insieme per Roma | Fini | 46.9 | Msi-Dn, Insieme per Roma |

| Caruso | 11.4 | Dc, Psdi, Un. di centro, Civiltà e progresso |
|---|---|---|
| Nicolini | 8.3 | Rifond. comun., Liberare Roma |
| Ripa di Meana | 1.5 | All. laica riformista |
| Germontani | 0.7 | Lega Italia federale |
| Pappalardo | 0.6 | Solidarietà democratica |
| Scalabrini | 0.5 | Verdi federalisti |
| Pozzi | 0.5 | Partito amore |
| Savelli | 0.2 | Movimento ind. Roma |
| Rossi | 0.2 | Nuova Italia |
| Pasquali | 0.2 | Partito crist. democrazia |
| Cece | 0.1 | Mov. eur. lib. crist. |
| Caccamo | 0.1 | Mov. pop. crist. uomo amb. |
| Olivieri | 0.1 | Alleanza umanista |
| Fiorelli | 0.1 | Diritti e doveri |
| Bartolomei | 0.1 | Dem. cor. libertà |

## Naples

| Candidates | % | Parties supporting candidature | Candidates | % | Parties supporting candidature |
|---|---|---|---|---|---|
| Bassolino | 41.6 | Pds, Rif. com., Fed. dei verdi, La-Rete-Mov.dem., Rinascita socialista, Alternativa Napoli | Bassolino | 55.6 | Pds, Rif. com., Fed. dei verdi, La Rete-Mov.dem., Rinascita socialista, Alt. Napoli |
| Mussolini | 31.1 | Msi-Dn | Mussolini | 44.4 | Msi-Dn |
| Caprara | 14.1 | Dc, Psi, Pli, Psdi | | | |
| Santangelo | 8.6 | Alleanza Napoli | | | |
| Garofalo | 1.2 | Servire Napoli | | | |
| D'Acunto | 1.1 | Lista arcobaleno | | | |
| Sommella | 0.9 | Progetto Napoli nuova | | | |
| Saggese | 0.7 | Noi per Napoli | | | |
| Dufour | 0.7 | Unione civica | | | |

## Palermo

| Candidates | % | Parties supporting candidature | Candidates | % | Parties supporting candidature |
|---|---|---|---|---|---|
| Orlando | 75.2 | La Rete - Mov. dem. | | | |
| Pucci | 16.3 | Forum | | | |
| Giordano | 6.1 | Unione di centro | | | |
| Raneli | 1.4 | Movimento democratico siciliano | | | |
| La Berbera | 1.0 | Unione lega Italia federale | | | |

*Source*: Salvato (1994: 291–3, Table B20a).

*Left*

clear that Communist Refoundation would have to be brought into the alliance. More centrally located forces such as the AD and C-S were unhappy with this but were obliged to accept it for it was plain that the RC's involvement was now essential to help the left win marginal colleges. In this way, the PDS managed to construct an alliance which stretched from the RC on its left, through the *Rete*, Greens, RS, PSI and C-S, to AD on its right. Meanwhile, for their part, the leaders of the RC found it that much easier from the outset to justify belonging to a coalition that stretched as far to the right as the AD to the degree that the coalition was necessary in order to oppose an alliance consisting of Berlusconi and the neo-fascists.

If the debut of Berlusconi and *Forza Italia* can be explained largely by the strategic manoeuvrings of the parties in the political context that had come to be created by the end of 1993, the question remains as to what it was that induced Berlusconi, as opposed to any other businessman with more or less clearly defined right-wing sympathies, to take on the task of uniting the right. The following observations may supply an answer. First, 'politics' was in no sense an 'alien' world to Berlusconi. Following university, he had begun his career as a building contractor at a time when the economic miracle and mass migrations had led to a dramatic rise in the demand for new housing. Consequently he was probably used, from an early stage, to operating on what in Italy had traditionally been an ill-defined border separating (or failing to separate) the world of politics from the world of economics (McCarthy, 1995: 57). Building is a line of business where the need for planning permission, permits and licences gives rise to frequent and continuous contacts with the public authorities and, in a context of *partitocrazia*, the fruitfulness or otherwise of these contacts would have depended quite closely on the quality of one's political connections. Although there is no evidence that Berlusconi was personally involved in illegalities, his first large-scale project, the construction of the satellite-town, Milano 2, gave rise to more than one accusation of the exchange of money for building permits and other kinds of political corruption (Ruggeri, 1994).

Second, his name was found to be on the list of the 900-odd members of the P2 masonic lodge published in May 1981. Besides being a consortium for a variety of shady business dealings, P2 also had a precise political objective: that of combating communist and left-wing influence by means which included helping selected politicians gain control of their organizations. In this way, P2 itself would become a sort of secret, cross-party, 'controlling' organization. What is most curious about Berlusconi's connection with P2 is the overlap between parts of the latter's plan of action, and steps which he himself took. Thus, if Berlusconi based *Forza Italia* on 'supporters' clubs composed of political activists and representatives of civil society who were, by temperament, open to politically pragmatic action and willing to give up the usual and rigid ideological dogmas', P2's 'plan for democratic renewal' had itself floated the idea of the launch of new political movements 'founded by an equal number of *supporters' clubs composed of political activists and representatives of civil society . . . by temperament open to politically pragmatic action and willing to give up the usual and rigid ideological dogmas'* (Fiori, 1995: 55–6).

Third, Berlusconi's association with Bettino Craxi had been a key factor in the growth of the former's media empire in the 1980s. In 1976, the Constitutional Court had decreed that the state's monopoly on the right to broadcast nationally had full constitutional legitimacy but that private broadcasting could take place on a local level, enjoining parliament to pass the legislation required to give the expression 'local level' the necessary legal definition. Notwithstanding this judgment, during the course of the 1980s, Berlusconi – forging ahead where others hesitated in the absence of the aforementioned legislation – managed to construct three national-level television networks. The relevant legislation was not forthcoming until 1990, a situation which suited Berlusconi since it placed him in a strong position to win advertising revenue in competition with smaller broadcasters whose interests would have been protected by a definition of 'local level' broadcasting. It was widely believed that a principal reason for the absence of legislation was a tacit understanding between Craxi and Berlusconi whereby the former used his party's coalition 'blackmail power' to prevent the legislation from being introduced, while Berlusconi continued to construct a media empire which, as far as the PSI was concerned, would give a friendly industrialist a position of dominance in a sector of vital importance for the formation of public opinion (ibid.: 103). Notoriously, in 1984, Craxi, as Prime Minister, was able to secure the passage of a decree law which sought to legitimize the position of Berlusconi's TV networks (despite their manifest unconstitutionality) pending the passage of more general legislation in line with the requirements of the Constitutional Court. He was then able to secure the decree's conversion into ordinary law[20] by what was widely judged to be a shameless manipulation of parliament's own standing orders, as well as by making the issue a question of confidence in his government.

What each of these three sets of observations illustrate is the way in which the overlap between economic and political power mentioned above could lead to the emergence of veritable clans whose purpose was nothing other than mutual assistance in the management and enhancement of the power of their members. Thus, as McCarthy (1995: 60) points out, Andreotti had a clan, comprising the chemicals industrialist, Nino Rovelli, the building contractors of the Caltagirone family, parts of the Catholic banking sector and numerous politicians such as Sbardella (responsible for Rome) and Salvo Lima (responsible for Sicily), while Berlusconi (who would hardly have been able to make his fortune without political support) belonged to Craxi's clan. Seen from this perspective, Berlusconi's entry into politics is much less surprising. It may be said to represent an attempt to fill the vacuum left by the collapse of the old political class, not with a new kind of power but with the nucleus of a new clan (ibid.: 61). Thus it may well be that Berlusconi's political debut was not only the result of a straightforward business decision – the mounting debts of his Fininvest group, according to this view, led the entrepreneur to conclude that he would not be able to survive the extinction of the political class, and especially of the CAF axis, that had assured him the subordination of legislators, ministerial bureaucracies and banks to his needs and interests – but that the disappearance of the CAF also raised the possibility of an even more grandiose project – that of *taking its place* (Fiori, 1995: 203).

If there is any truth in this view, then it throws a very large question mark over just what kind of novelty Berlusconi and *Forza Italia* could be held to represent. Novelty and political renewal were, of course, central themes of *Forza Italia's* campaign message in 1994. However, as Fiori (1995: 205–6) points out, almost half of *Forza Italia's* voters are totally uninterested in politics and less than a third of them read a newspaper every day. Voters such as these can be told all kinds of fairy tales. They can be told that Berlusconi has never been the leader of a party before, and so is 'new'. They can also be told that *Forza Italia* is 'new' because it didn't exist before – all of which completely overlooks the deals struck under Craxi's protection, the close relations with the CAF axis, as well as the ex-*Craxiani*, the ex-*Andreottiani* and the ex-*Forlaniani* recycled within the ranks of *Forza Italia*. Just how much really *has* been new in the period since *Forza Italia's* victory in 1994 is the subject matter of the next three chapters.

## Notes

1    This tradition has roots which extend back to the end of the last century when Italian politicians looked to the British example in order 'to assess the extent to which it was possible to remain faithful to the liberal tradition of the Risorgimento without being overwhelmed by the processes of democratisation' (Cammarano, 1992: 310).

2    The Acerbo law, passed in 1924, had helped the fascists come to power by stipulating that 65 per cent of the seats in the Chamber of Deputies were to be assigned to the electoral list which obtained a simple (but not necessarily an absolute) majority of the vote. The so-called *legge truffa* ( or 'swindle law') was passed in 1953 and stipulated that two-thirds of the seats were to be assigned to whichever coalition of parties succeeded in obtaining at least 50 per cent of the votes. Designed to consolidate the hold on power of the Christian Democrats and their allies, the law was repealed in 1954 after the Christian Democrats, the Social

Democrats, the Republicans and the Liberals had failed by the very narrow margin of 57 000 votes to reach the magic 50 per cent at the general election held a year earlier.

3  With a Socialist President, Pertini, occupying the *Quirinale* (the President's official residence) it is possible, as Galli argues, that DC opposition to Craxi as premier would have resulted in the office being conferred on the PCI as the largest of a group of left-wing parties (the other being the Radicals and Proletarian Democracy) which had more seats than the DC. Assuming the failure of a Communist prime minister-designate to construct the necessary majority, the likely alternative – a dissolution and fresh elections – would have seen the DC having to confront the electorate from a position of considerable weakness. It therefore had little choice but to accede to the PSI's demand for the premiership (see Galli, 1991: 230–33).

4  Craxi was reasonably successful in this endeavour. His first government (August 1983–June 1986) was, at 1060 days, by far the longest-lasting in the history of the Republic to that point; the improving health of the economy during his premiership was widely hailed as a 'second economic miracle'; and he pushed important measures through parliament by using decree powers or by attaching votes of confidence to bills. On the other hand, there has, as Daniels (1988: 266) points out, been a tendency to eulogize Craxi's record. Craxi's unusually long incumbency had more to do with the lack of any feasible alternative to the *pentapartito* (five-party) coalition than to any real change in the nature or style of Italian government; it is difficult to say how much improvement in the health of the economy was due to the government and in areas like unemployment and the public debt, the record was not a success; Craxi's assertive use of decree powers and parliamentary procedures was by no means a new phenomenon and was not, in any case, based on a coherent long-term strategy.

5  The term 'lay parties' was traditionally used to refer to the group of small 'centre' parties that had existed since the beginning of republican Italy and that included, besides the Socialists, the Liberals (PLI), the Republicans (PRI) and the Social Democrats (PSDI). The Republicans had provided the premier, in the person of the widely respected academic, Giovanni Spadolini, between July 1981 and December 1982, and at the 1983 elections had seemed to benefit from an incumbency effect when their vote rose from 3.0 per cent to 5.1 per cent – their best performance ever.

6  This seems first to have been realized by the Radicals whose charismatic leader, Marco Pannella, had developed the theory that the referendum instrument could be used to bring together, especially around civil rights issues, coalitions of forces opposed to the Christian Democrats, and in this way to create pressure for a change in the mechanics of the party system in a bipolar, left–right, direction. Referenda with this objective had been promoted by the Radicals on a number of civil liberties issues in the late 1970s and early 1980s.

7  Italian law in fact establishes three stages for the organization of referenda. First, the half-million signatures required for referenda to be held at all have to be collected within a period of 90 days. Then the signatures have to be validated by the Court of Accounts. Finally, the Constitutional Court has to give a judgment on the admissibility of the referenda proposals (Donovan, 1995: 54). The proposal on the Senate electoral law was declared inadmissible on the grounds that it would impede the smooth functioning of Senate elections; the proposal on communal elections was declared inadmissible on the grounds that it did not offer voters a choice that was univocal (Fusaro, 1995: 47).

8  The organizations' activities were coordinated by COREL – the Committee for Electoral Reform – chaired by Segni himself. The need for such a coordinating committee stems from the sheer size and complexity of the task involved in

gathering half-a-million valid signatures (Donovan, 1995: 54; Pasquino, 1991a: 52).

9    Parliament was dissolved and elections announced (for 5 April) on 2 February 1992. The tenth legislature's mandate was due to expire on 2 July and that of the President on 3 July, while Article 88 of the Constitution prohibits presidents from dissolving parliament during the last six months of their terms (an arrangement known as the *'semestre bianco'* (or 'white semester'). Therefore, a special ad hoc constitutional law had to be passed in order to allow the 1992 dissolution to take place (Pasquino and Hellman, 1993: 42).

10   The constitutional lawyer, Zagrebelsky, argued – with considerable justice one feels compelled to add – that the formation and operation of *Gladio* amounted to high treason (Ferraresi, 1992: 90) – this on the grounds that it was a secret military organization, serving political ends, controlled by a foreign power, and formed through an international treaty kept secret from parliament, when Article 80 of the Constitution places on parliament the responsibility for ratifying such treaties. By combining attacks on the judiciary and the parliamentary commission investigating *Gladio* activities with attacks on the functioning of state institutions *tout court*, the President presumably hoped to pose as a reformer and thus shore up his position with the popular support that might have been expected to flow therefrom.

11   On 3 February 1992 the head of the Rome Prosecutor's Office requested that the *Gladio* case be closed (*archiviato*). The Rome Prosecutor's Office had for long been known as the 'foggy port' for the large number of judicial proceedings it had succeeded in 'burying' over the years without the accused in such proceedings being properly brought to trial.

12   On 16 January 1993.

13   With the exception of the drugs law proposal: 'only' 55.3 per cent of voters were in favour.

14   The fact that the 'no' vote (at 17.3 per cent) was slightly larger than the combined vote of these parties at the previous election (15.7 per cent) suggested that their efforts at persuasion were not *entirely* without effect (although exit polls suggested that only about one half of their own nominal supporters had heeded their invitation to vote 'no') (Corbetta and Parisi, 1994: 152; Newell and Bull, 1993: 612).

15   Amato's position was also effected by the fact that he had, on several occasions, vigorously expressed the view that referenda on the electoral laws were 'highly unconstitutional' (*'incostituzionalissimi'*). He was, as Pasquino and Vassallo (1994: 70) put it, a man whose feet were firmly planted in the old system.

16   The relevant formula was the d'Hondt system of highest averages. This formula, together with the relatively large size of the electoral districts, meant that the proportionality of the system was rather pure (Bull and Newell, 1996: 54).

17   This is a procedure which begins with the computation of a 'quota' (q) given by:

$$q = v/s + 2$$

where:

v = total valid votes cast
s = number of seats to be distributed.

Each party's vote was then divided by the quota and the party awarded as many seats as there were whole integers in the resulting quotient. This formula, together with the existence of a 'national pool' for the distribution of any unallocated seats meant that – aside from the occasional anomaly resulting from the finer details of its working – this was a rather pure system of proportional representation too (Bull and Newell, 1996: 53–4).

18  Although care must be taken to avoid reading too much into this since the councils concerned were not a representative sample of all the councils in Italy (Di Virgilio, 1994a).

19  This was the significance of Berlusconi's famous remark, on 23 November, that if he were an elector in Rome he would have no hesitation in voting for Fini.

20  Under Article 77 of the Constitution, governments are empowered to issue decree laws which, however, cease to have effect if they are not 'converted' by parliament into ordinary legislation within 60 days. The large number of decree laws that governments were in the habit of issuing until recently was widely held to fly in the face of the intentions of the Constitution's Founding Fathers, since Article 77 goes on to limit the sphere of legitimacy of decree laws to 'exceptional cases of need and urgency'.

# 6 The New Party System

Up to now we have argued that the transformation in Italian party politics that began after 1989 can be explained in terms of three broad sets of factors, each of which was stimulated to some degree by the collapse of communism: the exposure of corruption; the emergence and growth of the Northern League; and the success of the referendum movement in forcing a change in the electoral laws. Corruption, we have seen, had deep roots in the partitocratic character of the Italian state and spread via the self-generating mechanisms inherent in it. With the end of the communist question, investigating magistrates were encouraged to launch an anti-corruption drive secure in the knowledge that, in so doing, whatever damage they inflicted on the governing parties could no longer play into the hands of an opposition PCI. Corruption had so undermined the solidity of the governing parties' membership bases and organizational structures that its exposure led to their complete disintegration.

Meanwhile, with traditional forces anchoring voters to the established parties – clientelism, ideological conflict and the political subcultures – having lost much, if not most, of their strength by the beginning of the 1990s, the way was paved for an organization such as the Northern League to step in and exploit the growing conflict of interests between the needs of northern small businesses and those of the DC in seeking to maintain its southern clientele bases. Dubbed by commentators as an earthquake, the 1992 election saw the League emerge as the fourth largest party at national level while the traditional parties suffered record-breaking losses. Having prepared the ground well through the shrewd exploitation of its own resources, the League was the principal force able to inflict further electoral damage on the established parties as the anti-corruption drive took off in the aftermath of 1992. If the exposure of corruption and the activities of the Northern League acted as catalysts in the *de*composition of the party system, the latter was then subject to the *re*composing effects of political actors' reactions to the referendum movement's success in forcing the adoption of a new electoral law and to the anticipated consequences of this law. This, in essence, summarizes the story so far.

113

In this chapter we seek to do three things: first, to analyse the immediate causes and consequences of the outcome of the 1994 elections which put the final seal on the old party-system's collapse; second, to describe in detail the precise ways in which the party system since the 1994 elections has differed from the one which characterized the first half-century of republican Italy's existence; and, finally, to ask whether these changes, though still continuing, amount to a change in the essential nature of the Italian party system.

## The 1994 Election

The 1994 elections were fixed by President Scalfaro on 13 January for 27 March after parliament had passed, on 20 December, the necessary legislation establishing the boundaries of the single-member colleges provided for by the new electoral law. Apart from the success of the Freedom Alliance/Alliance for Good Government and the failure of the Progressive Alliance, the most striking and significant results were the emergence of *Forza Italia* as the largest party (with 21 per cent of the Chamber of Deputies proportional vote), the slippage in support for the Northern League, and the startling growth of the MSI–AN.

Most observers agreed that the organizational and communication resources that Berlusconi was able to bring into play were crucial to the success of *Forza Italia* and to the alliances built around it. Central was the assiduous exploitation of the electronic media made possible by virtue of Berlusconi's ownership of Italy's three largest private television stations. The use of television was central, not in the sense of crude manipulation but in the sense that it allowed *Forza Italia* to communicate its message speedily and efficiently at a critical moment. On the other hand, the short time available to establish itself in the electoral marketplace acted in its favour by legitimizing it to the voters in a context in which the connotation of novelty was a positive electoral advantage.

Although the League more or less held its position in aggregate (winning 8.4 per cent of the Chamber proportional vote as compared to the 8.7 per cent it won in 1992), a considerable number of its 1992 supporters switched to *Forza Italia* (see Table 6.1). The desire to minimize the impact of this flow of votes largely explains why Bossi had agreed to an electoral alliance with Berlusconi in the first place. The degree of overlap in the nature of the two parties' electoral appeals and images meant that the new voting system almost dictated an alliance. To have run alone, forcing voters to choose between the two parties for the 75 per cent of the seats distributed according to the plurality formula would have been to dice with political death. On the other hand, once Berlusconi had entered the fray, his agreement with the League – a 'new' formation, untainted by association with the traditional political system – meant that these connotations were transmitted to his own movement. The League, then, was no longer the only outlet available to those dissatisfied with *partitocrazia* and the old political system.

Table 6.1    Electoral flows 1992–94

| | Vote April 1992 (%) | | | |
|---|---|---|---|---|
| Vote March 1994 | DC | PDS | League | PSI |
| Greens | 2.3 | 3.9 | 1.9 | 3.8 |
| League | 4.0 | 1.9 | 54.9 | 8.2 |
| AD | 2.0 | 2.3 | 0.5 | 3.0 |
| PPI | 26.5 | 0.6 | 1.1 | 3.1 |
| PDS | 3.9 | 75.3 | 3.2 | 12.1 |
| Network | 0.9 | 1.3 | 0.4 | 1.8 |
| *Forza Italia* | 32.8 | 7.3 | 28.0 | 35.0 |
| *Patto Segni* | 14.2 | 0.6 | 1.5 | 6.1 |
| AN | 9.2 | 1.4 | 5.8 | 10.2 |
| RC | 0.5 | 4.0 | 0.6 | 1.2 |
| Pannella/others | 3.7 | 1.4 | 2.1 | 15.5 |
| Total | 100.0 | 100.0 | 100.0 | 100.0 |

*Source*: Data supplied by Directa, srl, Milan.

Likewise, novelty, moderation and the other images projected by *Forza Italia* were a significant element in the success of the AN (whose share of the Chamber proportional vote rose from 5.4 per cent to 13.5 per cent). For if Berlusconi's agreement with the League meant that his own movement could take on the connotations of novelty and originality of that formation, then the process of 'contagion' could also work the other way round, and the AN undoubtedly benefited from Berlusconi's reassuring and moderate image which, for the first time, made the party a realistic proposition for sections of the electorate which might otherwise have been deterred by the party's (real and imagined) connections with the country's fascist past.

On the other hand, it was the fact of 'the past' and the *absence* of any connotations of novelty which, most observers agreed, lay at the root of the failure of the left to win the elections. Given the inevitable prominence of the PDS within the Progressive Alliance, the left was compromised by being associated too closely with the old assumptions of Italian politics. 'Old' in this context meant three things. First, though mostly innocent of the grossest acts of corruption, the PDS had nevertheless been involved with the old political class and the process of *lotizazzione* ('sharing out') by means of *consociativismo* – the practice whereby, given the overall shape of the Italian party system and the structure of opportunities set by parliament's internal rules of procedure, the communist opposition had been able to bargain with the government majority in ways which blurred the distinction between the two.[1] Second, it has been suggested that, although the PCI–PDS had long internalized the norms and values of parliamentary democracy and persuaded large numbers of voters that it had done so, it had never been entirely able to shake off the stigma of its authoritarian past. Third, for significant proportions of voters, hostility to the practices of *partitocrazia* had apparently led to a profound suspicion towards the institution of party itself. Therefore, because the Progressives were unable to construct a leadership group that was the consequence of something other than negotiations between party elites, the left was consequently delegitimized in the eyes of voters.

In many respects, the 1994 election was marked by strong continuities with the past. First, while one of the objectives of the previous year's electoral reform had been to improve voter choice by forcing parties together around competing programmes for government before polling occurred, it would be difficult to argue that the 1994 election comprehensively achieved this. Certainly, there were pressures on the parties to find allies in order to survive, but the resulting electoral cartels were more 'opportunistic' alliances to win an election than a meeting of minds around common programmes among which voters could then make a choice. First, the alliance around Berlusconi was really *two* alliances (the 'Freedom Alliance' and the 'Alliance for Good Government') and in no part of the country were voters able to choose candidates backed by the entire range of parties which subsequently went on to form the government. Second, since the parties were campaigning separately for the proportionally distributed seats, they maintained the prominence of their own programmes over the common proposals of each alliance – which, far from *improving* the choices offered to voters, muddied them. Third, to the extent that genuinely common programmes for each cartel existed, these resembled more a series of objectives and declarations of intent than policies for government and were further obscured by the invective displayed, not just between alliances but within the alliances themselves (Bull and Newell, 1995: 85).

A second continuity with the past was shown by the voters' responses to the parties' appeals. Considering the 1994 choices of the supporters of the 1992 parties (Table 6.1) leads to the conclusion that a large proportion (possibly the majority) of voters behaved in ways that were entirely predictable given the range of choices with which they were presented.[2] Hence, although aggregate volatility – at 37.3 – was higher than at any time in the post-war period,[3] this was almost entirely explicable in terms of the change in the structure of choices put before the electorate. Voters may have shown 'unprecedented availability' (D'Alimonte and Bartolini (1997b: 121) but they had already begun to show signs of growing availability from the mid-1970s onwards. That the change in the nature of the political demand was less striking than the change in political supply was not surprising, for electors do not make their voting decisions afresh every time; rather, they arrive at the polling booths with already formed and deeply held attitudes that are the product of the ongoing influence of their social, cultural and ideological backgrounds.

Of the PDS voters some three-quarters remained loyal to their party – a proportion well within the range that political scientists would expect for a large established party. DC voters, too, showed loyalty of a kind, since, far from distributing their votes randomly after their party's demise, some three-quarters opted for one of the three parties (the PPI, the Segni Pact and *Forza Italia*) which had direct affinities with the old DC, either in terms of their appeals – as in the case of *Forza Italia* which, among other things, sought during the campaign to stress its 'functional equivalence' to the old DC by emphasizing the notion of anti-communism – or in terms of organization and personnel – the PPI and the Segni Pact.

The distribution of support of ex-PSI voters was remarkably consistent with what was already known about their attitudes. Research, such as that of Natale (1994), had suggested that they could be divided into three broad categories: those with sympathies towards the League and the traditional 'lay parties' of the centre (30–40 per cent of the total); those animated by progressive ideals (20–30 per cent); and the remaining 'exchange voters', who supported the PSI based on a calculation of the material resources and personal benefits that were likely to accrue from such a decision. A remarkably similar distribution emerges from the figures contained in Table 6.1: taking switches to *Forza Italia* and the League to represent those in the first category and switches to the parties of the Progressive Alliance to represent those in the second, it would appear that roughly 43 per cent belonged to the first category in 1994, and approximately 22 per cent to the second.

Regarding, finally, the League, Table 6.1 suggests that up to a third defected to *Forza Italia* in 1994. Again, this was quite consistent with the predominant attitudes among League voters: underlying their demand for greater autonomy for the North was not so much the sense of territorial identity as such as a feeling of dissatisfaction towards the traditional parties and the desire to defend specific economic interests, particularly in the matter of taxation. Support for the League was therefore instrumental, rather than ideological, and thus intrinsically fragile. Were another party to attempt to compete with it on the same, or similar, ideological territory it would be in particular danger of losing votes. This in fact happened: major planks of Berlusconi's platform were privatization of health care, local fiscal autonomy and tax reductions, all of which were also distinctive themes of the League's campaign.

More significant than changes in electoral behaviour for the further evolution of the party system were the effects of the new electoral law: first and foremost, its penalization of the centre parties (which, squeezed between left and right, ended up with 46 Chamber seats despite taking 15.7 per cent of the proportional vote); second, its penalization of the Progressive Alliance, only two of whose parties (the PDS and RC) managed to clear the 4 per cent threshold for the distribution of Chamber proportional seats with the result that 3 million (over a fifth) of its votes were wasted; and, third, its effect on the distribution of seats among the parties which subsequently went on to form the government. The largest of these parties was the Northern League with a total of 117 seats in the Chamber of Deputies. However, as it was only the fifth largest party in terms of popular support (as measured by the Chamber proportional vote) it probably owed a large part of its parliamentary strength not only to the geographical concentration of its support but also to FI votes as a result of the stand-down arrangements in the single-member colleges.

This was of crucial significance as far as the consequences of the election were concerned for it posed a mortal threat to the League (and thus helped ensure that Berlusconi's government would be shortlived). The emergence of *Forza Italia* had forced Bossi to work hard to maintain his party's separate identity; and the fact that so many League deputies owed their positions to the electoral alliance with Berlusconi threw a question mark over their loyalty from the new parliament's very start. Dark hints by representatives of *Forza Italia* that League deputies would be able to conduct more or less the same battles in association with Berlusconi and that they should decide their attitude to the government on the basis of their own personal electoral fortunes only encouraged Bossi to struggle even harder against 'Berlusconi's stifling embrace' as he called it, with the result that, from the moment it took office, the governing coalition proved as brittle and unstable as any of those of the so-called 'First Republic'.

All in all then, the election results gave every reason for anticipating that the party system would be as fluid as subsequently proved to be the case: the right had been unable to form a univocal alliance and the one it had formed gave no indications of solidity; the centre had had to acknowledge that its future was highly uncertain if it refused to be courted by the left or right; the parties of the left were forced to come to terms with the fact that their entire alliance strategy needed rethinking. Yet the period since has also revealed a number of significant breaks with the old party system (D'Alimonte and Bartolini, 1997b: 130). These breaks are analysed in the following two sections.


## Party System Transformation

Since the crisis of 1992–94, it has become clear that, though continuing in a state of fluidity, the party system has undergone a rapid and fundamental transformation (Daniels, 1999). The precise nature of this transformation can best be gauged by considering the debate over how the old party system was best characterized in order to appreciate what the system has evolved from.

In 1966 Giorgio Galli argued that Italy's party system could be understood as an 'imperfect two-party system' in which only two of many parties had 'a hegemonic and unmistakable role . . . that of directing the government (the DC) and that of directing the opposition (PCI)' (Galli, 1984: 66). This was an *imperfect* two-party system in the sense that it consistently lacked the two features essential to the efficient functioning of representative democracies – namely, 'a parliamentary majority sufficiently cohesive and able to govern for a period sufficiently lengthy (usually an entire legislature) as to allow it to attempt to implement its manifesto and legislative programme, and a minority able to present itself as an alternative at the next election' (ibid.: 44). The absence of these two features was essentially the consequence of the PCI's ineligibility for government. The most serious problem with this model was that it did not suggest any rules for counting – that is, any criteria for deciding – when a party was to count as being *relevant* to the classification of a party system as a 'two party' or as some other type. Sartori addressed this problem in his model.

For Sartori (1966, 1976), parties count if they have coalition or blackmail potential – that is, if they are necessary for coalition formation or if their presence encourages particular coalition alliances among their opponents. Then, in addition to number of parties, a second criterion for the classification of party systems is the ideological distance between the parties. On this basis, Italy could be regarded as an example of 'polarized pluralism'. That is, it had a party system with a large number (six–seven) of 'system-relevant' parties spread over a maximum ideological distance. According to Sartori, polarized pluralist systems have seven further and consequential features:

1  relevant 'anti-system' parties (parties which undermine the legitimacy of the regime they oppose);
2  bilateral oppositions;
3  one or more centre parties occupying the centre of the ideological spectrum;

4    a 'likely prevalence of *centrifugal drives* over the centripetal ones'
     caused by the occupation of the centre (Sartori, 1976: 136) – in other
     words, a loss of votes by the more centrally placed parties to the
     extreme ones and thus a prevalence of extremist over moderate
     politics;[4]
5    ideological rather than pragmatic appeals;[5]
6    'irresponsible oppositions' brought about by the permanence in
     office of the centre party, or parties, and the absence of alternation:
     since the extreme parties do not expect to govern or to have to
     implement what they promise (and since even governing-oriented
     parties may have only a secondary role in government so that their
     responsibility goes undetected) such parties have no incentive to
     make responsible promises;
7    since they have no incentive to make responsible promises parties
     make irresponsible ones, with the result that polarized pluralist
     systems are characterized by a 'politics of outbidding'.

'Polarized pluralism' seemed to characterize the Italian case less
perfectly as time went on. Taken to its logical conclusion, this process
would lead one to anticipate eventual political disintegration as the
centrifugal drives, implying persistent losses of votes to one or both of
the extreme ends, lent such strength to the anti-system parties that
sooner or later they would be led to attempt a *coup d'état*; yet, by the
late 1970s the system had already survived for far longer than the two
other principal examples of polarized pluralism cited by Sartori –
Weimar Germany and Fourth-Republic France. Of course, it could
always be argued that these two systems had collapsed as a result of
their inherent weaknesses in the face of external crises – inflation in
the case of the former, the Algerian War in the case of the latter – and
that Italy had simply not yet had to face a crisis of such severity as
these (although this might be to overlook the left- and right-wing
terrorism of the 1970s). Nevertheless, the increasing, and increasingly
manifest, moderation of the PCI throughout the 1970s (the 'historic
compromise', the PCI's support of the 'National Solidarity' government
in 1978–79 and its hard line on terrorism), as well as electoral trends,[6]
seemed incompatible with the model's expectation of a predominance
of centrifugal drives within the system (Daalder, 1983). Meanwhile,
voters' left–right self-placements seemed to indicate a decline in
polarization.[7] As a description of the Italian case, then, the model of
'polarized pluralism' seemed to call for some refinement.
    Farneti consequently argued that tendencies towards disruptive
polarization had 'come up against counteracting forces capable of
holding political society together and moderating the tendency towards
head-on collision' (Farneti, 1985: 179). The existence of these
counteracting forces – first significantly manifesting themselves with

the PSI's entry into government in 1963 and later with the PCI's search for a governing accommodation with the Christian Democrats by way of the 'historic compromise' – was due to the fact that:

> ... the social and political centre, as a continuous reference point for any governmental majority, is fed by the heterogeneity, the contradictions and the tensions of the two poles of the system, namely the right and the left, that causes them to be feared as either 'National' Front or 'Popular' Front, and hence as non-viable and unacceptable governmental alternatives, by a great majority of the electorate. (Farneti, 1985: 182)

In other words, the presence of a large extreme right, supportive of monarchy, fascism and nationalism had prevented the formation of a large 'constitutional' right while favouring the formation of a large centre party. By the same token, the presence of a large extreme left, supportive of a Soviet-type regime, had prevented the formation of a large social democratic left while also encouraging the formation of a large centre party (ibid.: xxix). Thus, unable to come together to propose themselves as viable, potentially governing, coalitions of the right and left respectively, the parties located on each side of the left–right divide found that the only viable coalition partners available were located in the centre. And there was a real incentive to seek to forge an alliance with the centre since:

> ... the penalty for remaining in permanent opposition is, after all, higher than that of participating in a heterogeneous majority, or a government bill on which one has had to compromise, or the permanent dissatisfaction of the most purist or integralist of the groups within the competing parties in this effort to ally with the centre. (Ibid.: 184)

Farneti recognizes that moves towards coalition with the centre can be troublesome for parties causing them to lose support on their outside flanks (as, for example, the PSI's losses after 1963 combined with the PCI's gains) as predicted by the model of polarized pluralism, but his analysis of post-war voting patterns leads him to conclude that 'penalisation is not drastic, *it does not bring about a disappearance of parties*', and 'in the end, the electorate follows' (ibid.: 188). Thus he decides that centripetal pluralism was able to serve, in post-war Italy, as a functional alternative to that agreement on the fundamental rules of the political game which the otherwise polarized character of the system served to deny to Italian politics:

> The political forces of the Italian political spectrum have often sought formulae of legitimation *outside* the national boundaries, either in other, non-Italian political and philosophical traditions, or in the *future*, in some development to be implemented, precisely because these forces yearn for a

fundamental unity to be created, a core-set of values to be set up. The heterogeneity of these forces has in practice resulted in a search for unity through compromise rather than through polarisation and crisis of the whole system. (Ibid.: 184)

Despite their differences, each of the accounts just considered agree on identifying three characteristics as the *differentiae specificae* of the post-war party system: namely, the enormity of the ideological distance over which parties were spread; the ineligibility for government of the extremes; and the consequent permanence in office of the DC. The party system can clearly no longer be characterized in these terms, for the old anti-system parties, as well as the bilateral oppositions, have disappeared, and the centre is no longer occupied by one large party (D'Alimonte and Bartolini, 1997b; Morlino, 1996). In addition, the party system is more fragmented than it was in the past.

## Changes in the Party System

'The disappearance of the old "anti-system" parties' refers, of course, to the changes in the nature of the PCI and the MSI. 'Anti-system parties' may be difficult to identify since throwing doubt on the democratic credentials of particular parties is itself a partisan, and thus frequent, activity (Hine, 1990: 65) while, on the other hand, attempts by parties so labelled to show that they *do* have the necessary credentials can always be portrayed by opponents as mere accommodations to necessity rather than changes of *principle*, so that, ultimately, whether the parties concerned are or are not genuinely 'anti-system' may be unprovable one way or the other. For our purposes, the PCI and MSI were 'anti-system' in the sense that they were widely *perceived* as aiming at thoroughgoing and permanent change in the basic rules of the political game and were, for that reason, deemed permanently ineligible as coalition partners by the remaining political actors in parliament.

The PCI's shedding of its 'anti-system' status was, of course, intimately bound up with its transformation into a non-communist party with a new name in the wake of the collapse of the Berlin Wall. From the perspective of the party's own evolution, the transformation was not of great significance since it was in fact merely the culmination of a process of programmatic change and growing legitimacy for the party that had been taking place for a long time (Mannheimer and Sani, 1987: 110). But from the point of view of its implications for the party system as a whole, its significance could hardly be overstated. Prior to its transformation the party had tended to be perceived as presenting two contradictory faces to the world. On the one hand, its defence of the post-war constitution which it helped draw up and its insistence that the changes it wanted would only be sought through the winning of electoral majorities, lent it the appearance of a liberal-democratic party like any other.[8] On the other hand, its fundamental identity as a *communist* party carried the implication that the sort of change it would introduce if and when it won office would be both *structural* and *irreversible*. The party's transformation and change of name thus amounted to the final removal of this ambiguity. And with the removal of this ambiguity the way was thus prepared for the defusing of 'anti-communism' as an electoral weapon of the governing formations and hence for conferral on the party of eligibility as a coalition partner.

Since entering government in 1996, the party's attempts to establish an alternative, non-communist, identity for itself have been threatened by its need to defend government policies which it can influence but not control, while on the other hand having always to keep one eye firmly focused on *Rifondazione Comunista* to its left. This is a strategic dilemma reflected in what is currently the major ideological fault line in the party between those who envision a party anchored within the tradition of European social democracy and hold out the (at least theoretical) possibility that this could include *Rifondazione* and those who regard the social democratic traditional as obsolete and see in the *Ulivo* 'a "rough draft" of the future political formation' (Hellman, 1997: 92–3) and who wish to distance themselves decisively from *Rifondazione*. Yet despite these difficulties, the PDS remains 'by far the most solidly organised party in Italy' (Hellman, 1997: 85) and without serious challengers for its status as the fulcrum around which one of the two dominant poles of the political spectrum must inevitably be organized.

The MSI's escape from the political ghetto also involved the transformation of an identity, but was neither so traumatic nor so long drawn-out as that of the PCI. This was undoubtedly because it was more closely linked to the prospect of immediate electoral gains than that of the PCI. In fact, it was not until November 1993 and Berlusconi's famous declaration that if he were a resident in Rome he would vote for Fini that the party was formally invited to come in from the cold – by which time it was already clearly apparent that, with a general election just round the corner, the maintenance of party discipline could be expected to deliver that large reservoir of conservative anti-left voters whom the disintegrating DC was no longer capable of defending.

Like that of the PCI, the MSI's history could also be described as 'one of a gradual, albeit ambiguous *rapprochement* to the established political parties' (Ruzza and Schmidtke, 1996: 148) and, as in the case of the PCI, this gradual *rapprochement* sat alonside the maintenance of a fundamental (in this case neo-fascist) identity giving rise to an ambiguity which would have to be removed before full legitimacy could be conferred on the party. This was clearly illustrated by the reactions to the party's entry into the Berlusconi government in May 1994, something that gained widespread attention in the international press and was greeted by the passage of a European Parliament motion implicitly condemning the appointment of fascist ministers. It was not surprising then, that in the aftermath of its electoral breakthrough of March 1994, Fini decided to seek approval to dissolve the MSI into the less ideologically distinctive AN which had been set up days after Berlusconi's declaration (supposedly as a confederation of forces of the right, but in reality almost completely dominated by the MSI) and which was made to commit itself 'to the principles of liberal democracy, to the condemnation of any form of racism or anti-Semitism and to the (strongly contested) declaration that anti-fascism constituted an important part of the democratic renewal of the post-war order' (Ruzza and Schmidtke, 1996: 157). Thus, like the PDS, the AN constitutes a party whose new-found legitimacy makes it a central and indispensable element in the organization of one of the two dominant poles of the political spectrum.

The second fundamental change in the party system has been the disappearance of bilateral oppositions, a change that is inseparable from the third change – the disappearance of a single large party of the centre. In turn, the disappearance of a single large party of the centre was both cause and consequence of the transformation of the two parties at the ends of the political spectrum. On the one hand, the collapse of the DC and its role as a dam against the opposing extremes removed the most fundamental, and hitherto insurmountable, obstacle in the way of the MSI's overriding ambition of finding a partner or partners in the construction of a conservative, anti-left pole. On the other hand, it had been the PCI's transformation that had removed the last of the three pillars (Catholicism, clientelism and anti-communism) on which electoral support for the DC had traditionally rested, thus hastening that party's demise in the first place.

If the centre is currently the most fragmented area of the political spectrum, then the AN and the PDS have a common interest in ensuring that centre-inclined parties remain weak, and especially in preventing the re-emergence of anything resembling a single centre party, which would inevitably take votes from, and result in a diminished role for, both (Carioti, 1995: 89). Therefore, as long as the favour is reciprocated, each has an incentive to assist in the continuing legitimacy of the other. This explains why, unlike Berlusconi, the leaderships of the two parties have gone out of their way, in political contests, to avoid resorting to the old battle-cries of 'anti-communism' and 'anti-fascism' (which, after all, might otherwise have been expected to have a residual echo with voters in view of the origins and heritage of the two parties). From this perspective the failure of the *Bicamerale* in June 1998 (see below, p. 140) represented a considerable defeat for the two parties which reasonably expected to render their legitimacy irrevocable by being the founding parties of the 'Second Republic'.

In addition to the three basic changes just described, the party system has become more fragmented. Describing this heightened fragmentation is complicated by the effects of the electoral system in clouding the relevant units to be counted. Prior to 1994 there had been more or less complete overlap between the names and numbers of 'parties' – understood as formally organized political entities with an existence independent of Parliament – and the names and numbers of the political groups *within* parliament. After 1994 this was no longer so as parliament's standing orders – prescribing the minimum numbers that have to belong to groups for the latter to be recognized and thus be eligible to benefit from parliament's resources – forced the creation of 'composite groups' among the larger number of smaller parties that now won seats. The picture is further complicated by the existence of 'lists' – political formations, composed of one or more parties,[9] competing for the proportionally assigned seats in the Chamber of Deputies (Chiaramonte, 1997: 49) – and 'tickets' – coalitions of parties, such as *Progressisti 1996*, presenting common candidates in the single-member districts – as well as the broad electoral cartels, such as the *Polo delle Libertà* or *Ulivo-Rifondazione Comunista*, themselves.

There is a good case for arguing that the relevant units to be counted are the parties. The most obvious alternative is to take the electoral cartels as the basic units but neither in 1994 nor in 1996 did they offer voters, throughout the country, the choice of supporting a single array of parties grouped around a single programme. Even more fundamentally, the cartels appear to be too unstable to be regarded as the basic units of the system. Between 1994 and 1996 what had been the centre cartel disappeared to be replaced by a new 'centre' – the League – with an altogether different character. The left cartel changed by extending its range towards the centre. The cartel of the right shed one of its principal components. If cartels have been unstable, this is just as true of tickets and lists which have been formed as responses to immediate institutional imperatives to at least the same degree as the cartels.[10] The parliamentary groups are primarily responses to the imperative given by the standing orders for each chamber of parliament.[11] Only the individual parties have the semblance of entities having, in the intentions of their organizers, purposes and structures more fundamental and permanent than those deriving from the electoral needs of the moment. If, then, the relevant units are parties, the number of units in the system rose to 20 in 1994 and 24 in 1996. These compare with the figures given in Table 6.2 for previous legislatures.

Fragmentation is also a function of the relative sizes of the system's units. From Figures 6.1 and 6.2[12] we can see that the party system:

... seems to have moved from a standard 'imperfect bipartism' configuration, with two large parties a long way ahead of the medium and small groups ... to a configuration of equitable distribution, characterised by four or five medium-sized parties with little difference between them in strength' (D'Alimonte and Bartolini, 1997b: 117).

**Table 6.2   Number of parties in the Italian legislature**

| | Legislature | | | | | | | | | |
|---|---|---|---|---|---|---|---|---|---|---|
| | 1948–53 | 1953–58 | 1958–63 | 1963–68 | 1968–72 | 1972–76 | 1976–79 | 1979–83 | 1983–87 | 1987–92 |
| **Parties** | 10 | 9 | 11 | 10 | 9 | 9 | 11 | 12 | 13 | 14 |

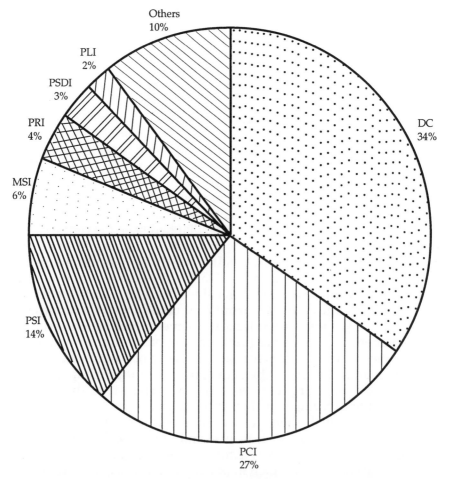

**Figure 6.1   Valid votes received by parties at the general election of 1987 (Chamber of Deputies) (%)**

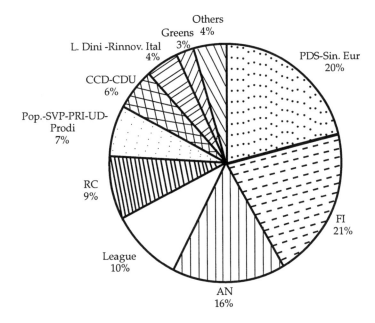

Figure 6.2   Valid votes received by lists at the general election of 1996 (Chamber of Deputies proportional segment) (%)

## A New Party System Type?

If the above changes amount to a *transformation* of Italy's party system, then it remains to suggest to what type the system now approximates. The most reasonable conclusion may well be, as Pappalardo (1996) argues, that despite its fragmentation, the system most closely resembles Sartori's (1976) model of 'moderate pluralism'.[13]

'Moderate pluralism' in Sartori's conception, results from a small number of relevant parties combined with a relatively small ideological distance between them. The absence of relevant anti-system parties allows all the non-governing parties to coalesce and present themselves as an alternative governing coalition 'and this means that the opposition will be "unilateral"' (Sartori, 1976: 179). Therefore, the party configuration will be bipolar with two coalitions competing centripetally for the allegiance of the median voter.

Pappalardo argues that the number of relevant parties in the Italian case can be set at five, or six at the most, and includes: the AN, FI, PPI, the League, the PDS and *Rifondazione*. Other parties are excluded on the grounds that they do not conform to the *presuppositions* that have to be made in order to apply Sartori's relevance criteria. In other words, the parties are excluded because they have not yet demonstrated sufficient consolidation to be regarded as 'true' parties – that is, sufficient consolidation to be regarded as more than mere labels or 'loose coalitions of notables that often change at each election and tend to dissolve from one election to another' (Sartori, 1976: 284). The League's status as a relevant actor is made unclear by its self-exclusion from left–right competition by means of its almost exclusive emphasis on the centre–periphery dimension, thus raising doubts about whether it meets the presupposition of actually being willing to engage with rival parties along a common competitive (left–right) dimension.

Pappalardo measures the ideological distance over which the parties are spread in terms of the mean left–right self-placements (on a ten-point left–right scale) of the supporters of each of the system-relevant parties. While the distance between the mean placements of AN and RC supporters in 1995 is, at 5.4 (8.1 minus 2.7), little different from the distance between the mean placements of MSI and PCI supporters in 1975 (5.8 – that is, 8.3 minus 2.5), a considerable reduction is apparent if one calculates the distance between the mean placements of the supporters of each of the two *poles* – that is, of the supporters of the centre-left parties (the RC, PDS and the PPI) and of the centre-right parties (the AN, FI and CCD) combined. This gives a distance of 4.2 (that is, 7.5 for the centre-right parties minus 3.3 for the centre-left parties) – a distance which is considerably shorter than the distance of 5.8 which, as referred to above, separated MSI and PCI supporters in 1975.

Finally, according to Pappalardo (1996: 129–30), a bipolar party configuration and centripetal competition are being given a strong stimulus not only by depolarization on the left–right dimension but also by depolarization on the religious dimension and the disappearance of a centre party with Church ties thus making available the vast majority of the (ex-Catholic) electorate of the centre to the appeals of the two 'lay' coalitions of left and right.

On the whole, Pappalardo's argument is convincing. He finds a decline in ideological distance in the system. In fact the decline may have been even greater than he suggests, for comparisons of distances between parties over time may be misleading if based on standard left–right self-placement scales which take no account of the fact that ideological space is elastic and can in principal be extended or contracted by the parties themselves. When asked to locate themselves on such scales, it may be assumed that voters' resulting self-placements will be influenced by their knowledge of the location of their favoured party relative to the locations of all the other parties. Therefore, supporters of the RC can hardly be expected *but* to place themselves towards the extreme left and supporters of the AN towards the extreme right, and this will happen irrespective of the fact that, in the meantime, other indicators give every reason for thinking that *the overall distance over which the parties are spread* has contracted considerably.

Better indicators of depolarization are given by the direct measurement of mass attitudes such as that reported by Morlino and Tarchi (1996). They argue that it is possible to distinguish between at least two forms of dissatisfaction: what they call 'pragmatic dissatisfaction' – 'an immediate . . . expression of discontent with the working of democratic institutions' – and a more extreme 'ideological dissatisfaction' connected with 'alternative cultural values' (ibid.: 47). Among the dissatisfied, the proportion of those falling into the seond category appears to have been declining over time.[14] With time, and particularly among voters for the two extreme parties – the PCI–PDS and the MSI–AN – there has been a decline in expressions of more extreme, ideological dissatisfaction and an increase in expressions of more moderate, pragmatic, dissatisfaction.[15] Morlino and Tarchi thus reinforce the view that there has indeed been a reduction of the overall extension of the ideological space brought about by the parties themselves.

The acid test of the direction in which the system is moving is given by evidence about whether competition is predominantly centrifugal or centripetal. One piece of relevant evidence is given by the characteristics of parties' messages as communicated via the mass media. On this, Sani and Segatti (1997) note how, during the 1996 election campaign, party spokespersons paid relatively less attention to potentially polarizing ideological principles and relatively more attention to specific policy issues as compared to previous campaigns. Another piece of evidence is offered by the content of parties' election programmes. On this, Sani and Segatti (1997: 15) suggest that, at the 1996 election, it was not, in fact, possible to speak of policy competition between the two main contenders – the *Ulivo* and the *Polo delle Libertà* – as their programmes not only agreed on the relative emphasis to be given to problems, but even went so far as to envisage substantially similar solutions. Further evidence is given by the goals of the RC and the AN as the two most extreme of the system-relevant parties: according to Sartori, in polarized pluralism, parties at the extremes of the ideological spectrum 'neither desire nor have much to gain, in competing centripetally [since t]heir goals are best furthered by tearing the system apart' (1976: 350). Whether the RC and the AN *do* have goals that are 'best furthered by tearing the system apart', and therefore a disinclination to compete centripetally, can best be discerned from party statutes and congressional documents, as their main purposes are precisely to allow the party to define for itself, and its members, its medium- and long-term goals.

The preamble to the RC's statutes describes the party's ultimate goals as being to:

> . . . work for the transformation in a socialist direction of society and the State. The communists: campaign to further and to affirm, in Italy, in Europe

and in the world, the demands of freedom, social justice, peace and international solidarity; commit themselves to the protection of nature and the environment; seek the supercession of capitalism as a condition for building a democratic society of free men and women offering the greatest potential for human diversity . . . .

That goals such as these are obviously 'best furthered by tearing the system apart' remains to be demonstrated. In the concluding motion passed at the last party congress held in December 1996, the party said that its goals for 'the coming months' were: a 10 per cent cut in tax evasion to finance a reduction in unemployment to below 10 per cent within one year; the introduction of a 35-hour week with no loss of pay; the recasting of IRI (*Instituto per la Ricostruzione Industriale*) as an agency for the sustainable development of the South; legislation to establish conscientious objection as a civil right; new legislation on trade union representation and a charter of workers' rights; monocameralism; legislative decentralization; decriminalization of minor offences; and legalization of soft drugs. None of these proposals would appear, on the face of it, to be unacceptable to significant sectors of that most moderate and centripetal of parties, the British Labour Party.

The AN's statutes describe the party as:

> . . . a political Movement whose purpose is to defend the moral dignity and the economic and social aspirations of the Italian people, respecting its cultural traditions and its tradition of national unity, in conformity with the values of individual freedom and social solidarity, through unwavering adherence to democratic principles and to the norms of representative institutions.

The 'theses' adopted at the party's most recent congress in February/ March 1998 declared that *Alleanza Nazionale* did not believe:

> . . . that the 'public hand' – which nevertheless has and maintains a significant role in protecting the less fortunate classes and in redistributing resources in the name of social equity – should take the place – except in specific cases of certified gaps in the provision of certain services recognised as indispensable – of individuals or social groups, their initiative, entrepreneurial skills or autonomous choices.[16]

Again, this does not look like a party hell-bent on overturning the Constitution at the first opportunity. The thesis that Italy is moving in the direction of moderate pluralism, then, has much to be said for it.

However, much in our assessment of the direction in which the party system is headed depends on our judgements of the degree of voters' 'availability'. In a 'polarized pluralist' system, that part of the electorate which occupies the centre ground refuses to move from its location out of fear of the extremes. 'Moderate pluralism', on the other hand, requires a certain critical proportion of centrally placed voters to be willing to shift between left and right coalitions (otherwise centripetal competition is unrewarding). Yet the results of the 1996 general election appear to suggest that there are far fewer voters available and willing to move than are necessary to make alternation between left and right a realistic possibility in most ordinary circumstances. The centre-left seems to suffer from a 'permanent structural deficit' of voters: it won not because of vote switching but because the *Progressisti* of 1994 extended their system of alliances towards the centre, and even then because, unlike the centre-right, its vote was not split by such disturbances as the League in the North and the *Fiamma Tricolore* in the South (Newell and Bull, 1996; D'Alimonte and Bartolini, 1997b).

Furthermore, if attention shifts to the parliamentary arena, the image of centripetal competition becomes decidedly blurred. The RC made it clear from the beginning of the Prodi government that its support for the latter would be conditional, with the availability of its voting strength in the Chamber being decided on a case-by-case basis. Since then, the RC has made the most of its indispensability to the maintenance of a government majority – 'making the government respond to its concerns on a variety of issues, such as slowing down privatisation, forcing more taxation and less social spending cuts, protecting pensions and so on' (Hellman, 1997: 89) – aware that, if it is responsible for the centre-left government's survival, the maintenance of internal party unity, on the other hand, makes a permanently critical stance obligatory. Perhaps, then, we should, as Bardi (1996) suggests, distinguish between an *electoral* and a *parliamentary* party system. However, if, for parties, election campaigning is a continuous activity, parliament is one of the arenas in which they campaign. And, as they are organizations with projects and policies of their own, they cannot compete merely by moving opportunistically to the position of the median voter, but must also attempt to induce voters to move towards them – something which, to a degree, requires a critical, 'centrifugal' posture as a means of protecting their distinct identities.

Thus, the party system remains fluid and the possibility of a return to the past is not entirely closed. It is for this reason that early 1998 saw the emergence of a new centre formation, ex-president Cossiga's *Unione Democratica per la Repubblica* (UDR), which hoped to exploit the fragility of the government's majority in order to create a pivotal role for itself as part of its long-term ambition to split the forces of the centre and of the left in the *Ulivo* as a prelude to the creation of a new, large centre party. The consequences of the UDR's emergence were seen at their most dramatic in June 1998 when in the face of the RC's refusal to vote in favour of NATO enlargement, the measure was passed with the help of the UDR – that is, with the help of a majority other than the one that had emerged victorious at the 1996 elections. As the editor of *la Repubblica*, Ezio Mauro pointed out on 24 June 1998, the episode appeared to open up the prospect of the *Ulivo* acting as an eternal centre by relying on varying majorities, and thus in fact acting as a *brake* on reformism despite its centre-left political complexion.

In this case it would be difficult to argue that responsive, responsible and accountable government had been achieved even after the emergence of a clear winner in the 1996 election. Yet, in the final analysis, for the ordinary citizen and for the quality of democracy, it is the possible *consequences* of party-system change, rather than the degree of change itself, that are of most importance. So what *have* been the most significant consequences of the change for the working of Italian democracy? It is to this question that Chapters 7 and 8 are dedicated.

## Notes

1   See Hine (1993: chs 3 and 6).
2   Strictly, Table 6.1 does not show the 1994 choices of *1992 supporters* of these parties because it excludes those who will have left the electorate for various reasons (for example, death). It also excludes those who said they would not vote. What Table 6.1 shows is the decisions of *1994 voters* who supported these parties in 1992. I do not think that this significantly affects the conclusions drawn in the text, however.
3   This is Pedersen's index, calculated as half the sum of the absolute differences in the proportion of the vote received by each party between one election and the next. See Pedersen (1979).
4   Centrifugal drives are likely to predominate over the centripetal ones because centre parties capitalize on the fear of extremism giving them a very strong appeal and bedrock of support which they then attempt to increase by expanding on both sides. The attempt of the centre party (or parties) to push outward may be counteracted by centripetal moves of the parties immediately to its (their) left and right; but these parties – the moderate left and the moderate right – are outflanked by other parties on their left and right respectively so that centripetal, as opposed to centrifugal, competition may be unrewarding for them. Finally, the most extreme left and right parties, though not exposed to outflanking, are likely to be discouraged from converging by their own ideologies which mean that they perceive themselves as having little to gain by competing centripetally: 'Their goals are best furthered by tearing the system apart' (Sartori, 1976: 350).
5   There are, according to Sartori, two reasons for this:

> The first is that if so many parties are to be perceived as justified in their separateness, they cannot afford a pragmatic lack of distinctiveness. The second reason is that in a situation of extreme pluralism most parties are relatively small groups whose survival is best assured if their followers are indoctrinated as 'believers'; and a law of contagion goes to explain why the largest party or parties is likely to follow suit. (Sartori, 1976: 138)

6   The combined votes of the MSI, the PCI and smaller groups to its left (that is, the PSIUP in 1968, PDUP in 1979 and DP in 1976, 1983 and 1987) at elections for the Chamber of Deputies were as follows: 1948: 33.0 per cent; 1953: 28.4 per cent;

1958: 27.5 per cent; 1963: 30.4 per cent; 1968: 35.8 per cent; 1972: 35.8 per cent; 1976: 42.0 per cent; 1979: 37.1 per cent; 1983: 38.2 per cent; 1987: 34.2 per cent.

7   For example, Morlino and Tarchi (1996: 51) refer to Eurobarometer data showing a decline from 16.2 to 14.3 per cent between 1973 and 1985 in the proportion of those placing themselves at the centre-right or right positions (that is, 7–10) of a ten-point left/right scale, while the proportion placing themselves at the centre (5–6) increased from 29.5 to 35.3 over the same time period (with those placing themselves at the left or centre-left positions (1–4) remaining unchanged).

8   Of the specific programmatic changes contributing to this appearance, arguably the most important was the 'historic compromise' declaration – representing as it did, the culmination of a process of 'social democratization' of the party's ideology. Its essence was the call for a governing accommodation with the Christian Democrats. How far the DC 'had to move before compromise could be struck remained open to question' and '[t]here is nothing in the documents of this phase to indicate that the PCI leadership had any answers' (Lange, 1980: 121). If social democracy has historically distinguished itself by an unconditional readiness to subordinate policy aims to the goal of winning office, then – its *marxisant* language notwithstanding – the historic compromise was a theoretical rationalization for just such a proposal. For, as Berlinguer had himself admitted in November 1971: '. . . in the relationship between reforms and alliances, the priority criterion by which to measure the validity of a [political] line must remain that of alliances' (Berlinguer, 1975: 383).

9   Such as, for example, the *PDS–Sinistra Europea* at the 1996 election which consisted of the PDS, the *Comunisti Unitari*, the *Cristiano Sociali*, the *Laburisti*, the *Lega Autonomista Veneta* and *la Rete*.

10  For example, the *Progressisti* ticket of 1994 became two in 1996: a metamorphosis whose purely electoral purpose was, if anything, emphasized by the parties concerned; the four lists within the *Ulivo* in 1996 themselves comprised parties which two years previously had presented their own lists (for example, *la Rete* and the *Patto Segni*) but which now did not do so in order to avoid the risk of being penalized by the 4 per cent threshold.

11  In the case of the Chamber, the standing orders stipulate that the constitution of a parliamentary group normally requires a minimum of 20 deputies; in the case of the Senate, a minimum of ten senators is normally required. The parliamentary groups are the principal bodies through which deputies and senators obtain the offices, facilities and funds made available by parliament for the execution of their duties. (For details see 'Regolamento della Camera dei deputati', http://www.camera.it/camera/funzto/fonti/regolam/ and 'Regolamento del Senato', http://www.senato.it/funz/reg/).

12  Figure 6.2 has had to be constructed taking the *proportional lists* as the basic units. Although a number of lists were composed of coalitions of parties and we have argued that parties constitute the basic units of the system, since a large number of parties winning seats did not present candidates under their own names (see Table 2.4), there was no alternative to using the lists.

13  As Sartori (1976: 282–93) himself points out, typologies are maps of complex reality so that any given, concrete, party system, if it is not a deviant case, (thus 'pointing to a lack of correspondence between the format of the class and the properties of the type' (ibid.: 286)), can be seen as either being of a given type, as being *in transit* towards a given type, or as being a mixed case. 'With respect to [the] mapping or charting purpose [of typologies], mixed cases are just as good and as helpful as the ones that fit into one cell' (ibid.: 290).

14  Using Eurobarometer data they calculate that, among those 'not very satisfied' or 'not at all satisfied' 'with the way democracy works', those wanting revolutionary change declines from 16 per cent in 1976 to 6 per cent in 1988. Meanwhile, those

wishing to '[defend] society against subversive forces' declines from a mean of 28 per cent in 1977–81 to a mean of 18 per cent in 1986–90 (Morlino and Tarchi, 1996: 49–50).

15  This is inferred from the changes over time in the proportion of each party's voters who declare themselves to be 'not very satisfied' and in the proportion declaring themselves to be 'not at all satisfied' 'with the way democracy works'.

16  Quotations from the RC's and AN's statutes and congressional documents have been taken from the relevant items downloaded from their Web sites: for the RC: http://www.rifondazione.it; for the AN: http://www.alleanza-nazionale.it/

# 7 Institutional Consequences

Despite the fact that the change in the party system does not yet seem to have come to a resting place, it would be surprising indeed if the destruction of the old system had not had significant political consequences: the political party is central to the functioning of the modern state and to the running of government, so that it is only natural to expect that party-system changes will have significant consequences elsewhere in political systems. To one degree or another we might expect party-system change of the magnitude Italy has witnessed to have affected: political institutions and the way they function; the social characteristics of those who staff those institutions; the nature of the public policies that are the consequences of institutions' functioning and the decisions of those who staff them.

Since institutions define the rules of the political game, their characteristics have profound implications for the distribution of political power. Therefore, as party systems change, bringing a concomitant change (permanent or otherwise) in the distribution of political power between contending forces, so institutional change is likely to come on to the agenda as a reflection of the new balance of power. Parties act as channels of political recruitment so that, depending on how they engage in competition with rival parties, some qualities, and thus social characteristics, of individual politicians will be encouraged, and others penalized. That the nature of public policy will be significantly affected by variation in the characteristics of party systems is suggested by the impact which these characteristics have on things like the degree of government stability and degrees of ideological conflict, each of which in turn affects the abilities of parties to direct and guide the policy-making process. The sheer range of possible consequences of party-system change makes it seem likely, then, that the quality of democracy overall (measured in terms of such factors as the responsiveness and accountability of government) will also be affected by party-system change.

In this chapter we shall examine changes in institutions: in the Constitution, in parliament, in the presidency and in subnational government. In the following chapter we discuss changes in the characteristics of politicians and in the nature of public policy. Then in the final chapter we use the material considered in this and Chapter 8 to draw some conclusions about the impact of party-system change on the overall quality of democracy in Italy.

## Constitutional Reform

Once it became clear in 1992–93, especially once the new electoral law had been passed, that the traditional governing parties were destined to disintegrate, it became widely taken for granted that Italy was undergoing a 'transition' of the entire polity. The reason was that, since the old parties had been so central to the functioning of the political system, their demise was viewed as the death of an entire regime. Hence, the terms 'First' and 'Second Republic' soon became common currency as a means of giving expression to the expectation that the old parties' extinction, together with the new electoral law, would result in a change in the political system's mode of functioning so profound as to amount, in practice, to the establishment of a new political system – even though the formal constitutional framework remained unchanged. As Ignazi and Katz (1995: 29–35) point out, the expectation was that, in place of the old system of government, based on unstable coalitions whose composition owed more to 'behind-the-scenes' negotiations after the votes had been counted than to citizens' voting choices, there would be a new system providing greater stability, accountability and responsiveness. By forcing parties to form electoral coalitions whose leaders would be natural candidates for the premiership, the new system would present voters with a straightforward choice between a coalition of the left and of the right, thus allowing them directly to determine both the composition of government and the identity of the prime minister who, by virtue of his popular mandate and competition from the opposition, would enjoy sufficient authority to be able to impose discipline on the governing coalition. All of this would in turn bring a number of substantive benefits such as: an end to the parties' colonization of public-sector agencies; an end to corruption; an increase in public-sector efficiency; and greater financial responsibility.

The outcome and aftermath of the 1994 election were such that these expectations were unrealized in the immediate term. First, although the election seemed to result in the installation of a government directly chosen by the voters, this was an illusion: in no part of the country had voters been able to vote for or against the entire coalition of parties that subsequently went on to form the government (Ignazi and Katz, 1995: 32). Second, by treating voters to the spectacle of litigious electoral coalitions and a government whose life was rather shorter than the 300-day average for post-war Italy, the campaign and its aftermath made it clear that electoral reform on its own could not deliver those clear voting choices and stable government that had been the ultimate objectives of the reform. Consequently, in both academic and political circles, institutional and constitutional reform now became regarded as an absolute priority: because it was assumed that Italy was undergoing a transition of the entire political system, the apparent failure of the new electoral law to live up to the hopes placed in it seemed to suggest that, until new constitutional rules were drafted, the transition could not be brought to a successful conclusion. From this perspective, the electoral reform of 1993 tended to be viewed as only the beginning of a process that now required completion (Ignazi and Katz, 1995; Pasquino, 1997).

Meanwhile, a number of more specific features of the 1994 election and its aftermath increased the pressure for institutional reform. First, in a context in which the themes of 'novelty', renewal and freedom from connections with the past seemed likely to bring significant electoral gains, the parties had a clear incentive to brandish institutional and constitutional reform as a means of associating these themes with themselves in voters' minds. Second, the election brought into government the Northern League with its ambition of a federal reform of the state – a reform that seemed likely to require a comprehensive range of complementary changes and which in one guise or another had, precisely *because* of the League's growth, by then become a *valence* issue for the parties. Valence issues are issues on which, as the students of electoral behaviour, Butler and Stokes (1974), explain, there is a virtual consensus on the values entailed by the different alternatives. The classic examples of such issues are peace and economic prosperity. 'Issues of this sort do not find the parties positioning themselves to appeal to those who favour alternative policies or goals. Rather the parties attempt to associate themselves in the public's mind with conditions, such as good times, which are universally favoured, and to dissociate themselves from conditions, such as economic distress, which are universally deplored' (Butler and Stokes, 1974: 292). As such, valence issues are to be distinguished from *position* issues on which the parties do appeal to rival bodies of opinion. Finally, if, as Pasquino pointed out, 'institutional and constitutional reform [had] been discussed intensely for more than ten years' (1997: 35), then there was a general presumption that the demise of the parties whose mutual vetoes had paralysed reform for so long meant that early institutional changes aimed at removing the perceived deficits of responsiveness and accountability in Italian democracy could, and would, be enacted.

Despite all of this, however, the Berlusconi government achieved virtually nothing. What it *did* do was appoint the so-called 'Speroni

Committee' (under the chairmanship of the Minister for Institutional Reform, the League Senator, Francesco Speroni) with the task of drafting proposals for reform of the 'form of government' and 'form of state' and for judicial and electoral reform.[1] However, the government fell the day after the committee presented its proposals (21 December 1994).

That more was not accomplished can probably be attributed to three factors: the short life of the government (it lasted 225 days); the profound divisions between the governing parties (not to mention the divisions between the latter and the parties of opposition) over the reforms to be pursued (for example, if the League wanted a strong form of federalism, the AN was largely opposed to it); the essential indifference to institutional matters (unless for purely opportunist motives), of Berlusconi who was fundamentally convinced that Italy's problems were due to the inferiority of the political to the entre-preneurial class and that the political system ought to be run like a corporation.

The Dini government's period in office marked a further delay in the reform process, and not for nothing was 1995 – with which the period of Dini's tenure essentially coincided – called the year of the 'stalled transition' (Caciagli and Kertzer, 1996). As a 'non-political' government of technocrats, without any electoral mandate, none of whose members sat in parliament (Pasquino, 1996: 175), Dini's administration inevitably had to be limited to the pursuit of a restricted number of predetermined objectives, and this, arguably, made it ill-equipped to pursue the kind of incisive reforms needed to facilitate the Italian transition. Indeed, when he took office in mid-January, Dini announced that his government was, in effect, an 'armistice' govern-ment, (one designed to cool the political tensions arising from the circumstances surrounding the fall of Berlusconi's administration); that it would remain in office only as long as was necessary to achieve four specific legislative projects (a supplementary budget, reform of the pensions system, a new electoral law for the regions, and a law governing access to televised election propaganda), and that, once these had been achieved, it would resign. Although the government ultimately remained in office until the end of the year, elections were therefore constantly expected, or hoped (depending on the party concerned), to be 'just around the corner', while the government's resignation, it seemed, was repeatedly postponed to allow it to complete yet another immediate-term project. The sheer brevity of the time horizons that politicians were consquently induced to work to was such as to impede the emergence of concrete proposals for the consideration of constitutional reforms which would inevitably require time and would risk being nullified if elections took place. Moreover, any substantial constitutional change would inevitably also require a minimum level of underlying, cross-party agreement to stand any chance of getting off the ground, yet such agreement as there was seemed to have been diminished even further as a result of the tensions arising from the fall of the Berlusconi government (see below).

Therefore, it was only towards the end of the year, with its legislative programme largely complete and the forces pushing for the government's resignation beginning more clearly to outweigh those arguing for its prolongation, that serious attention began to turn to the issue of how to tackle institutional and constitutional reform. Having managed, in mid-December, to avoid defeat in a motion of no-confidence tabled by the *Polo* by promising to resign immediately after parliamentary approval of the budget, Dini, echoing the President of the Republic, raised the prospect, as an alternative to elections, of his government being followed by a grand coalition (*'un governo di larga intesa'*) whose purpose would be precisely that of bringing about a constitutional overhaul. Since the attempt to form a government of this kind failed (apparently as a result of intransigence on the part of the AN's leader, Fini), the issue had to wait upon the outcome of the April 1996 elections that were the consequence of this failure.

By producing a (reasonably) clear winner, the elections separated 'the issue of who should govern from the larger question of institutional reform' (D'Alimonte and Nelken, 1997: 18) and seemingly reduced the possible approaches to the latter to two: either the election of a 'constituent assembly' or the creation of a parliamentary commission with the task of producing proposals that would then be debated by the two chambers. Quite apart from the legal objections to it,[2] the constituent assembly idea had the distinct disadvantage that it was likely to undermine the government's authority, especially if the balance of political forces within it turned out to be distinctly different from that within parliament. However, similar problems could be foreseen with the parliamentary commission: its proposals would inevitably have to have broad, cross-party support, yet this would mean parliament having to rely on different majorities for its activity – one for ordinary government, another for the definition of new constitutional rules – and it was not at all clear whether the latter would be able to withstand the tensions arising from the former. Nevertheless, parliament decided in favour of the parliamentary commission option and passed a constitutional law[3] giving life to a bicameral 'Parliamentary Commission for Constitutional Reform', under the chairmanship of the PDS leader, Massimo D'Alema, composed of 35 deputies and 35 senators, and with responsibility for drafting, by 30 June 1997, proposals for revision of Part II of the Constitution.

The law institutive of the *Bicamerale* stipulated the procedure by which its proposals were to be considered.[4] Within 30 days following their presentation, each deputy and senator was to be allowed to present amendments to the proposals. Such amendments were to be considered by the *Bicamerale* and a final set of proposals presented (something which took place on 4 November 1997). The proposals were then to be considered by parliament and would have to be passed twice by each House at an interval of not less than three months. An absolute majority of each House would be required at the second vote and then, in partial derogation of Article 138 of the Constitution,[5] the proposals would have to be approved in a referendum in which the participation of a majority of electors and a majority of valid votes would be required for the proposals to pass.[6]

In fact, parliament never managed to complete its first deliberation of the proposals because FI withdrew its support for the entire project on 2 June 1998, ostensibly over the issue of the powers of the president to dissolve parliament. The proposals that had been agreed by the *Bicamerale* allowed the president to dissolve only in the case of a government's resignation, and FI now wanted to introduce amendments to make dissolutions possible even in the *absence* of a resignation – and made its continued support for the entire project conditional upon acceptance of this point. The AN, not wishing to risk a breakdown of the *Bicamerale* over the issue, but not wanting to risk a split with FI either, stated that it would not continue to support the project in the absence of FI's support for it. This was enough to bring the reform process to a halt, since the law institutive of the *Bicamerale* had made clear that the final act was to be an obligatory referendum, and it was difficult to envisage the latter succeeding with the two major opposition parties (not to mention, in all probability, the League and the RC) opposed to the proposals.

In fact, the *Bicamerale* failed for reasons that went far beyond the relatively technical question of the president's powers of dissolution. Fundamentally, the breakdown seems to have occurred because by the time the *Bicamerale* began its work – almost five years after the 1992 elections had revealed the first major cracks in the old 'regime' – much of the enthusiasm for institutional reform, on the part of both the public and politicians, had already passed its peak. Opinion polls regularly indicated very low levels of awareness of, and even lower levels of concern for, the *Bicamerale*'s activities.[7] Partly because of this there was an absence of any really deeply held vision – either within, or common to, the parties – of the essential nature of the polity the reforms ought to be designed to achieve.[8] As a consequence, the proposals and their outcome could not be disconnected from the short-term interests of the parties responsible for developing them and were thus bound to fall victim to their mutual vetoes, just as previous attempts at reform had done. As Stefano Rodotà put it:

> The highly ambitious aim, not of revising but of re-writing the whole of Part II of the Constitution, is not matched by any grand project for politico-

institutional transformation, but rather is based on the acceptance of the abstract models of political scientists. There is no clash of projects or ideas, and this makes the process of constitutional revision mediocre, leaving it constantly exposed to the winds of circumstance, to the risk that this or that new piece of constitutional architecture will be exchanged for voting support on quite another issue. (Rodotà, 1998: 15)[9]

If one then asks what *were* the short-term interests of the parties that the reforms fell foul of, one is immediately confronted with the widespread belief that the most significant of these concerned the various judicial investigations into allegations of bribery, false accounting and illegal party financing in which Silvio Berlusconi had been publicly involved as one of the principal suspects since 1994. According to this line of reasoning, Berlusconi saw in the work of the *Bicamerale* a means of solving his legal difficulties. It offered him the opportunity to exchange a willingness to cooperate (something that would also help the Prodi government survive) for legislation – or, as was more frequently suggested, constitutional changes – that would in some way shelter him from legal responsibility for the offences he had been accused of. When it became clear that cooperation in the *Bicamerale* was not capable of delivering the gains he had expected, Berlusconi decided to break with it.

This view is not without plausibility. Claiming that the judges' investigations were part of a politically motivated campaign designed to discredit him, Berlusconi and his collaborators made no secret of the importance they attached to the achievement of major changes in the judicial field, such as separation of the careers of judges and public prosecutors and measures which would allow, *de facto*, for a higher degree of political control of the judiciary.[10] Berlusconi was, of course, careful to insist on a clear separation between his *personal* legal difficulties and the demands he was making: 'It's not a personal issue, it's a question of the system of justice, "and if this knot is not confronted, the reforms will not resolve the problems of our democracy"' (*la Repubblica*, 14 May 1998: 6). Yet Article 129 of the 4 November text, for example, established the principle that 'A person who has committed an act which is defined in law (*previsto*) as an offence, shall not be found guilty if the act has not resulted in concrete injury' – a principle that might be thought to be of considerable help to one facing charges such as false accounting or illegal party financing (Rinaldi, 1998: 55). Whatever the degree to which Berlusconi's demands were in fact motivated by his personal interests, and whatever the degree to which constitutional change might, objectively, have been expected to help him, there can be little doubt that provisions concerning the justice system were the source of considerable tension between FI and the DS in particular and that, if necessary, FI was willing to break over the issue. As Giuliano Ferrara, one of Berlusconi's collaborators, wrote on 16 April:

> Berlusconi is a practical person. If D'Alema decides to give him a hand in preventing politicised and partisan judges throwing him off the stage because of grotesque tales about corrupt functionaries belonging to his group and illegal financing of parties, then fine, he'll agree. If not, no. Why? Because it's not worth his while. (Quoted by Rinaldi, 1998: 56)

Why did Berlusconi decide to break when he did? A major role, it would seem, was played by the encouraging vote for FI in the provincial and communal elections held on 24 May. These suggested that if FI did threaten to withdraw from the *Bicamerale*, the other parties would not realistically be able to blackmail it with the threat of fresh elections. On the other hand, if a break was to be made, it was probably better to do it sooner rather than later when the process of reform would have reached an advanced stage and when it could therefore be assumed that breaking would carry a much higher electoral penalty. Parliament was, at this time, considering Article 70 of the 4 November text, concerning the president's powers of dissolution. Berlusconi must have calculated that insisting on his proposed amendment to the Article was almost bound to produce breakdown since, because a directly elected president had already been agreed to, allowing the president to dissolve even in the *absence* of a governmental resignation was, as D'Alema argued (*la Repubblica*, 27 May, 1998: 2), a potential recipe for recurring institutional crises, if not constitutional chaos.

Despite all this, however, in the weeks and months following Berlusconi's break the reform process did not appear to be completely dead: on 2 June it went into a coma rather than being killed off completely. For one thing, as was pointed out in the immediate aftermath of 2 June, reformers were still able to pursue the *Bicamerale's* proposals by using the ordinary procedure for constitutional reform laid down by Article 138.[11] For another thing, the *Bicamerale* did not cease to exist upon presentation of its proposals to parliament and so could be reconvened, while in the event of a *rapprochement* between the political parties, parliament's consideration of the proposals could be resumed at the point where they left off. On the other hand, it did seem likely that reform would be extremely difficult as long as Berlusconi remained one of the major players, for if successful constitutional change was difficult to imagine without the support of the principal opposition party, virtually all Berlusconi's political moves in the weeks immediately following the *Bicamerale's* failure – from the accusations of subversion against the *Tangentopoli* magistrates and FI's parliamentary walk-out on 4 June,[12] to his demand, in early July, for a Parliamentary Commission of Investigation into *Tangentopoli*[13] – added to the impression that here was a clan leader who was simply not interested in reform unless it could be used to achieve objectives difficult for his interlocutors to support simply because they were so blatantly designed to serve Berlusconi's personal interests and of such doubtful legitimacy. However, if by the summer of 1998, attempts at constitutional overhaul had come to a (possibly temporary) halt, in other areas, such as parliament, the potential for change still seemed to exist.

## The Parties in Parliament

One of the features of legislative behaviour which had most struck observers of the so-called 'First Republic' was its apparent tendency towards what had been pejoratively called *consociativismo* – that is, the tendency, quite unexpected in the light of the profound ideological divisions running through the Italian polity, towards convergence through the frequent joining of government and opposition votes, in the passage of legislation. This was decried by political commentators for two basic reasons. First, it seemed to betoken a degree of complicity of the Communist opposition in the maintenance of *partitocrazia*. For example, much of the earlier-mentioned micro-distributive legislation which helped the governing parties and especially the DC maintain clientele ties with their voters tended, as we saw in Chapter 3, to be passed in the relative privacy of parliamentary committees acting in *sede deliberante*. Now Article 72 of the Constitution enables parliament to pass a great deal of legislation via this 'committee-only' route – except that it can be overridden at the request of one-tenth of the whole House, in which case the bill in question must be referred back to the plenary session. 'This gave the opposition considerable concealed power over the government since it could, if it so desired, choke the work of the whole chamber by demanding that all legislation be subject to the full legislative procedure' (Hine, 1993: 178). So the fact that the passage of micro-distributive measures continued unhindered notwithstanding the availability of procedures to delay, if not defeat, them, caused many understandably to suspect that there was a degree of hidden collaboration going on between the leaders of the DC and the PCI whereby the former got the micro-distributive measures they wanted, the latter support for legislative initiatives and other measures that would assist it in its quest for legitimacy. Second, *consociativismo* was thought to be fundamentally undemocratic because, by undermining 'the ordinary political division of labour between government and opposition' (Giuliani, 1997: 67), it had a negative impact on the effective accountability of politicians and parties through the mechanism of elections: by blurring the distinction between government and opposition, it made it difficult for voters to locate responsibility for given policies. Finally, therefore, *consociativismo* was thought to be fundamentally unnatural because it was held to contradict the electoral interests of opposition parties in concentrating on criticizing, and publicly highlighting, the shortcomings of majority legislation.

In fact, the more sophisticated observers (for example, Follini, 1996; Sartori, 1974; 1976) noted that precisely because visible ideological divisions in the Italian polity were so deep, it was quite likely that there would be something of a gap between this visible level and a less visible level of more cooperative politics, for political élites understood that there was ultimately no other way in which ideological disagreement could be reconciled with system continuity.[14] As Marco Follini put it, *consociativismo* bought social peace, offering 'the PCI the status of a privileged opposition in exchange for the prohibition on its access to government' (1996: 873). But if this helped explain *consociativismo*, it could not justify it from a normative point of view. Moreover, since the complaints of its detractors are difficult to refute, it is important to know to what degree it has survived the collapse of the old party system.

A number of considerations lead to the expectation that much lower levels of consensual policy-making are likely to be found in the new party system. One is that if *consociativismo* really was a form of less visible party interaction consequent on more visible, ideological, divisions in the polity, then the effective evaporation of ideological conflict (which was one of the basic reasons for the old system's collapse) will have removed the fundamental rationale for it. A second, and related, consideration stems from Cotta's theory, mentioned above. As we have seen, Cotta observes that the level of policy competition between parties was very low, the parties' abilities to take policy initiatives being effectively compromised by their heavy involvement in the passage and implementation of micro-level distributive measures (thus creating vast networks of sub-party and intra-party vetoes) and by their reluctance to jeopardize agreement at the ideological level by seeking electoral mandates on the basis of contrasting policy platforms. Since ideological conflict has largely evaporated, and since, therefore, we would expect to be able to observe a heightened level of *policy competition* in the years following the old party system's collapse, by that token should we also expect to observe a decline in levels of consensus in legislative behaviour. Third, if the new system is both competitive[15] and predominantly bipolar in comparison to the old system, this would also lead to expected heightened levels of policy competition: in competitive, bipolar systems the fortunes of each line-up are, in effect, inseparable from their abilities to offer the most attractive package of policies to voters. Thus, again, we would expect to find a reduction in levels of consensual legislative behaviour as a concomitant of heightened levels of policy competition. What does the empirical evidence tell us?

Looking at the proportions of each of the major parties' bills that were also sponsored by parliamentarians of a party or parties belonging to an antagonistic ideological block in the eighth to the twelfth legislatures, Marco Giuliani (1997) finds that there may actually have been an *increase* in rendezvous between opposing parties and MPs during this period. If there really has been an impact of party-system change on levels of consensual law-making, it ought to show up through a comparison of the percentages which Giuliani provides for the twelfth legislature with corresponding percentages for the first two years of the thirteenth legislature. During the twelfth legislature, party government was effectively in abeyance for half of its life owing to the incumbency of the Dini technocratic government. Therefore, during this legislature – by its nature without clearly defined majority and opposition roles for much of the time – it might be unreasonable to expect any unambiguous evidence of decline in consensual law-making. The first two years of the thirteenth legislature, with their relatively clearly defined majority and opposition roles, have removed this ambiguity.

By providing figures for rates of co-sponsorship of bills among deputies belonging to the four largest parliamentary groups in the twelfth and thirteenth legislatures – that is, the Progressive Federation (the Democratic Left in the thirteenth legislature), FI, AN and the Northern League – Table 7.1 allows the relevant comparisons to be made. The table should be read by following the rows. The figures in the diagonal cells sloping down from left to right give the number of bills sponsored by each group *alone*, while the figures in the far right-hand column give the total number of bills sponsored by each group. The remaining cells in each row give the numbers of bills sponsored by the relevant party that were *also* sponsored by parliamentarians of the party indicated at the head of the corresponding column. For example, of the 1820 bills which, at the time of writing, had been sponsored by parliamentarians belonging to the Democratic Left in the thirteenth legislature, 352, or 19.3 per cent of those bills, had also carried the signature(s) of one or more parliamentarians belonging to FI.

The figures in Table 7.1 are quite striking and indicate a significant decline in consensual law-making. Thus, the proportions of bills presented by each party alone, without the signatures of parliamentarians belonging to other groups, have risen in every case, while in most cases the percentages of bills also carrying the signatures of parliamentarians belonging to rival parties have declined. In some instances, these declines are remarkable. Thus, while over 30 per cent of the bills presented by members of *Forza Italia* in the twelfth legislature

**Table 7.1    Co-sponsorship of bills in the twelfth and thirteenth legislatures**

**Twelfth legislature**

|  | Prog Fed | Forza Italia | Alleanza Nazionale | Lega Nord | Total |
|---|---|---|---|---|---|
| Progressive Federation | 899 54.8% | 274 16.7% | 255 13.6% | 317 19.3% | 1642 |
| *Forza Italia* | 274 30.9% | 316 35.6% | 400 45.0% | 288 32.4% | 888 |
| *Alleanza Nazionale* | 255 18.0% | 400 28.2% | 881 62.2% | 261 28.4% | 1417 |
| *Lega Nord* | 317 31.6% | 288 28.7% | 261 26.0% | 532 53.0% | 1003 |

**Thirteenth legislature (situation as at 15 February 1999)**

|  | Democratic Left | Forza Italia | Alleanza Nazionale | Lega Nord | Total |
|---|---|---|---|---|---|
| Democratic Left | 1034 56.8% | 352 19.3% | 292 16.0% | 142 07.8% | 1820 |
| *Forza Italia* | 352 20.7% | 849 49.9% | 660 38.8% | 234 13.7% | 1702 |
| *Alleanza Nazionale* | 292 13.1% | 660 29.5% | 1499 67.0% | 200 08.9% | 2237 |
| *Lega Nord* | 142 14.9% | 234 24.6% | 200 21.0% | 685 72.0% | 952 |

*Sources*: Giuliani (1997: 77, Table 2) and own calculations based on Senate data.

also carried the signatures of members of the Progressive Federation, only a fifth of *Forza Italia* bill submissions so far in the thirteenth legislature have also been sponsored by parliamentarians belonging to the Democratic Left.

However, it could be argued that what really counts so far as the issue of consensual law-making is concerned is not the co-sponsorship of bills by parliamentarians belonging to different *parties* (one might, indeed, expect *some* co-sponsorship, for parties belonging to the same coalition would use it as a means of maintaining and enhancing coalition solidarity); rather, it might be said that what counts is the extent of co-sponsorship by parliamentarians belonging to different *ideological blocks*. Furthermore, the apparent decline in the former could be masking a situation of no change, or even of increase, in the latter. Table 7.2, which groups the parties into 'centre-left', 'autonomy/mixed' and 'centre-right' ideological groupings, was drawn up to test for this possibility.[16] In fact, however, the table essentially confirms the earlier impression. Thus, so far in the thirteenth legislature, the proportion of bills sponsored by parties of the centre-right which were not *also* sponsored by parties outside this block, is higher than the corresponding figure for the twelfth legislature. The same is true of the proportion of bills sponsored by the autonomy/mixed parties alone. Both the parties of the centre-right (broadly corresponding to the parties of the opposition 'Freedom Alliance') and those belonging to the autonomy/mixed block (dominated by the League) appear less keen now than they were in the previous legislature to seek support for their

Table 7.2 Co-sponsorship of bills by parties belonging to different ideological blocks in the twelfth and thirteenth legislatures

| Twelfth legislature | Centre-left | Autonomy/Mixed | Centre-right | Total |
|---|---|---|---|---|
| Centre-left | 1842 74.4% | 458 18.5% | 479 19.4% | 2475 |
| Autonomy/ Mixed | 458 37.7% | 602 49.6% | 458 37.7% | 1214 |
| Centre-right | 479 21.2% | 458 20.2% | 1631 72.0% | 2264 |

| Thirteenth legislature (situation as at 16 February 1999) | Centre-left | Autonomy/Mixed | Centre-right | Total |
|---|---|---|---|---|
| Centre-left | 1902 69.3% | 649 23.6% | 594 21.6% | 2746 |
| Autonomy/ Mixed | 649 30.4% | 1338 62.6% | 548 25.7% | 2136 |
| Centre-right | 594 17.0% | 548 15.7% | 2745 78.7% | 3488 |

*Sources*: Giuliani (1997: 81, Table 4) and own calculations based on Senate data.

proposed measures outside their respective blocks. So the idea that party-system change has led to a real decline in the practice of *consociativismo* is again confirmed.

Nonetheless, it could still be objected that the figures presented here have not captured the practice successfully – this time because *consociativismo* was not just about the sponsorship of *proposals* but, more significantly, about collaboration during *subsequent stages* of the law-making process. To address this issue we looked at the proportion of bills approved in committee rather than the legislature as a whole in the thirteenth as compared to earlier legislatives. As Giuliani points out, such a proportion constitutes a rather good indicator of consensual law-making, for, as we noted earlier, the committee-only route can be blocked if it is opposed by as few as one-tenth of the members of the chamber in question. This means that trends in the proportion of measures passed in committee should yield a fairly clear picture of changes in the willingness of parties to collaborate with each other. From the base of our calculation we naturally have to exclude those types of laws for which the full legislative procedure is obligatory.[17] When we do this we find that 68 per cent of the remaining laws which, by February 1999, had been passed by the thirteenth legislature had been approved in committee. In the twelfth legislature, the corresponding proportion had been 71 per cent; in the eleventh legislature, 95 per cent; and in the tenth – the last legislature before the collapse of the old parties – 89 per cent (Giuliani, 1997: 87–8). So, again, we seem to have robust evidence of a clear move away from *consociativismo* consequent on the party-system change.

## The Presidency

If the collapse of the old party system has thrown a question mark over traditional legislative practices, it has likewise thrown a question mark over the traditional role of the presidency. The president is elected for seven years by members of the Chamber of Deputies and the Senate and three representatives of each regional council (with the exception of Valle d'Aosta which has one representative). The most important of the president's constitutionally prescribed duties are to dissolve and to convoke parliament and to appoint the prime minister and other members of the cabinet. In performing these duties, presidents have often played a substantive, rather than a merely formal, role – a circumstance that has arisen from a combination of imprecision in what the written rules of the Constitution specify,[18] together with the relative complexity and unpredictability of Italian political life, which has effectively prevented the emergence of 'long-term, consistent, and stable patterns of presidential behaviour which [would allow the identification of] clear-cut conventions which fill out the written Constitution in each of the real-world situations in which a President may find himself' (Hine and Poli, 1997: 170).[19] This means, therefore, that the real powers of the presidency have tended to vary in magnitude with changes in the political situation.

It also explains why, '[i]n all those areas in which the institution has hitherto been of significance, its role has been increased' by the uncertainties created by the party-system changes since the early 1990s (ibid.: 169): in a situation in which an entire political class was disintegrating under the weight of corruption scandals, the presidency gained a heightened authority as public utterances articulating the mood of public outrage ensured a transfer of legitimacy from the parties and politicians to the presidency (ibid.).[20] This in turn created room for hitherto unprecedented levels of 'presidential interventionism' of which the appointment of the two technocratic governments under Ciampi and then Dini were the most conspicuous examples. Taking place independently of the balance of forces within parliament, their appointment provides an excellent illustration of how the crisis of the parties increased the presidency's political significance. When there is a high level of agreement among a group of parties clearly able to command a parliamentary majority, the president is said to play a 'notarial' role (Calandra, 1986: 56), his choices of prime minister being *de facto* limited to those individuals whose names emerge during the intense rounds of consultations which presidents hold with the party leaders following the collapse of a government – a situation that could hardly be otherwise given that governments must have the confidence of the two houses of parliament if they are to survive. However, when – as following the 1993 referenda and the consequent resignation of the Amato government – the parties do not have the necessary authority to dictate the composition of governments,[21] or where – as following the collapse of the Berlusconi government – the parties themselves are unable to indicate an acceptable governing formula, the room for presidential discretion becomes much wider.

But the heightened significance of the presidency since the old party system's collapse has not been confined to the appointment of governments; it has extended to government stability. For, once governments have been appointed, the above-mentioned transfer of legitimacy has allowed the head of state to use the resulting popular authority to help sustain the governments in office by means of regular pronouncements (known in Italian constitutional law as *esternazioni*, meaning, literally, 'disclosures') indicating his active support. In the case of the Amato government, this had the paradoxical consequence that, although the government was composed of the parties that had resisted change for so long, it was relatively free of their influence and thus able to act as a reforming government, initiating measures destined to reduce the parties' overwhelming economic and political power, especially through measures of privatization (Hellman and Pasquino, 1993: 49–50). In the case of the Amato, Ciampi and Dini governments, the transfer of legitimacy meant that the president was able to exercise considerable 'behind-the-scenes' influence over their programmes (De Fiores, 1995).

With the outcome of the 1994 election, expressing, as it apparently did, a clear party majority, the president's role initially seemed set to decline in significance. In fact, the presidency remained influential, both as a result of the support it lent in moments of difficulty,[22] and, later, as a result of a number of procedural disagreements with the government which led a number of actors, including the president himself, to take the view that the adoption of a majoritarian electoral system had reinforced the need for a sort of presidential counterweight to check the threat of majority tyranny (ibid.).[23]

The most important of the procedural disagreements arising with the Berlusconi government concerned the dissolution of parliament following the government's collapse. Berlusconi and his supporters maintained that the FI–AN–League electoral coalition that had come to power the previous March had, by virtue of the new electoral system, in effect received a Westminster-style mandate and that, since one of the coalition partners (the League) was no longer willing to respect that mandate, the latter ought to be passed back to the electorate for fresh conferral in new elections.[24] The fact that the president was able to resist this line of reasoning[25] was evidence – if not, as FI maintained, of a 'bloodless coup' – at the very least that the new electoral law had in no way diminished existing levels of presidential discretion in matters of early dissolution and in so far as the president decided against dissolution despite the impossibility of finding a stable majority among the parliamentary parties, that this discretion had possibly increased.[26]

Since then, the *Bicamerale* has sought to formalize a more high-profile role for the presidency. The proposals which the *Bicamerale* passed to parliament on 4 November 1997 provided for a president directly elected by the double-ballot method, and who would: chair a 'Supreme Council for Defence and Foreign Policy';[27] nominate the prime minister, taking account of the results of the Chamber of Deputies elections; authorize the presentation to parliament of government bills; and have the authority to ask the prime minister to submit to a vote of confidence by the Chamber. The text authorized the president to dissolve the Chamber of Deputies once upon his election and thereafter in cases of a government resignation. The likely effects of these provisions must inevitably be largely a matter of speculation, depending, as they do, on the assumed effects of related provisions (such as the electoral system)[28] and any constitutional conventions they might give rise to.[29] But there can be little doubt that direct election may lead to a considerable strengthening of the presidency, especially if it is combined with government instability consequent upon a failure of possible future electoral law reform to provide sufficient incentives for parliamentarians to identify with their coalition as well as their party (Vassallo, 1998).

By the summer of 1998, therefore, the institution of the presidency was standing at a crossroads. On the one hand, if the exceptional circumstances associated with the party-system change had given heightened significance to traditional presidential functions, nevertheless, from a purely constitutional point of view, the president's position had remained largely unchanged; and since the return of party government in April 1996, the pendulum of presidential power had, to some degree, swung back again (Hine and Poli, 1997). Conversely, however, it seemed likely that the experience of 'presidentialism' during the party-system crisis had influenced the thinking of members of the *Bicamerale*, whose proposals had placed the possibility of a permanent change in the president's position more firmly on the agenda of Italian politics than it had ever been before.[30]

### Central–Local Relations

Another institutional arena in which processes of change appeared to have reached a crossroads by the summer of 1998 was centre–periphery relations. Here there had been new legislation as a direct result of the disappearance of the old parties in the political upheavals of 1992–94. This development should not be altogether surprising, for as Pitruzzella argues:

> . . . laws governing local-level competences are, in effect, the laws which govern the interface between society and the state so that it is natural that as soon as a new regime begins to establish itself new legislation concerning local competences comes into force as a consequence of the relationship which the regime intends to establish with the surrounding community. (Pitruzzella, 1994: 473)

If this legislation has distinctly improved the quality of subnational government, it has also interacted with the demise of the old parties themselves to result in 'a strengthening of the local level as a political force capable of better resisting the intrusion of the national level' (Dente, 1997: 188).

The first significant item of legislation was Law no. 81 of 1993. Introduced under the direct pressure of the referendum movement and growing concern over local-level party behaviour, it was an integral part of the party-system crisis. The law principally provided for the direct election of mayors but also sought to increase the efficiency and effectiveness of local and provincial governments through concentrating power in the hands of their chief executives. From now on directly elected mayors and provincial presidents with absolute majorities to back them were able to appoint and dismiss members of their executives without reference to their legislatures, were free to appoint such members from among non-elected experts, and could try to force the adoption of policies by threatening resignation (since this would lead automatically to the dissolution of the council). Since these changes took place in tandem with a decimation of the old political class by the *Tangentopoli* investigations, the outcome was, as Dente points out, 'spectacular':

> Between 1992 and 1993, the class of municipal politicians was completely renewed through the election of mayors who were either new to politics (e.g. Castellani in Turin, Sansa in Genoa, Illy in Trieste and Di Cagno in Bari) or different to the usual politicians (e.g. Cacciari in Venice, Rutelli in Rome, Orlando in Palermo and Bianco in Catania). Furthermore, the composition of the executives ('personally selected' by the mayors), combined with the transfer of power away from local authority legislatures, completely transformed local policy making by substantially depoliticising it. (Dente, 1997: 184)

The momentum created by this success has since stimulated further reform legislation. The following year saw the definitive introduction of the *imposta comunale sugli immobili* (local property tax, ICI), giving local councils the power to tax property values and hence a considerably enhanced level of financial autonomy;[31] then, in March and May 1997 parliament sought to remove the threat to local government autonomy and effectiveness posed by centrally imposed bureaucratic controls and procedures through the passage of two major pieces of legislation (Law nos. 59/97 and 127/97) known after their sponsor, the Minister for Regional Affairs and Public Administration, as Bassanini 1 and Bassanini 2.[32]

Impressive though they were, these legislative innovations were by themselves insufficient to produce the enhanced autonomy and effectiveness of local government that has been apparent since the early 1990s: the decisive factor has been the simple collapse of the old party system itself. Under the old system, whatever the formal autonomy of subnational government, in reality, there was almost nothing in the way of a distinct subnational level of politics that was not subject to the traditional practices of clientelism and *lottizzazione*, and hence not subjected to the overall process of negotiation within and between parties at national level.[33] This was only to be expected: in a 'partito-cratic' system in which the parties had tried to compensate for their inability to control policy processes *in depth* by extending the *range* of their control (Cotta, 1996: 18–19), it was largely through intraparty clientelistic networks that the centre integrated the regions and localities, and through party networks that local-level politicians gained access to Rome. This meant that the old system's collapse freed subnational politicians from their subordination to the demands of national-level intra- and interparty power-broking. If nothing else, the larger number of smaller parties in the party system, with their relative lack of organizational and power resources, made central control more difficult to exercise than with the previous larger ones. Regional-level politicians and the mayors of large cities were not slow to take advantage of their new freedom, attempting, whenever possible, to build power bases independent of the national-level structures of their parties. A very clear example of this was the so-called 'Mayors' Party', the Movement for Constitutional Reform, which came to prominence in the aftermath of the 1996 elections.[34]

Finally, the *Bicamerale* tried to underpin the subnational government *renaissance* with a new constitutional relationship between the centre and periphery. It envisaged a new set of Title V articles, 'The Federal Organization of the Republic', designed to change existing constitutional practice in two fundamental ways. First, existing constitutional practice, whereby the areas in which the regions are empowered to legislate are set out in Article 117, was to be reversed. Instead, the areas reserved to the central authorities were to be listed with the regions being empowered to legislate in all areas not so listed. Second, the regions' legislative powers in these areas were to be exclusive and not merely concurrent. Implied in this was the abolition of the existing constitutional machinery which, through the government commissioners and the mechanisms set out in Article 127, gives the government, with parliamentary approval, an effective power of veto over items of regional legislation.

For these reasons, the *Bicamerale*'s proposals represented a fundamental break with what had hitherto been the dominant conception of the nature of central–local relations within the political class. In other words, the need to guarantee equality before the law – that is, to guarantee to each citizen that they be treated in accordance with a uniform body of law, impartially applied – had as its concomitant the need to provide standardized services to be delivered according to standardized procedures whose application is supervised through tutelage and a prefectoral model of government. In this conception, any decentralization can amount, at most, to the decentralized application of policies whose fundamentals continue to be decided elsewhere, with regional and local governments remaining, in essence, agents of the central authorities, rather than organs whose primary purpose is the representation of local communities conceived of as autonomous entities which only *then* concede to a more remote level of government the power to provide those services which each is unable to provide for itself – the so-called 'partnership model' (Allen,

1991: 81). In reversing the presumption that decentralization would take place by identifying those competences to be transferred rather than by identifying those to be retained, in affirming the relevance of such principles as 'subsdiarity', and in raising the prospect of dismantling large parts of the machinery of supervision from above, the *Bicamerale* represented a significant step towards such a model.

As the process of constitutional reform has come to a halt, the likelihood of this shift of perspective becoming actuality is, at the time of writing, uncertain. Uncertain too, however, is the degree to which the quality of government would improve even if it *were* to become actuality. The currently widespread assumption that decentralization is an essential prerequisite for such improvement is far from having been conclusively demonstrated.[35] In the final analysis, the quality of government is likely to be as much a function of the qualities of individual politicians and the specific policy choices they make as of the institutional framework within which they operate. It is to changes in the qualities of politicians and of policies that our attention turns in Chapter 8.

## Notes

1   In Italian constitutional law, the terms 'form of government' and 'form of state' refer respectively to: the nature of the relations between the principal organs of the state, especially parliament, the cabinet and the head of state; and the way in which society is organized as a political entity (Neppi Modona *et al.*, 1995: 207).

2   A number of constitutional lawyers argued that the election of a body called a 'constituent assembly' which then presumed, on its own authority, to be able to change the constitution, would in fact be illegal, for it would be to confuse the *constituent power*, whose exercise can take place only once and for all time with the *power of constitutional revision* – the procedure for whose exercise is clearly laid out in Article 138 of the Constitution. See Neppi Modona *et al.* (1995: 464–71); Barile (1998a).

3   A constitutional law is one which, although not itself an article of the Constitution, has the same legal status. Hence, it is a law which can be introduced only by following the same procedure required for proposed revisions of the Constitution itself – that is, the procedure laid down by Article 138 of the Constitution. This stipulates:

> Amendments to the Constitution and other constitutional laws must be passed twice by each House at an interval of not less than three months. An absolute majority of each House is required in the second voting.
>
> These laws are submitted to referendum when, within three months of their publication, a demand shall be made by one-fifth of the members of either House or by five hundred thousand electors or by five Regional Councils.
>
> A law submitted to referendum shall not be promulgated unless approved by a majority of valid votes.
>
> No referendum is possible if the law has been approved in both Houses at the second voting by a majority of two-thirds of the members of each House. (Hine, 1993: 365)

4    For a detailed overview of the work of the *Bicamerale*, see Vassallo (1998).

5    See note 3 above.

6    Article 138, by contrast, does not make a referendum compulsory (see note 3). Article 5 of the law made explicit that attempts to revise the proposals once they had been finally approved would require the normal constitutional procedures. In other words, the procedures specified in the law were to apply only to the proposals produced by the *Bicamerale* and, once they had become part of the revised Constitution, there would, in effect, be a 'reversion' to the normal procedures for constitutional change. (From a legal point of view, Article 5 was, arguably, redundant.)

7    For example, early in 1998, an opinion poll carried out by Explorer for the newspaper *la Stampa* found that only 5 per cent thought that constitutional reform was 'the most important and urgent problem' (Rinaldi, 1998: 54).

8    This might have been less true of the League than of the other parties, but the League had decided to defend its distinctiveness from what it called '*Roma Polo'* and '*Romo Ulivo'* by largely boycotting the *Bicamerale* from the outset.

9    See also Follini:

> The fact is that the long debate over the Second Republic and its rules has been progressively reduced to a technical question, almost a kind of political and legislative virtuosity. We have disagreed over presidentialism, over federalism and over electoral representation without ever managing to link institutional solutions to any conception of the country, its identity or its mission. (Follini, 1997: 681)

10   For example, both the 30 June text (Article 125) and the 4 November text (Article 122) proposed to take responsibility for disciplinary proceedings against members of the judiciary away from the *Consiglio superiore della magistratura* and to vest it in a nine-member 'Court of Justice of the Magistracy' three of whose members would ultimately be chosen by the Senate.

11   See note 3 above.

12   This was a result of the request made by the public prosecutor on 3 June in the 'All Iberian' trial (in which Berlusconi was facing a charge of illegally financing Craxi's PSI) for a sentence of five-and-a-half years' imprisonment against the media tycoon. The profound constitutional implications of Berlusconi's reaction to the request (which related to a period long before he entered politics) are succinctly analysed by Paolo Flores d'Arcais (1998a).

13   This demand posed serious risks for the independence of the judiciary. See, for example, the observations of Barile (1998b). One of its objectives seemed to be to highlight just how widespread the corruption uncovered by the *Tangentopoli* investigators had been. Thereby, it would have been possible to argue that since everyone had been guilty, then no one was guilty.

14   Perhaps it is this that accounts for the lexicographical overlap betwen the terms *consociativismo* and 'consociational democracy' – even though, as Giuliani (1997: 66) points out, the two have quite different referents, the former being a political practice, the latter a type of polity.

15   The doubts about this have been mentioned in the previous chapter: see above, pp. 130–32.

16   The groupings are constructed as follows. In the twelfth legislature, the centre-left block includes: RC, *Progressista Federativo, Sinistra Democratica, Verdi-Rete, Laburisti, Democratici,* PPI; the autonomy/mixed block includes: *Lega Nord* and *Lega Italiana Federalista,* the 'mixed' group; the centre-right block includes: CDU, CCD, Democratic Liberals, *Forza Italia, Alleanza Nazionale.* In the thirteenth legislature, the centre-left block comprises: RC, *Sinistra Democratica,* PPI, *Verdi, Rinnovamento Italiano;* the autonomy/mixed block includes: *Lega Nord,* the

'mixed' group; the centre-right block consists of: *Forza Italia, Alleanza Nazionale,* CCD, UDR.

17   That is, we have to exclude: constitutional laws; finance legislation; laws ratifying treaties; legislation conferring delegated law-making powers; and laws converting decree laws into ordinary legislation.

18   For example, Article 92 of the Constitution states simply, without any further specification, that 'The President of the Republic appoints the President of the Council of Ministers and the Ministers who are proposed by him', thus leaving unanswered the fundamental question of how much discretion the president is authorized to exercise in making his nominations and therefore what the constitutional position would be were a president's preferences to conflict with those of other significant political actors.

19   This is most abundantly clear in relation to the president's power to dissolve. In most parliamentary regimes, the power of dissolution is only formally vested in the head of state. In Britain, for instance, the monarch's power to dissolve can only be formal since any real power for the monarch in the timing of dissolutions would undermine the institution of the monarchy itself by involving an unelected head of state in the making of real political decisions. In Italy, by contrast, coalition instability has prevented the development of a clear and unambiguous constitutional convention limiting the head of state's discretion; on the contrary, coalition instability means that dissolutions cannot be granted automatically and that presidents have to consider requests for dissolution very carefully. Clearly, if, for example, every resignation of a government were followed by a dissolution, such perpetual resort to elections would quickly lead to the breakdown of the entire political system.

20   As well as to the other institutions (for example, the investigating magistracy) whose purposes include acting as guarantors of the proper functioning of democracy.

21   Following the referenda of April 1993, the then imminent collapse of the old party system, together with the bitter unpopularity of the governing parties, in effect gave the president sufficient latitude for a more or less literal interpretation of Article 92 of the Constitution. As Pasquino and Vassallo (1994) point out, in effect, the outcome of the April 1993 referendum on the electoral law was capable of being interpreted as a demand for a greater influence of ordinary voters on the formation of executives. Therefore, if the party secretaries no longer had the necessary authority to decide the composition of governments, and if ordinary voters were not yet able to do it, then the person to assume this responsibility had to be the president given the constitutional requirement that he 'represent the unity of the nation'.

22   The most conspicuous example of this came just after the new government had been installed, when it seemed that its legitimacy would be undermined by the European Parliament's motion implicitly condemning the inclusion of fascist ministers in the Berlusconi cabinet. The president replied to the motion the same day saying: 'The history of Italy's allegiance to the values and principles that are the foundation of the construction of Europe is transparent and unquestioned and requires neither reminders nor teachers.'

23   For example, in July 1994, the president used his constitutional powers to require the government to reconsider decree legislation which was widely thought to be unconstitutional in so far as it would have had the effect of transferring control of the state television company, *Radiotelevisione Italiana*, from parliament to the government.

24   The claim that the Berlusconi government had received a mandate directly from the electorate was, of course, incorrect since, as mentioned earlier, in no part of the country had voters been able to vote either for or against the entire

coalition of parties that subsequently went on to form the government (Ignazi and Katz, 1995: 32).

25 However, as Pasquino points out, the president did not *ignore* the implications of the new electoral law:

> Scalfaro declared himself unable to sanction the formation of a new government majority made up of the Northern League plus other groups, such as the Progressives and *Popolari*, which had lost the 1994 elections. He maintained his firm opposition to the solution that Berlusconi had immediately chastised as a *ribaltone* (an overhaul of majorities). As a consequence, he asked Berlusconi to suggest a person acceptable to him who was capable of forming and leading a government for a relatively short, perhaps pre-defined period of time (Pasquino, 1997: 41–2).

26 Legally, early dissolutions should be distinguished from the type of dissolution involved when a legislature reaches the end of its natural life and there is no presidential discretion. And the power of early dissolution (which, though circumscribed by a range of legal requirements and constitutional conventions, gives the 'last word' to the president) should be distinguished from other powers such as those involved in the promulgation of laws where the president can exercise a 'suspensive veto' but where the 'last word' lies elsewhere (see Baldassarre, 1994). Certoma suggests that, by convention, at least one of three different sets of circumstances have to exist in order for a decision to dissolve early to have the necessary legitimacy. That is, an early dissolution can be decided on 'when the Parliament is no longer representative of the actual political forces in the country; when it is impossible to form a stable parliamentary majority; and when there is an irremediable political conflict between the two Houses' (Certoma, 1995: 143).

27 This body, together with its functions, was to be established by ordinary law and was designed to give the presidency executive powers in the field of foreign policy. To that extent it represented a step back from the original semi-presidential option voted on on 4 June which provided for the president to chair cabinet meetings. The decision to retain a presidential role in the field of foreign policy derived largely from the traditionally consensual character of policy in this area and from the president's responsibility, laid down in the immediately preceding article (Article 65) of the text, to represent 'the unity of the Nation and to ensure its independence and integrity'.

28 It was recognized from the beginning of the *Bicamerale*'s life that it made little sense to discuss constitutional changes, and especially changes to the 'form of government', without also agreeing on the nature of the electoral system. Since discussion of the electoral system – as a non-constitutional matter – fell outside the remit of the *Bicamerale*, the leaders of the PPI, PDS, FI and AN reached agreement at a private meeting held at the house of one of Berlusconi's advisers, Gianni Letta, on the evening of 18 June. Rumour had it that the agreement was struck over supper as the leaders were eating dessert – as a result of which it quickly became known as the *patto della crostata*. It provided for a rather complicated double-ballot system whereby, at the first ballot, 25 per cent of the seats would be distributed proportionally, and 55 per cent according to the single-member, simple plurality system. At the second ballot, voters would make a choice between alternative coalitions and the remaining 20 per cent of the seats would go entirely to the coalition winning the largest number of votes.

29 As Cesare Salvi pointed out during the plenary session of the *Bicamerale* held on 28 May, the very experts and academics who had testified before the *Bicamerale* had 'not only not provided univocal answers', but on the contrary had, 'in some cases shown a polemical virulence exceeding that of the Parliamentary forces

themselves in defending their positions and attacking those of others' (!). http://www.camera.it/parlam/bicam/rifcost/ressten/ed028r.htm

30   For example, on 12 June, ten days after parliament stopped considering the *Bicamerale*'s proposals, President Scalfaro launched the idea of a directly elected president but with the currently existing powers. The idea was received favourably both by the PPI and the DS and by the UDR (*la Repubblica*, 13 June 1998: 7).

31   A circumstance that was welcomed by some as restoring what they regarded as a desirable link between taxation and spending decisions.

32   Bassanini 1 empowered the government to pass legislative decrees conferring upon the regions and local authorities, administrative responsibilities in all areas 'related to the protection of the interests and the promotion of the development of their respective communities', except those areas listed in the law itself. Among a wide range of provisions, Bassanini 2 places limits on the powers of the Regional Control Commissions. These are the bodies, based one in each regional capital (comprising three members elected by the regional council, one member nominated by the government commissioner and a judge drawn from the regional administrative court (*Tribunale Amministrativo Regionale*, TAR)) which exercises supervisory powers over the measures of provinces and communes. Their supervisory powers extend to the legitimacy and, where legislation stipulates, also to the merits of provincial and communal measures. Besides limiting the types of measures subject to Regional Control Commission supervision, Bassanini 2 provides that those measures which remain subject to supervision will become operative in any event if Commissions fail to deliver judgments within 30 days of communicating measures to them. For details see Newell (1998).

33   For example, in the aftermath of the regional elections of 1980, the Social Democratic Party apparently sought to enhance its prospects of re-entering the national-level coalition of which it was not then a member, by offering to exclude the PCI from power in three regions – Liguria, Lazio and Marche – where negotiations were proving difficult (Graziano *et al.*, 1984: 437).

34   The aim of the 'Mayors' Party' – a loosely organized cross-party structure surrounding the charismatic mayor of Venice, Massimo Cacciari – has been to try to cut the ground from under the League by campaigning for decentralizing reforms on an explicitly cross-party basis. Cacciari was worried that, while the 1996 election had, for the first time, produced a governing majority which could 'really oversee a process of federalisation' (De Vito, 1996: 63), there were many in the *Ulivo* who, unconvinced of the need for reform, would be likely to drag their feet.

35   Indeed, there are a large number of instances in which the opposite is likely to be the case. The inhabitants of regions with high levels of organized crime are unlikely to look favourably on proposals for devolving policing functions. Streamlining centrally imposed bureaucratic procedures also risks reducing the number of legal controls on activities potentially damaging to human life and the environment.

# 8 Policy Consequences

To what extent has the change in the party system brought with it a change in the kinds of politician typically found in the legislature and in the nature of public policy? This chapter explores these questions in three sections. The first section explores the turnover of members of parliament and the changes in their social, political and other characteristics that took place as a consequence of the 1994 and the 1996 general elections. The second explores the extent to which there has been a change in the balance between 'meso-policy' outputs and the (formerly predominant) 'micro-policies' of narrow scope, similar in character to patronage. The third section starts from the observation that at the 1994 and 1996 elections the parties were apparently more willing to compete in terms of policies as opposed to the ideologial distinctions of the past. The question asked in the third section therefore is: 'What has been the rate of pledge-fulfilment of the governing coalitions of the changed party system?'

## The Turnover of Parliamentary Personnel

In view of the old parties' collapse, in view of the fact that, at the height of the *Tangentopoli* investigations, as many as a third of the Chamber of Deputies members had been under judicial investigation (Bull and Newell, 1995: 74), and in view of the emergence and growth of new parties, such as the League and *Forza Italia*, which sought to emphasize their incommensurability with the political assumptions of the past, it was reasonable to assume that any election held in the wake of this turmoil would see a very high level of turnover of parliamentarians. This proved to be the case: 71.3 per cent of deputies (and an almost identical proportion of senators) elected in 1994 had never sat in parliament before, compared with an average of 34.4 per cent for the three previous legislatures (Verzichelli, 1994: 717). On the other hand, this change in the level of turnover did not necessarily mean that the sociological characteristics of the new parliamentarians would differ much from those of the past – in other words, quantitative change would not necessarily give rise to a corresponding qualitative change (Mastropaolo, 1994b: 462).

The principal changes in the characteristics of parliamentarians as compared to the period prior to 1994 were as follows. First, there was a larger proportion without a 'political background'. One of the most characteristic features of Italian parliamentarians had traditionally been their long political careers in party, and party-related, organizations, and their relative lack of other professional experience, prior to entering parliament (Cotta, 1979; Mastropaolo, 1994b). However, the proportion of 'professional politicians' among those elected in 1994 halved (Mastropaolo, 1994b: 466); only 25.9 per cent of the deputies elected in 1994 had had previous experience in the national-level bodies of their parties, and only 41.3 per cent (down from 65.1 per cent in 1992) experience of elective office at the local level (Verzichelli, 1994: 730). Reflecting this, there was a marked change in the occupational profile of parliamentarians. Thus, while the proportion of profesional politicians declined, there was a dramatic increase in entrepreneurs and managers (rising threefold as compared to 1987) and in other professionals (whose numbers doubled from those of 1987). The number of lawyers and notaries, journalists, teachers and university professors remained largely stable. There was a slight decline in the average age of deputies – down to 47.1 from an average of almost 50 for the tenth and eleventh legislatures (Mastropaolo, 1994b: 464; Verzichelli, 1994: 724). Finally, the proportion of female deputies rose – from 8.4 per cent for the eleventh legislature, to 15.1 per cent – due largely to the PDS and RC (26.2 per cent and 22.9 per cent of whose deputies were women respectively) and to the new electoral law.[1]

Needless to say, these overall changes concealed divergent characteristics and tendencies between parties. For example, whereas 90.4 per cent of *Forza Italia* deputies had never sat in parliament before (Verzichelli, 1995: 141), the League and the AN, while also contributing large numbers of first-time deputies (69.5 per cent for the League; 77.5 per cent for the AN), also returned to parliament significantly sized proportions of outgoing deputies, because they each won so many more seats in 1994 than in 1992. On the other hand, the PDS and the PPI although in both cases fielding rather fewer established leaders than in the past, returned below-average proportions of first-time deputies because they failed to achieve that significant overall improvement in terms of seats achieved by the parties of the *Polo*. Among the parties with clear links with the past – that is the AN, the PDS and the RC – the proportion of deputies with prior political experience, either within their parties or in elective local office, was significantly higher than among wholly new parties such as the League and *Forza Italia*. Similarly, dramatic differences were noticeable in the proportions of professional politicians among deputies belonging to the wholly new parties as compared to those parties having links with the past (Verzichelli, 1994). At the same time, however, these proportions were also largely in *decline* for the latter group of parties, all of which suggests that such parties found themselves confronted with conflicting imperatives: on the one hand, the need to demonstrate political renewal by means of novel recruitment mechanisms; on the other hand, the need to continue to provide places for those having worked their way up through the traditional party channels.

In the aftermath of the 1994 election it was possible to suggest that the recruitment of parliamentarians via the traditional mechanisms, tightly controlled from the centre by mass parties, was being supplemented by additional, partially new, channels of recruitment. One was represented by the deputies of *Forza Italia* with their very much higher than average proportions of entrepreneurs, managers and independent professionals, and their very low levels of prior political experience, many of whom had professional or other ties with Berlusconi himself.[2] This suggested a model of recruitment via careful, highly centralized, selection whereby illustrious members of the professional bourgeoisie were being prevailed upon to lend their skills of 'action' and 'efficiency' to politics in response to Berlusconi's call. The profile of League deputies suggested yet another model of recruitment. Younger and of generally lower social extraction than *Forza Italia* deputies, small businessmen and artisans as opposed to senior managers and the owners of large companies, relatively inexperienced in terms of prior elective office, these deputies were highly dependent, for election to the Chamber, on the organization and support of their party – a party which, as we saw in Chapter 4, controls the selection of personnel, their entry to and exit from positions, according to centrally defined and strictly applied criteria.

The 1996 election witnessed a further relatively high level of turnover of parliamentarians, due both to interparty factors (the growth in numbers of seats won by the centre-left and the decline in numbers won by the centre-right) and intraparty factors (especially the low numbers of outgoing League and *Forza Italia* parliamentarians running again). Of those elected in 1996, 44.8 per cent of the deputies and 40.3 per cent of the senators had never sat in parliament before (Verzichelli, 1997a: 147). This did not represent the return of the old 'political class': only 62 deputies and 36 senators had been first elected before 1990 (Verzichelli, 1997a: 150). The changed occupational profile of parliamentarians – within, as well as across, parties – registered in 1994 was also largely confirmed in 1996. Thus, for example, *Forza Italia* deputies continued to be characterized by higher than average proportions of entrepreneurs and managers, and League deputies by higher than average proportions of artisans and independent professionals.

On the other hand, the 1996 election also saw a reversal of many of the changes in the social characteristics of parliamentarians that had seemed to be set in motion two years earlier. Hence, the proportion of female deputies, which had grown so remarkably in 1994, declined to 11.3 per cent, thus confirming that halt in their growth which had been registered with the 1992 election,[3] and confirming too that the 1994 rise had been largely an 'artefact' of the new electoral law (Verzichelli, 1997b: 325).[4] Similarly, the decline in age of deputies was reversed – a mean of 48.1 years signalling a return to that average of 49–50 years that had characterized the tenth and eleventh legislatures.

Particularly striking was evidence of a return to past tendencies for deputies to be drawn predominantly from among those with established party-political careers: the decline of 1994 went into reverse in 1996. The proportion of deputies with an established party career went up for all parties except the RC. The proportion of deputies having held a party office before being elected to parliament was at least 40 per cent for all parties except *Forza Italia* and, in most cases, the proportions were much higher (Verzichelli, 1997b: 336–7). When the figures showing a rise in the proportion of deputies with prior experience of elective local office are added to this, the evidence seems to point away from the dismantling of those traditional channels of recruitment characteristic of the 'First Republic' that had been suggested by the election results of 1994.

It is probably fair to agree with Mastropaolo that 'after four years of debilitating turmoil, the Italian polity and Italian society [had reaffirmed] a political class that [it was] difficult to describe as new' (1996: 507). Certainly, confirmation in 1996 of the novel and distinctive profiles of League and *Forza Italia* parliamentarians suggested new models of recruitment and thus the appearance of a new type of parliamentarian: in the case of the League, this was a parliamentarian whose small-business background gave him deep roots in a circumscribed locality and a record of party commitment which made him ideally suited to an isolated movement, little disposed to compromise; in the case of *Forza Italia* it was a parliamentarian whose social visibility and status would help him retain voting support and make him a reliable member of the parliamentary contingent (Verzichelli, 1997b). But the overall rise in levels of prior political experience and activity among the 1996 intake suggested the possibility that there had been a re-admission to the 'election circuit' of a conspicuous portion of politicians socialized by the old parties of the 'First Republic'. And if this was the case, then it could be anticipated that there would be little change in the nature of public policy by sole virtue of parliamentary personnel turnover. As described in the following section, structural change in the characteristics of the party system itself provided more solid grounds for expecting significant changes in the nature of public policy.

## Implications of Structural Change

These grounds are essentially based on the implications of Cotta's (1996) theory linking structural features of the pre-1989 party system to the polity's tendency towards policy outputs of a predominantly small-scale, patronage-type. Cotta's argument is that, before the change, parties found it difficult to take policy initiatives – which would come on to the agenda most often as the result of some external event to which the government would be required to respond. The parties' input into the policy-making process would then usually be of a negative, reactive, kind whereby they would seek to defend particularistic interests by exercising a power of veto. The reason for the parties' incapacity to direct and guide policy-making was to be found in the nature of party competition, which could be thought of as taking place on three levels:

1 the level of 'meta-policies' – that is, policies concerning the fundamental characteristics of the political regime, the economic and social system or the location of the country in systems of international alliances;
2 the level of 'meso-policies' – that is, policies involving significant proposals and changes in the areas of economic, social, foreign or institutional policy;
3 the level of 'micro-policies' – that is, policies concerning the management and defence of the interests of some specific category of persons (and which often overlap with patronage).

In post-war Italy before 1989, meta-level competition between the governing parties on the one hand and the PCI on the other led to the relative atrophy of competition at the meso level, partly because meso-policy disagreements would tend to metamorphose into ideological disputes and partly because the governing parties avoided competition between themselves at that level in order to maintain solidarity at the meta level. Therefore, what competition there was tended to take place at the micro level, as unlike competition at the meso level, this would not jeopardize agreements reached at the meta level. At the same time, while micro-policy competition was encouraged by the system of preference voting in force until 1991 (see Chapter 3), it also further discouraged meso-policies because of the antithetical criteria for resource distribution which each involved – particularistic in the one case, universalistic in the other. Meanwhile, since the parties neither sought nor obtained mandates for proposals of a meso kind, their capacity for policy-making at this level was further diminished, for they were consequently neither legitimized, nor regarded as accountable for action, at this level.

Cotta's theory is evidently intended to highlight certain *tendencies*, not to suggest that the parties were incapable of initiating *any* meso-level policies in post-war Italy. However, the changes in those party-system characteristics which Cotta highlights as having been responsible for these tendencies lead to the expectation of a significant shift in the balance between meso- and micro-policy outputs when compared to the past. First, competition at the meta level has essentially ceased since the collapse of communism: with this and the consequent trans-formation of the PCI into a non-communist party of the left, the fundamental characteristics of the political regime and of the economic and social system, as well as the location of the country in the system of international alliances, are all matters of consensus, not conflict, for the great majority of the political forces represented in parliament. Second, there now appears to be none of the avoidance of meso-policy competition hypothesized by Cotta: specific and readily identifiable policy disagreements do exist, both between the governing parties themselves and between these and the parties of opposition. Third, if as Cotta argues, the parties neither sought nor obtained mandates for proposals of a meso kind because the perceived anti-system character of the PCI made it essentially unnecessary for the governing parties to seek a following on the basis of their policies, the parties do now seek mandates on the basis of alternative policy programmes: even at the 1994 election, the one closest in time to the old system, the election manifestos presented by some of the parties 'showed an interesting change as compared to the past' (Segatti, 1995). Judging by their content, some parties apparently intended to compete more on the terrain of the things to be done than on that of eternal ideological identities' (Sani and Segatti, 1997: 14). Moreover, the end of the party system's 'blocked' character and its bipolar logic would seem to make such competition a necessity: to maximize its chances of winning an absolute majority of parliamentary seats, each of the electoral coalitions is required to attempt to outdo its rivals by offering a package of policy proposals sufficiently attractive as to be able to court the median voter. Fourth, since as Cotta points out, the criteria for resource allocation implied by meso- and micro-policies are antithetical, it seems likely that the imperative to compete on policy proposals (and achievements) will have reduced the 'room' available for initiatives of a micro kind. Finally, and perhaps most significantly, the room available for the latter will also have been decisively reduced by the change, if not in the characteristics of the party system itself, yet in a factor intimately connected with it – namely, the degree of latitude available with regard to the size of the public-sector deficit. Before the signing of the Maastricht Treaty, the parties had a leeway to avoid the political costs associated with (increasingly intense) competition at the micro level, by refusing to raise taxes while allowing levels of public debt to rise.

The convergence criteria for Economic and Monetary Union meant that this option was no longer available, and the advent of the single currency will ensure that it remains so.[5]

What evidence is there, then, for a shift in the balance from micro- to meso-policies as a proportion of the total policy outputs of the government and legislature? And what evidence is there that any such shift can be attributed to a heightened initiating role of the parties? To answer these questions it seems sensible to focus on the activities of the permanent committees of the Chamber of Deputies and the Senate. These committees, as we noted in Chapters 3 and 7, have the power to act in *sede deliberante* – that is, they have full powers to enact legislation on their own authority. It seems likely that much, if not most, legislation of the micro kind will be enacted in, and through, these committees (Table 8.1) rather than via the full legislative procedure, for they have traditionally been the principal fora for the consideration of those *leggine* mentioned earlier – namely, laws of narrow sectoral scope usually concerned with very specific issues affecting very restricted numbers of people. That such laws have traditionally been

Table 8.1   Permanent committees of the Chamber of Deputies and Senate

| Chamber of Deputies Committee no. and area | Senate Committee no. and area |
|---|---|
| I    Constitutional Affairs | I    Constitutional Affairs |
| II   Justice | II   Justice |
| III  Foreign Affairs | III  Foreign Affairs and Emigration |
| IV   Defence | IV   Defence |
| V    Budget | V    Budget |
| VI   Finance | VI   Finance and Treasury |
| VII  Culture | VII  Education and Cultural Resources |
| VIII Environment | VIII Public Works and Communications |
| IX   Transport | IX   Agriculture and Food Production |
| X    Trade and Industry | X    Industry, Commerce and Tourism |
| XI   Labour | XI   Labour and Social Security |
| XII  Social Affairs | XII  Hygiene and Health |
| XIII Agriculture | XIII Land, the Environment and |
| XIV  European Union | Environmental Resources |
| Also: Special Committee for Anti-corruption Measures. | |

*Source*: http://www.camera.it/cam ... ss/leg 13/lavori/home.htm;
           http://www.senato.it/bd/comp/i_commi.htm

dealt with by the committees can be explained by their large number – the committee-only route helps streamline the work of parliament as a whole – and by the other advantages offered by the committees: they publish minutes, although these are not readily available to the public; television cameras, allowed into the full assembly, do not cover their proceedings; difficult matters may be delegated to small subcommittees – and *their* deliberations take place entirely outside the public domain. 'So the activities of the committees . . . take place almost entirely outside the public gaze' (Furlong, 1994: 183). Micro-policies are, by definition, policies of very narrow sectoral scope and, since the committee route is only available when, as Article 92 of the Chamber of Deputies' Standing Orders puts it, the proposal 'does not have special relevance of a general nature' (ibid.: 139), a good indicator of the weight of micro-policies in total policy outputs should be provided by the proportion of legislation that has been enacted by committee. As we saw in Chapter 7, excluding those for which the full legislative procedure is obligatory, the proportion of laws enacted by the committee-only route has declined from 89 per cent and 95 per cent in the tenth and eleventh legislatures respectively, to 71 per cent and 68 per cent in the twelfth and thirteenth legislatures.

The drawback of this indicator is that, although much committee legislation may be narrow in scope, this does not automatically mean that it is the product of patronage or clientelism. Traditionally, many *leggine* have been the consequence not of the patronage concerns of parliamentarians but, as Furlong points out, simply of the careless drafting of previous legislation, which thus requires an 'extension of rights already granted in favour of one group to another similar group' (ibid.: 132–3). Second, a micro-policy agenda may be pursued as much through a simple *failure* to take measures as through the positive *promotion* of measures. Indeed, taking into account the multiple pressures on ministers to be *in*active, this may traditionally have been the predominant mode by which micro-policies were made.[6] Third, therefore, it is possible that it was through means other than formal items of legislation that the predominantly micro character of the policy competition between the pre-1989 parties took place. Certainly, when it comes to clientelist political activities, most of these have traditionally taken place much more frequently within the framework of *existing* procedures, far away from parliament, at subnational level, rather than through changes in the procedures themselves.

A better indicator of the significance of micro-policies may perhaps be provided by the extent of party involvement in appointments to the range of public agencies making up the 'administrative system', broadly conceived. To the extent that micro-policies entailed the distribution of public resources to specific sectoral interests such as small farmers, the provincial self-employed and so on, they required appointments to public agencies to be made on a party basis, since it was through control of organizations such as the *Federconsorzi* in agriculture, the state-holding companies, IRI (*Istituto per la Ricostruzione Industriale*, Institute for the Reconstruction of Industry), ENI (*Ente Nazionale Idrocarburi*, National Hydrocarbon Corporation) and others (as well as control of the ministries to which they were directly or indirectly responsible), that control over the resources necessary for the pursuit of micro-policies was ultimately exercised.[7]

Hard evidence about the extent of party involvement in appointments in the public sector is difficult to come by. First, it is obviously a normal and accepted part of political life in liberal democracies that public officials be appointed and held accountable through parties.[8] What was apparently anomalous about the Italian case was that, in addition to all this, the political affiliations and reliability of candidates became criteria of appointment, even at the cost of failing to appoint people better technically equipped, with the parties 'sharing out' available positions according to the bargaining power of each (a system, as we noted in Chapter 2, known as *lottizzazione*). Yet this, of course, creates the problem of knowing how one can be certain, in the case of any given appointment, that political criteria really *have* prevailed over objective criteria of competence or vice versa.

Judging from a range of secondary sources and specific incidents, the evidence for the Berlusconi government would seem to indicate 'a retreat from the ideal of separating clearly the executive from the administration, not only in the sectors traditionally most affected by political influence (such as the RAI broadcasting agency), but also for autonomous or nominally independent groups, such as the Bank of Italy' (della Cananea, 1997: 202). First, in June 1994 the government had attempted to introduce a decree renewing financial aid for the heavily indebted RAI but stipulating that the government could dismiss its management board if the Minister of Posts and Telecommunications deemed its rescue plan inadequate. President Scalfaro had refused to countersign the decree (on the grounds that it appeared to remove control of the RAI from parliament in violation of the Constitution) and insisted that control of the board be vested in the speakers of the two houses of parliament. Later, the speaker of the Chamber of Deputies, Irene Pivetti, revealed that Berlusconi had tried to influence nomination of the RAI board, telling her that it 'should answer to the government'. Equally, when the RAI board came to nominate the directors of the three television channels, many claimed that these had been delivered, lock, stock and barrel to Berlusconi and Fini, Bossi in particular complaining loudly that his party had been excluded from the share-out (Gundle, 1995: 241). Second, the government had tried to compromise the traditional independence of the Bank of Italy by replacing Director General Lamberto Dini, who had become Treasury

Minister, with one of its own nominations in opposition to the central bank's choice. In the autumn it had announced that it intended to introduce legislation revising the bank's statute, ending, in particular, the system of lifetime appointments for governors – a change that would make them more amenable to political control. Third, one of the referenda of April 1993 had struck down the legislation allowing the Treasury to appoint directors within the largely state-owned banking system, while the role of supervising the system had been given to the Bank of Italy. Out of an apparent desire to bring the system back within the orbit of the government parties, the Berlusconi administration had wanted to transfer these supervisory functions to the Treasury. Fourth, the government had presided over a series of delays in implementing the privatization programme – delays which, according to Filippo Cavazzuti (1995: 206) (who became an under-secretary at the Treasury on the election of the *Ulivo* government), were almost always due to political, rather than technical causes, and not least to the AN's tenacious defence of the state holdings in whose command positions it had attempted to place its own people. Finally, according to della Cananea (1997: 202), the priority given to adminis-trative reforms by previous governments was downgraded as the governing parties' main preoccupation had shifted to the acquisition and occupation of existing institutional positions.

Evidence of a reduction in the extent of party interference in public appointments seemed more likely to be found for the *Ulivo* government since honest and open government had been a key element of the image which the *Ulivo* – and especially Prodi – had sought to project at the 1996 election. *Ulivo* politicians had, indeed, presented themselves to voters in 1996 as the 'armed guard of merit and competence, as the vestal of integrity', and they therefore had 'an image to defend' (Padellaro, 1996: 54). In the search for such evidence we looked at every issue of the weekly news magazine *L'Espresso* from the date of the election of the *Ulivo* government onwards: well known for its centre-left sympathies, but also for its willingness to pursue the powerful of whatever political shade, *L'Espresso* seemed a likely source of any available evidence of change in party involvement in public appointments. That nothing had changed with the election of the *Ulivo* government must have seemed so striking and obvious to most contributors to the magazine in this period as to make the citing of specific instances seem largely superfluous. For if Antonio Padellaro, to give one example, could accuse the governing parties, on 11 December 1997, of wanting to compete for the blanket occupation of the available positions (1997: 69), it is striking just how few concrete examples of 'political appoint-ments' are actually given in the magazine during this period.[9]

If this was undoubtedly due to the problem of inference mentioned above rather than to some unaccountable virtue on the part of the *Ulivo* parties, nevertheless, at least two considerations lead to the view that *lottizzazione* has almost certainly declined as compared to the pre-crisis party system. First, if privatization had been resisted by important sections of the old governing parties so that it had been necessary to 'await the XI legislature and with it the . . . crisis of the party system . . . in order to witness the realisation of privatisations of any substance' (Cerboni and Cotta, 1996: 259–60), the programme now seems to be proceeding smoothly[10] and with the active *support* of the governing parties.[11] Since the state holding companies (but not only they) have traditionally provided the core resources by which *lottizzazione* could be carried on, their continuing disposal almost certainly betokens a decline in the desire to engage in *lottizzazione* itself. Second, *lottizzazione* is one among a set of political practices which have become clearly labelled in the news media as defining features of what continues to be called the 'First Republic': the political system as it was up until the disintegration of the old governing parties. The implication of this seems clear, namely, that these are practices of the past; that their appearance is not *expected* in a 'post-First Republic' world; and that their appearance will therefore be the subject of reproof. For example, the appointment of Enrico Testa and Franco Tatò as, respectively, president and managing director of ENEL, were greeted by Padellaro (1996: 53) in July 1996 with the assertion that:

> . . . the enormous power of D'Alema, decisive in the appointment of the well-regarded Tatò as managing director of the electricity giant, and Veltroni's support for the appointment of Enrico Testa as president . . . have all the flavour of the old and deprecated *lottizzazione*, even though garnished with a sprinkling of *Ulivo*.

But if what look like examples of *lottizzazione* excite comment, then this is likely to be because they are in fact perceived as being less widespread than in the past when the practice was all but institutionalized.

### Do Party Systems Make a Difference?

If, as seems to be the case, then, there has been a change in the balance of policy outputs away from micro-policies towards a greater reliance on meso-policies, to what degree does this signify a changed relationship between politicians and citizens and, specifically, a greater responsiveness and accountability on the part of government? Under the pre-1989 party system, the *conventio ad excludendum* and lack of alternation were the principal factors responsible for both patronage-type, micro-policies and low levels of accountability to the electorate at large for the broader policies under which patronage activities were carried on. Where permanent exclusion of the second-largest party was a basic assumption of politics, micro-policies provided the only terrain on which the remaining parties could safely compete; at the same time, the *a priori* exclusion of the second largest party undermined the need for responsiveness by artificially limiting the influence that election outcomes could have on government formation. If the changes in the party system have led to somewhat greater levels of policy competitiveness than in the past, then they should also have resulted in more accountable government. For if the emergence of two coalitions, each competing for an overall majority of seats, means that they have to compete for the median voter, and if competing for the median voter means that they have to try to present the most attractive package of policies, then by the same token it also means that they have to respond to what voters appear to want of governments: if a coalition wins an election without doing what voters want at least some of the time, then, all else being equal, it can expect its chances of winning at the next election to be much reduced. One of the ways of measuring responsiveness in this sense, then, is to see to what extent winning coalitions keep their election promises. And if the upheavals in the Italian party system really have resulted in more accountable government, then this should be discernible in rates of pledge fulfilment since the 1992–94 crisis.

Even in a country like the UK where election outcomes and a relative absence of constitutional checks and balances usually give authority over all of government to a single party, there are formidable obstacles in the way of pledge fulfilment. As Richard Rose puts it:

> Those who step aboard the ship of state find that they are subject to powerful currents, and are not taking command of a passive or easily manoeuvred vessel. Upon entering office, a party becomes subject to demands from pressure groups that it might ignore in opposition. It must also confront international forces, economic as well as diplomatic, that greatly constrain government. (Rose, 1984: 14)

Yet parties typically act on the great bulk of manifesto commitments – up to 90 per cent – when they achieve office (ibid.: 65) and, indeed, from a cross-national comparative perspective, pledge fulfilment sems to be more the rule than the exception.[12] In examining the Italian case, the *Ulivo* government under Romano Prodi has been chosen for analysis as it represents the longest period of uninterrupted party government following a general election since 1992–94: if despite especially unfavourable conditions, notably the absence of a stable majority in the Chamber of Deputies, it is possible to uncover evidence that rates of pledge fulfilment now approximate those achieved elsewhere, we will have further *prima facie* evidence that something very significant has happened as a result of the party-system upheavals of the early 1990s.

If rates of pledge fulfilment are typically measured by reference to election manifestos, the relevant document in the present case is the *Tesi per la definizione della piattaforma programmatica dell'Ulivo* (Theses for the Definition of the Programmatic Platform of the Ulivo) published on 6 December 1995. This, as Romano Prodi's introduction put it, was intended to provide the foundations of the legislative programme of an *Ulivo* government. As might be expected, it was very much a compromise document, drawn up following the decisions, in the spring of 1995, that the PDS deputy, Veltroni, would in effect act as Prodi's deputy and that the leaderships of the 12 parties comprising the *Ulivo*, would meet regularly to discuss the movement's strategy and tactics (Gilbert, 1996: 127). Running to some 43 000 words, it was also a substantial document (as a counterexample, the British Labour Party's manifesto for the 1997 general election ran to some 17 600 words), a feature which clearly stemmed from the fact that its authors were attempting to use it to meet two different needs at the same time. Since the *Ulivo* was a novel political formation, it needed 'an idealised and relatively timeless statement' of how the country should be governed and of what a well-governed Italy would look like; on the other hand, government and elections are concrete, so the document also had to specify a number of specific measures that could be implemented during the lifetime of a parliament (Rose, 1984: 52).

This double characteristic poses particular problems for analysing the document. Clearly, one has to disregard 'statements that are so vague or general that it is impossible to tell, after the event, whether or not they have been accomplished' (ibid.: 62), but with a document that wishes to be both a manifesto and a statement of a movement's founding values and ideals, the line between a vague statement and a verifiable pledge is not always clear. In British party manifestos, verifiable pledges are often signalled by certain standard phrases, such as sentences beginning, 'The Labour government will . . .'. However, when, for example, 'Thesis no 22' of the *Ulivo* document says, 'In every area the police, *carabinieri*, municipal police and the other forces of law and order must be coordinated . . . . The number of police cars present on the streets each evening and night must be increased' it is not immediately obvious how the accomplishment of the first aim can easily be verified, and neither is it obvious whether it and the second aim are, in fact, promises of specific pieces of legislation or mere statements of aspirations without specification of the means by which they might be realized. This is very different from the statement in 'Thesis no. 23' which states, unequivocally, that 'a new law on usury will be approved'. In the analysis, therefore, only statements promising specific legislative action are counted. Excluded too are those statements referring to proposals for constitutional change, for they would inevitably require the support of the opposition parties as well as the parties of government in order to be passed. In relation to these proposals, the mandate the *Ulivo* was asking for was, as Thesis 1 put it, merely a mandate to initiate 'a free and frank discussion', not a mandate to implement 'unilateral conclusions'.

Applying these criteria to analysis of the document threw up a total of 72 specific pledges (see Table 8.2), a figure that bears comparison with the numbers of pledges typically made in party-platform documents in other liberal democracies.[13] Most pledges fell in the area of 'government, administration and social/legal matters', with 'the economy and taxation' following a close second. But, in general, the pledges covered – as one would expect – the entire range of policy areas.

Table 8.2  The number and subject of *Ulivo* programme pledges, 1996

|  | No. | % | Acted upon | Ambiguous |
|---|---|---|---|---|
| The economy and taxation | 15 | 21 | 9 | |
| Education | 9 | 13 | 3 | |
| Government, administration, social/legal matters | 19 | 26 | 8 | 2 |
| Foreign affairs and defence | 3 | 4 | 2 | |
| Health and social security | 9 | 13 | 1 | |
| Environment | 3 | 4 | 2 | |
| Industry and the labour market | 11 | 15 | 1 | 1 |
| Entertainment and sports | 3 | 4 | 0 | 1 |
| Total | 72 | 100 | 26 | 4 |

In order to assess the extent to which steps had been taken to fulfil these pledges we compared them with the texts of bills enacted since the start of the thirteenth legislature.[14] This allowed us to compute the proportion of pledges for which there was at least some evidence of legislative action having been taken. In fact, the resulting proportion constitutes a rather stringent measure of pledge fulfilment since, clearly, some pledges can be fulfilled without legislation, merely by the exercise of administrative discretion (Rose, 1984: 64) so, if anything, our measure *understates* the degree of government activism in pursuit of its programme.

What we find is that, shortly after two years into a potential term of office of five years,[15] the *Ulivo* government (and despite the absence of a majority in one of the houses of parliament) is able to demonstrate unambiguously that it has acted upon 36 per cent of its pledges – a proportion which, in our view, compares very favourably with rates of pledge fulfilment elsewhere. It compares, for example, with the 90 per cent of pledges for which there was evidence of action at the end of the British Conservatives' period of office (with an absolute majority) between 1970 and 1974, and it compares too with the 73 per cent of pledges on which there appeared to have been action at the end of Labour's five-year term between 1974 and 1979 (Rose, 1984). Again, it is a proportion which appears significant in the light of Rallings' (1987) finding of average rates of pledge fulfilment of 64 per cent and 72 per cent for British and Canadian governments between 1945 and 1979 and in the light of Kalogeropoulou's (1989) finding of a 71 per cent rate of pledge fulfilment for the Greek PASOK government between 1981 and 1985.

So we think that there has been a fundamental change in the relationship between the electors and elected as a result of the transformation in Italian party politics since 1989. The *Ulivo* government *is* carrying out its contract with the electorate and, to that degree, has brought the functioning of the Italian polity more closely into line with those theories of representative democracy which say that parties gain power on the basis of election pledges which they then have a mandate to put into effect. In 1996, more so than in 1994, two competing sets of parties each stood on recognizably common platforms; one of the party coalitions achieved an unambiguous victory and then set about putting its programme into effect. Certainly, as an electoral coalition, the incoming *Ulivo* government's position was anomalous as compared to what would be prescribed by most normative theories of democracy: it took office as a result of stand-down arrangements with the RC although the two presented no common programme, and despite the persisting absence of programmatic agreement as the parliament got underway (the RC preferred specific agreements on single issues), the alliance prevented the government from having recourse to variable majorities by seeking support to its left and its right on an ad hoc basis. But it also has to be acknowledged that the expectations that party-system change would being significant improvements in the functioning of Italian democracy seem not to have been misplaced. An attempt to summarize the continuities and changes in the quality of Italian democracy overall constitutes the subject matter of our concluding chapter.

## Notes

1   Until, in September 1995, the relevant provisions were declared unconstitutional, this stipulated that lists presented for the distribution of the proportionally allocated seats were to contain both male and female candidates whose names were to appear in alternating order.

2   In addition to the many other *Forza Italia* deputies with less direct ties to Berlusconi, it was possible to count at least ten managers of *Publitalia '80* and *Fininvest* elected to the Chamber of Deputies in 1994.

3   Then the proportion of female deputies had declined to 8.4 per cent from 13.2 per cent (Verzichelli, 1994: 725).

4   This is because the clause which made obligatory the alternation of male and female candidates in the party lists presented for the distribution of proportional seats in  Chamber of Deputies elections was struck down by the Constitutional Court in September 1995 (see note 1 above).

5   On the other hand, it may be wondered how difficult the parties still find it to play anything other than a reactive role, and to initiate policy of a meso kind, when their leading echelons continue to be largely separate from the leading echelons of government. Of the four largest individual formations responsible for sustaining the government in office after the 1996 election (the PDS, the PPI, the RC and *Rinnovamento Italiano*), only one (*Rinnovamento*) had a leader in the cabinet (Lamberto Dini) while the other three, in conformity with past trends, remained (until the autumn of 1998) outside. As Cotta points out, 'Overlap between government membership and party-leader positions has tended to exist in Italy for only limited periods and even then to be true only of the minor parties . . .' (1996: 21) As in the past, the tendency of party leaders to stay out of the cabinet may make it difficult for the parties to take policy initiatives by undermining the authority of their actions (which come to be seen as an illegitimate interference in the conduct of public affairs). Periodic public spats between Massimo D'Alema and Romano Prodi (who consciously and explicitly identified with none of the parties making up the governing coalition he headed) were perhaps emblematic of this state of affairs. Moreover, in conformity with the tendency begun with the Amato government, the cabinet continues to feature non-party technocrats in key positions (such as Carlo Azeglio Ciampi at the Treasury, Giovanni Maria Flick at Justice, and, before his resignation, Antonio Di Pietro at the Ministry of Public Works).

6   For example, ministers have traditionally reached practical compromises with the senior officials in their ministries whereby, in exchange for non-interference in established working practices and existing power relationships, they have not been obstructed in the pursuit of their political goals. As Furlong notes, 'The easiest way for a Minister to make this compromise work is not to have strategic goals which differ from the consensus within the individual *Direzioni*, but rather to interest himself or herself in the much more manageable business of patronage and to leave the rest to normal administration' (1994: 105–6).

7   Traditionally, analysts have attempted to make sense of the variegated nature of the administrative system by distinguishing, besides the departmental ministries, three types of public agency. The first covers the *amministrazioni autonome* which derive a substantial part of their revenue from the provision of commercial services and are responsible to a given ministry, although effectively independent in terms of day-to-day management. The second covers the *enti pubblici* of which there are approximately 54 000 and many of which are organized on a local level to provide welfare and other services (such as local bus services) to a limited sectional group. Finally, there is the group consisting of the state holding companies which,

following the example of IRI established in 1933, emerged in order to manage state-owned shareholdings in private companies which could thereby be used as tools of industrial policy. The state stands at considerable remove from day-to-day operations, in so far as the typical arrangement is for a state holding company to own further, subsidiary holding companies, while the individual enterprises at the base of the pyramid operate in accordance with their legal status as private companies, the shares of which may be only partly owned by the state. The Byzantine complexity of the structure of public administration can be appreciated by considering that the Ministry of Communications 'has ultimate responsibility for the conduct of the public radio and TV service, operated on permanent concession by RAI [*Radiotelevisione Italiana*, the state television network], which is actually a subsidiary of the state-owned public sector company IRI, itself responsible formally [until 1993] to the Ministry of State Participation' (Furlong, 1994: 100).

8    This is, of course, one of the defining criteria of 'party government' as formulated by Richard Katz (1987).

9    Of course, examples were not entirely *absent*. One was the appointment of Enrico Testa as president of ENEL (said by Claudio Rinaldi (1996: 53) to lack the necessary experience and to have been appointed – against the will of Treasury minister Ciampi – because of his 'red–green' past); another was the appointment of Lucia Annunziata as Director of Tg3, the third channel's news programme. But this provides yet another example of how real evidence apparently seemed superfluous. If Cristina Mariotti (1996) and Giampaolo Pansa (1996) both hinted that Annunziata may have got the position by ingratiating herself with Massimo D'Alema, this was hardly sufficient to warrant Pansa's suggestion that in matters of public appointments, 'Every day we increasingly discover that "the left" in power is not very different to the others' (1996: 43).

10   Following the *Telecom Italia* privatization (the largest to that date) in October 1997, the government announced that it intended to push ahead with plans to reduce its industrial holdings as a means of increasing efficiency and reducing public debt. Included in its plans were the sale of a fourth tranche of ENI, the sale of its stake in the *Banca Nazionale del Lavoro*, and the sale of the motorway concessionaire, *Autostrade*, the national airline *Alitalia*, the ferry company *Finmare* and parts of the defence and engineering group, *Finmeccanica* (Economist Intelligence Unit, 1998: 20–21).

11   It seems at least marginally less plausible to argue now than it has been until recently that privatization is a policy undesired by the governing parties – one they have had to submit to rather than one they have been able to direct (Cerboni and Cotta, 1996). For if the privatization programme which finally took off during the eleventh legislature had largely been imposed by the requirements of deficit reduction and European integration, the programme is now continuing even after a large number of these requirements (and all but one of those associated with EMU) have been met.

12   See, for example, Rose (1984) on Britain, Rallings (1987) on Canada and Kalogeropoulou (1989) on Greece.

13   For example, Rose (1984) found the British Conservative and Labour parties making 96 and 83 pledges respectively at the 1970 general election, and 105 and 126 respectively at the two 1974 elections. The fact that the number of *Ulivo* pledges fell short of these figures is almost certainly to be explained by the fact that its document had, of necessity, to embody a compromise. Also important, in all probability, was a desire to avoid giving hostages to fortune – or, in other words, a desire to avoid including a number of pledges that might subsequently be revealed as excessive in light of the limitations imposed by the parliamentary arithmetic. (For example, analysing Canadian and British manifestos between 1945

and 1979, Rallings found that the former tended to contain fewer pledges than the latter – unsurprisingly in view of the fact that four out of 11 Canadian governments which took office during this period lacked an overall majority.)

14   Such material can be conveniently acccessed via the Italian Parliament's web site: http://www.parlamento.it/

15   The analysis was carried out in September 1998.

# 9 Conclusion: The Vices and Virtues of Italian Democracy

My purpose in writing this book has been to understand the sea-change that has taken place in Italian politics since 1989. In order to achieve this understanding it seemed necessary to try to pinpoint *what* had changed, *why* and with *what consequences* – a task that seemed to be made the more urgent by the change versus continuity debate which has tended to dominate recent analyses of Italian political developments. Since this debate has tended to focus on 'Italian politics' *tout court*, it has thereby drawn attention away from the possibility that the recent period can be characterized as both one of rupture with the past and as one of ongoing transition, depending on the area looked at. So, since some sort of rupture undoubtedly *seems* to have taken place, the most sensible initial question appeared to be: 'Can we specify in what area, precisely, the rupture is located?'

I decided early on that the rupture was located within the area of 'party politics', by which I mean parties, voters, their behaviour and the institutional rules prescribing their behaviour. Within this area, the disintegration of the parties which governed Italy for nearly half a century after the end of the Second World War, and the continuing upheavals in the party landscape, have been associated with the elimination of what were the *differentiae specificae* of the old party system. That is, the old extremes of left and right have shed their pariah status; there has been an end to bilateral oppositions and the old tripolar format; the centre is no longer occupied by one large party.

This then raised the question of *why* these changes had taken place. My answer to this question was that they had come about, in essence, as a result of three sets of factors: namely, the spread of corruption; electoral change and the growth of the Northern League; and the success of the referendum movement in bringing about the passage of a changed electoral law in 1993. Each of these sets of factors operated at a different level within the sphere of party politics: *within* the parties among their members; *below* the parties at the level of the mass electorate; and *above* the parties at the level of institutions.

Within the parties, the spread of corruption was encouraged by a well established clientelistic mode of managing power relationships because, clientelism, by its very nature, tends to undermine confidence in the even-handed application of the universalistic criteria that can otherwise act as barriers against corruption. The spread of corruption in turn undermined the parties by discouraging the ideologically committed member while encouraging the venal one, thus leaving the parties with membership bases that were increasingly brittle. When *Tangentopoli* cut off the flow of resources from above, a predominantly venal membership simply melted away.

Below the parties, voting choices had traditionally been stable, both for ideological reasons and because of clientelism which had made it worthwhile to support this or that party from the point of view of one's *individual* interests, even while generating contempt for the parties as providers of *collective* goods. But with economic and social change came a weakening of ideological attachments and a heightened contempt, especially in the North where there emerged a growing conflict between what was required for the successful pursuit of clientele politics and what was required in order to meet the needs of the growing small-business sector for efficiently provided collective goods. If the collapse of communism removed the final ideological barrier against desertion of the old parties, by the same token it also meant that voters could support the judicial investigators' moves against these parties' leaders and swing behind a Northern League whose efforts were even more explicitly directed at the removal of the old political class than were those of the judicial investigators.

Finally, above the parties, at the level of institutions, reformers such as Mario Segni were convinced that the root of Italy's problems lay in an absence of stable and effective government whose prospects could only be enhanced by institutional reform involving appropriate changes in the mechanisms for converting distributions of votes into distributions of legislative seats. Confronted with the reform paradox they were able to find a way out of it by making use of the constitutional provision for abrogative referenda. The effects of this were to further party-system change by altering the opportunities and constraints given to parties by the electoral system, opportunities and constraints to which they would have to adapt in the run-up to 1994.

If these were the *causes* of change, then there were a number of theoretical reasons for expecting there to be significant *consequences* of both an institutional and policy kind. With regard to institutions, parties had been so central to institutional functioning in post-war Italy that it would have been strange not to have found some change in the way they worked after the old parties collapsed. With regard to public policy, it seemed likely that the move away from 'peripheral turnover' towards bipolarity would result in at least a reduction in the output of micro-policies and in more programmatically-based government.

Institutionally, the effects of party-system change have been apparent in at least four arenas: the Constitution, parliament, the presidency and in subnational government. In terms of the Constitution, there has been a major attempt at renewal. The fact that is has not so far succeeded does not alter the fact that it has been the most sustained and thorough-going attempt in the whole of Italy's post-war history. In terms of parliament, the behaviour of parties has clearly shifted away from a style of law-making which blurred the roles of governing and opposition parties towards one in which the parties are more willing to confront each other. In terms of the presidency, the disintegration of the old parties considerably raised the political profile of the office and it has placed the possibility of a permanent change in the role of the presidency more firmly on the agenda of Italian politics than at any time since the Second World War. In terms of subnational government, the process of party-system change was directly responsible for a number of reforms that have considerably improved the efficiency and effectiveness of government at this level. With regard to policy, change, if not improvement, in the quality of legislation is suggested by the significant changes in the social characteristics of parliamentarians that have been apparent since 1994, by the evidence pointing to a decline in particularism and patronage in legislation and elsewhere, and by the evidence of an increase in the responsiveness of parties to voters through the parties' implementation, once in office, of the programmes on which they were elected.

Yet it is typical of the unpredictability of the current phase of Italian politics that this straightforward picture of the consequences of party-system change was thrown into doubt as soon as the foregoing paragraphs were written. At the beginning of October 1998 the Prodi government lost a confidence vote arising out of the inability of the RC to back a number of clauses contained in the annual Finance Law. Prodi resigned and was replaced as prime minister by Massimo D'Alema who now led a government that was sustained in office by the votes of Cossiga's UDR in place of those of the RC. However, the UDR had made it clear from the beginning that it would not simply be to the D'Alema government what RC had been to the Prodi government. Rather, its support was effectively conditional on the 'death of the *Ulivo*' – that is, on the understanding that the coalition that was taking office was something other than one formed by the *Ulivo* plus the UDR. Such an understanding was essential from Cossiga's point of view since otherwise his party risked being reduced to the status of the *Ulivo*'s 'spare wheel'. So, when, at the beginning of 1999, there was a meeting of the *Ulivo* leaders, designed to renew the alliance organizationally and programmatically, the UDR threatened to withdraw its ministers from the government. Although this did not actually happen, the episode did give the impression, perhaps, that an unambiguous break with the past and a new era of stable governing majorities was still a long way off. Certainly, Cossiga's actions suggested that he was much more interested in old-style power-broking than in effective government and political renewal.

What conclusions can we draw from all of this for the quality of Italian democracy? First, there is no escaping the fact that there is a widespread feeling of disappointment with the results of Italy's period of party-system change. Thus, Mauro Calise (1998: IX) has written recently of the 'naive optimism' that the 1993 referenda could bring lasting political stability, while the journalist Giovanni Valentini, evidently still optimistic about the potential of referenda, could be found, at the beginning of 1999, welcoming the Constitutional Court's decision to give the go-ahead to a new referendum designed to abolish the proportional element of the voting system – on the grounds that it met the expectations of 'the many citizens of all persuasions who are increasingly disillusioned by the poverty of daily politics . . . and therefore attracted by the siren-call of abstentionism' (Valentini, 1999: 18). Yet disappointment with the outcome of Italy's period of change is not really justified since Italian democracy is more healthy than most observers have been willing to admit.

It is true that the belief that electoral reform could reduce party fragmentation and put an end to weak executives has so far turned out to be illusory. But fragmentation and weak executives are in no sense unique to Italy. On the contrary, these are qualities that are shared with the Scandinavian countries of Norway, Denmark and Sweden, among others – countries that are often held up as examples of successful democracies. It is also true that there are features of Italian culture which have acted as a fetter on democracy in that country: mistrust; the absence of mutual respect between citizens and the state; and a lack of civic awareness. But other countries also have cultural impediments to democracy (in Britain, one could cite the culture of deference, for example) and the outbreak of the *Tangentopoli* investigations spoke to the existence of an official morality, supportive of democracy, universalism and the rule of law, which has always acted as an important counterweight to the aforementioned features of Italian culture.

Political systems that are called 'democratic' are often thought to merit this label because they have a variety of mechanisms in place for ensuring effective accountability of the governors to the governed. That is, they provide overall political stability and they have fair electoral systems providing for a clear impact of electoral outcomes on government formation. There is, in addition, effective accountability of the executive to the legislature, and decentralized forms of government are adequate to ensure government sufficiently close to the people that the potential influence of each citizen is maximized. On each of these counts, Italy fares well.

In the post-war period to the end of the 1980s, the great paradox of Italian politics was that overall political stability was guaranteed precisely by the existence of two such all-embracing and implacably opposed subcultures as the Catholic and the Marxist. On the one hand, the subcultures made for the internal cohesion of the two major parties, the DC and the PCI, and thus brought electoral stability. On the other hand, they forced élites, by virtue of the sheer intensity of the ideological conflict they symbolized, at least to find a *modus vivendi*. Thereby, the élites were forced to internalize the rules of pluralist democracy and, in so doing, to school the mass citizenry in the rules of democratic life (Mastropaolo, 1994a: 73). Meanwhile, clientelism provided a further element of political stability, for it is basically a *conservative* phenomenon – that is, it represents an alternative to the search for collective solutions to common problems and thus strengthens those who already occupy positions of power within the political system.

Since, and partly because of, the changes in party politics of the early 1990s, political stability has, if anything, increased. For one thing, the changes have brought the demise of the ideological extremes. So if it is true to say that the changes have had little resonance at the level of mass attitudes, and if therefore, the changes have had little impact on those classic features of Italian culture of 'relatively unrelieved political alienation and of social isolation and distrust' (Almond and Verga, 1963: 402), then what they *have* done is to eliminate the availability of 'destabilising mass movements' (ibid.: 490) as potential outlets for citizen frustrations. As we have seen, in the past two general elections not even the largest parties have succeeded in garnering more than 20 per cent of the vote each (hardly more than the Liberal Democrats in Britain) and there is extreme fragmentation. We have also seen that one of the reasons why comprehensive constitutional reform has so far failed is precisely because there is no wholesale ideological vision available which can provide the point and purpose of any project for large-scale reform. So if anything, then, the traditional responses of Italians to political alienation and dissatisfaction seem likely to have been reinforced. That is, instead of increasing the availability of citizens for 'involvement in destabilising mass movements' (ibid.: 490) alienation and dissatisfaction now, more than ever, produce responses akin to resignation (seen in growing electoral abstention and declining party membership) along with others of an essentially individualistic kind.

Within the sphere of party politics, individualism and the continuing absence of a well developed sense of civic awareness are particularly symbolized by Silvio Berlusconi and his 'business-party' *Forza Italia*. As Paolo Flores d'Arcais (1998b) points out, the fact that Italy has, as its largest party of the right, a party of *this* kind is ultimately due to a 'historical absence' – namely, the lack of a strong bourgeoisie able rigorously to apply the distinctive bourgeois values of law-and-order, responsibility and competition, and thus able to mediate, in the general interest, the short-sighted rapaciousness of its single components. Because of this 'historical absence' and because the main party of the right is a party of the stamp of FI rather than another kind, effective and coherent governance could well continue to elude Italian reformers despite the profundity of the changes in its party system. For in continuing to insist that the regular prosecution of the court cases that were pending against him before he entered politics would amount to a political witch-hunt, Berlusconi reinforces that deeply rooted particularlistic strain in Italian culture according to which law and its enforcement is ultimately assumed to be negotiable (LaPolombara, 1987). This can only perpetuate corruption and other acts of impropriety for, while it is in the interest of citizens collectively that an overall state of legality prevails, if politicians and parties tolerate *illegality*, then individual citizens will begin to find that their own interests are in fact best served by acting illegally themselves.

The second feature of political systems that are called 'democratic' is that they have electoral systems that are recognizably fair in the sense that they are designed to give all votes as nearly as possible equal weight and that they ensure a proper degree of popular influence over the partisan composition of governments. The first of these features can be assessed in terms of the correspondence between vote and seat distributions resulting from the operation of the electoral system, and thus measured in terms of the Loosemore–Hanby (1971) index, D, which is calculated as half the sum of the absolute percentage differences between votes and seats received by each party at a given election:

$$D = \frac{1}{2} \sum_i |v_i - s_i|$$

This gives values of 18.3 and 11.9 for the 1994 and 1996 elections if we compare the parties' list votes with their overall seat totals. While higher than the corresponding values for the earlier elections held under the proportional system, these figures are no higher than those for recent elections in Britain where electoral system-induced disparities between vote and seat distributions have traditionally been notorious.

One of the arguments for changing the electoral system was that it would allow for a more direct relationship between voting outcomes and the party composition of governments. While the new system *has* had this effect (with the caveats noted earlier) it is not true, as is often claimed, that the previous electoral system prevented it. True, it coexisted with a multi-party system in which no party had an overall majority and coalition-building took place after, rather than before, elections. But the electoral system cannot have been responsible, for it was highly proportional in the sense that it was, by definition, a 'no effects' system (Sartori, 1986): in other words, it translated vote distributions into seat distributions with a minimum of distortion. Nor was it correct to suggest that electoral pressures failed to affect coalition behaviour: clearly they *must* do in a parliamentary democracy (Pridham, 1983: 224). Although electoral shifts always failed ever to result in alternation – that is, in a 'pendulum swing' from government based on the DC to an alternative coalition formula centred around the main party of opposition – this was a consequence not of the electoral system but of the *conventio ad excludendum* which was a reflection more of the Cold War and of a long tradition of foreign, mainly American, interference in Italian electoral politics than of the country's 'incompleteness' as a democracy. For the fact was that the *conventio* was underpinned by a strong basis of popular consent in terms of the widespread acceptance of anti-communist attitudes.[1]

The third feature of countries that are said to be properly 'democratic' is that, if their form of government is parliamentary, as Italy's is, then there is effective accountability of the executive to the legislature. Traditionally, the mechanisms for ensuring this accountability have not been very strong in Italy. Before the old parties collapsed it was written that the structure of incentives operating on individual legislators did not encourage them to give oversight activities a particularly high priority; for 'vigorous participation in formal Parliament business [was] likely to preclude the kind of network-building which [was] required for junior members if they wish[ed] to ensure their re-election and to place themselves well in a strong faction' (Furlong, 1990: 62). Most importantly, pressures to ensure proper mechanisms of accountability were effectively undermined by the cabinet's weakness *vis-à-vis* the parties and parliamentary groups. First, cabinet ministers would tend to be beholden to the party secretaries who, as we have seen, would themselves rarely occupy cabinet positions, with the result that the cabinet itself was unable to function as a collegial decision-making body, most important decisions being taken elsewhere within the arena of so-called 'majority summits' of the party secretaries. Second, government legislation had no special place within the parliamentary timetable (which would be decided on at meetings of the parliamentary group leaders) and this resulted in a growing recourse over the years to decree legislation whereby governments would attempt to bypass parliament altogether. Con-stitutionally, government decrees have to be converted, by parliament, into ordinary law within 60 days in order to retain their validity, but governments even developed the habit of trying to circumvent this obstacle by the constant reissuing of decrees whose terms were about to expire.

The party-system changes that we have analysed contain signs of a likely considerable improvement in this situation. Under the old system, as we have seen, the PCI's status of permanent opposition drew it into a system of *consociativismo* and consensual law-making as part of its quest for legitimacy. But in a system, such as the one that has come to be created, in which the opposition can always hope to become the government, the incentive is to demarcate oneself from the latter by following the principle that 'the duty of the opposition is to oppose'. And this is most effectively done not only by offering a clear-cut set of alternative policies, but also by being assiduous in scrutiny activities and ready to pounce at the first scent of government blood. In a largely bipolar system with clear-cut government and opposition roles, the fate of individual governing parties, and of the coalition as a whole, is more closely tied to cabinet decisions than in a system of permanent opposition and peripheral turnover such as the old one. It therefore suggests a growing authority of cabinet that, although front-ranking party leaders generally continue to remain outside it, 'majority summits' are largely a thing of the past. Finally, pressure towards the emergence of a stronger, but more accountable, executive has recently been added to by a decision of the Constitutional Court which in 1996 effectively outlawed the reissuing of emergency decrees altogether. Despite this, two years into its life, the *Ulivo* government had succeeded in enacting a large part of its programme, as we have seen.

Finally, decentralized government is an important means of ensuring accountability in so-called 'democratic' regimes because it maximizes the influence of local people on local decisions. Although, under the old party system, subnational and local government was caught up in the network of power relations woven by the parties at national level, Italy has always been far ahead of countries such as Britain in terms of the potential it affords for localized decision-making. This is because subnational tiers of government are presumed to have general competence within the law (meaning that the onus is on parliament to show that they have acted in ways that are *ultra vires*) whereas in Britain subnational tiers have no general competence in law (meaning that the onus is on them to find their powers in specific Acts of Parliament).

As we have seen, the disintegration of the old parties of government between 1992 and 1994 has brought considerable improvement in the potential for effective localized decision-making. On the one hand, the collapse of the old parties and, with it, the breaking of the vertical clientele networks that linked national- to local-level politicians within party factions has freed the latter from *de facto* control from above in terms of how they exercise their competences. On the other hand, the same dissatisfaction with the performance of government that contributed to the crisis of the old party system has brought with it a series of reforms designed to improve the quality of that exercise of competences. Together, the reforms can fairly be described as a transformation which 'has, generally speaking, been welcomed by the Italian public' (Dente, 1997: 186). Finally, the deliberations of the *Bicamerale* have held out the prospect of a new constitutional autonomy of subnational entities from the centre.

And so we come full-circle, back to the point that I made at the beginning. There are, to be sure, enough continuities in Italian politics to give the lie to the notion that the events of recent years amount to anything like a generalized qualitative break. But recognition of this fact must not be allowed to obscure the revolution that has taken place in Italian party politics or the very real improvements in the quality of Italian democracy that have been its consequence. The 'Second Republic' may yet be unborn; the 'First Republic' is, equally obviously, dead.

## Note

1   As late as 1985 surveys were still finding as many as 39 per cent of the Italian electorate saying that they would never vote for the Communist Party (a figure that rose to 57 per cent if 'don't knows' and refusals were excluded). These proportions are slightly lower than those that had been revealed by surveys carried out during the 1960s and 1970s, although comparison is difficult owing to changes in the way the question was asked. For details see Mannheimer and Sani (1987: 108–113).

# References

Agosta, Antonio (1994), 'Maggioritario e proporzionale', in I. Diamanti and R. Mannheimer (eds), *Milano a Roma. Guida all'Italia electtorale del 1994*, Roma: Donzelli.

Allen, H.J.B. (1991), 'Central/Local Relations', in Vernon Bogdanor (ed.), *The Blackwell Encyclopaedia of Political Science*, Oxford: Basil Blackwell.

Allum, Percy A. (1973a), *Italy – Republic Without Government*, London: Weidenfeld and Nicolson.

Allum, Percy (1973b), *Politics and Society in Post-War Naples*, Cambridge: Cambridge University Press.

Almond, Gabriel A. and Verba, Sidney (1963), *The Civic Culture: Political Attitudes and Democracy in Five Nations*, Princeton, NJ: Princeton University Press.

Baccetti, Carlo (1990), 'La multiforme esperienza della Nuova Sinistra', in Mario Caciagli and Alberto Spreafico (eds), *Vent'anni di elezioni in Italia. 1968–1987*, Padova: Liviana.

Bagnasco, A. (1988), *La costruzione sociale del mercato*, Bologna: il Mulino.

Balboni, Enzo (1992), 'Presidente della Repubblica, giudici e Consiglio superiore della magistratura: cronaca di un aspro conflitto costituzionale', in Stephen Hellman and Gianfranco Pasquino (eds), *Politica in Italia: I fatti dell'anno e le interpretazioni*, 1992 edition, Bologna: il Mulino.

Baldassarre, Antonio (1994), 'Il Capo dello Stato', in Giuliano Amato and Augusto Barbera (eds), *Manuale di diritto costituzionale*, Bologna: il Mulino.

Banfield, Edward C. (1958), *The Moral Basis of a Backward Society*, New York: The Free Press.

Bardi, Luciano (1996), 'Change in the Italian Party System', *Italian Politics and Society*, No. 46, Autumn.

Bardi, Luciano and Morlino, Leonardo (1994), 'Italy: Tracing the Roots of the Great Transformation', in Richard S. Katz and Peter Mair (eds), *How Parties Organize: Change and Adaptation in Party Organizations in Western Democracies*, London: Sage.

Barile, Paolo (1998a), 'Costituente Illegale', *la Repubblica*, 2 June 1998, p.1.

Barile, Paolo (1998b), 'Conflitti tra poteri dello Stato', *la Repubblica*, 10 July 1998, pp. 1, 6.

Bartolini, Stefano and D'Alimonte, Roberto (1996), 'Plurality Competition and Party Realignment in Italy: The 1994 Parliamentary Elections', *European Journal of Political Research*, **29** (1), January.

Bartolini, Stefano and D'Alimonte, Roberto (1997), 'Il maggioritario dei miracoli', in Roberto D'Alimonte and Stefano Bartolini, *Maggioritario per caso*, Bologna: il Mulino.

Bellu, Giovanni Maria and Bonsanti, Sandra (1993), *Il crollo: Andreotti, Craxi e il lor regime*, Roma and Bari: Laterza.

Berlinguer, Enrico (1975), 'La nostra lotta per l'affermazione di una alternativa democratica', (November 1971), in Enrico Berlinguer, *La 'questione comunista'*, Roma: Editori Riuniti.

Biorcio, Renato (1990), 'La nascita dell'elettorato verde', in Mario Cacigli and Alberto Spreafico (eds), *Vent'anni di elezioni in Italia. 1968–1987*, Padova: Liviana.

Biorcio, Roberto (1997), *La Padania Promessa: La storia, le idee e la logica d'azione della Lega Nord*, Milano: il Saggiatore.

Bossi, Umberto (1991), 'Tutte le colpe di Agnelli &c.', *la Repubblica*, 25 April.

Bourricaud, François (1974), 'Partitocrazia: consolidamento o rottura?', in Fabio Luca Cavazza and Stephen R. Graubard (eds), *Il caso italiano*, Milano: Garzanti.

Bull, Martin J. (1991a), 'The Unremarkable Death of the Italian Communist Party', in Filippo Sabetti and Raimondo Catanzaro (eds), *Italian Politics: A Review*, Vol. 5, London and New York: Pinter.

Bull, Martin J. (1991b), 'Whatever Happened to Italian Communism? Explaining the Dissolution of the Largest Communist Party in the West', *West European Politics*, **14** (4), October.

Bull, Martin J. (1995), 'Il fallimento dell'Alleanza progressista', in Piero Ignazi and Richard S. Katz (eds), *Politica in Italia: I fatti dell'anno e le interpretazioni. Edizione 95*, Bologna: il Mulino.

Bull, Martin J. (1996a), 'The Roots of the Italian Crisis', *South European Society and Politics*, **1** (1), Summer.

Bull, Martin J. (1996b), 'The Reconstitution of the Political Left in Italy: Demise, Renewal, Realignment and . . . Defeat', in R. Gillespie (ed.), *Mediterranean Politics: Volume 2*, London: Pinter.

Bull, Martin J. and Daniels, Philip (1990), 'The New Beginning': The Italian Communist Party under the Leadership of Achille Occhetto', *The Journal of Communist Studies*, **6** (3), September.

Bull, Martin J. and Newell, James L. (1993), 'Italian Politics and the 1992 Elections: From "Stable Instability" to Instability and Change', *Parliamentary Affairs*, **46** (2), April.

Bull, Martin J. and Newell, James L. (1995), 'Italy Changes Course? The 1994 Elections and the Victory of the Right', *Parliamentary Affairs*, **48** (1), January.

Bull, Martin J. and Newell, James L. (1996), 'Electoral Reform in Italy:

When Consequences Fail to Meet Expectations', *Representation*, **34** (1), Winter 1996–97.

Bull, Martin J. and Rhodes, Martin (1997), 'Between Crisis and Transition: Italian Politics in the 1990s', in Martin J. Bull and Martin Rhodes (eds), *Crisis and Transition in Italian Politics*, London and Portland, OR: Frank Cass.

Butler, David and Stokes, Donald (1974), *Political Change in Britain: The Evolution of Electoral Choice*, second edition, London: Macmillan.

Caciagli, Mario and Kertzer, David I. (eds) (1996), *Italian Politics: The Stalled Transition*, Oxford and Boulder, CO: Westview Press.

Calandra, Piero (1986), *Il governo della Repubblica*, Bologna: il Mulino.

Calise, Mauro (1993), 'Remaking the Italian Party System: How Lijphart Got It Wrong by Saying it Right', *West European Politics*, **16** (4), October.

Calise, Mauro (1994), *Dopo la partitocrazia. L'Italia tra modelli e realtà*, Einaudi: Torino.

Calise, Mauro (1998), *La costituzione silenziosa: Geografia dei nuovi poteri*, Roma-Bari: Laterza.

Cammarano, Fulvio (1992), 'Il modello politico britannico nella cultura del moderatismo italiano di fine secolo', in Renato Camurri (ed.), *La Scienza Moderata: Fedele Lampertico e l'Italia Liberale*, Milano: Franco Angeli.

Carioti, Antonio (1995), 'Dal ghetto al palazzo: l'ascesa di Alleanza nazionale', in Piero Ignazi and Richard S. Katz (eds), *Politica in Italia: I fatti dell'anno e le interpretazioni*, Bologna: il Mulino.

Cartocci, Roberto (1990), *Elettori in Italia: Riflessioni sulle vicende elettorali degli anni ottanta*, Bologna: il Mulino.

Catanzaro, Raimondo (1993), 'Un anno di svolta nella mafia e nell'antimafia', in Stephen Hellman and Gianfranco Pasquino (eds), *Politica in Italia: I fatti dell'anno e le interpretazioni*, Bologna: il Mulino.

Cavazzuti, Filippo (1995), 'L'incerto cammino delle privatizzazioni', in Piero Ignazi and Richard Katz (eds), *Politica in Italia: I fatti dell'anno e le interpretazioni*, Bologna: il Mulino.

Cazzola, Franco (1988), *Della Corruzione: Fisiologia e patologia di un sistema politico*, Bologna: il Mulino.

Cazzola, Franco and Morisi, Massimo (1996), *La mutua diffidenza. Il reciproco controllo tra magistrati e politici nella prima Repubblica*, Milano: Feltrinelli.

Cerboni, Alessandro and Cotta, Maurizio (1996), 'Le privatizzazzioni: i partiti e la crisi finanziaria', in Maurizio Cotta and Pierangelo Isernia (eds), *Il gigante dai piedi di argilla*, Bologna: il Mulino.

Certoma, G. Leroy (1995), *The Italian Legal System*, London: Butterworths.

Chiaramonte, Alessandro (1997), 'The General Elections of 21 April 1996', in Roberto D'Alimonte and David Nelken (eds), *Italian Politics: The Centre-Left in Power*, Oxford and Boulder, CO: Westview Press.

Colaprico, Piero (1996), *Capire Tengentopoli*, Milano: il Saggiatore.

Corbetta, Piergiorgio and Parisi, Arturo M.L. (1994), 'Ancora un 18 aprile. Il referendum sulla legge elettorale per il Senato', in Carol Mershon and Gianfranco Pasquino (eds), *Politica in Italia: I fatti dell'anno e le interpretazioni*, Bologna: il Mulino.

Corbetta, Piergiorgio, Parisi, M.L. Arturo and Schadee, Hans M.A. (1988), *Elezioni in Italia: Struttura e tipologia delle consultazioni politiche*, Bologna: il Mulino.

Cotta, Maurizio (1979), *Classe politica e parlamento in Italia*, Bologna: il Mulino.

Cotta, Maurizio (1996) 'La crisi del governo di partito all'Italiana', in Maurizio Cotta and Pierangelo Isernia (eds), *Il gigante dai piedi di argilla*, Bologna: Il Mulino.

Cotta, Maurizio (1998), 'Introduzione', paper presented to the conference 'Lavori in Corso: il sistema politico italiano dopo il terremoto dei primi anni novanta: polity, politics, policies', Centre for the Study of Political Change, University of Siena, 19–21 February 1998.

Crispi, F. (1890), *Scritti e discorsi politici*, Roma.

Daalder, Ivo H. (1983), 'The Italian Party System in Transition: The End of Polarised Pluralism?', *West European Politics*, **6** (3).

D'Alimonte, Roberto (1995), 'La transizione italiana: il voto regionale del 23 aprile', *Rivista Italiana di Scienza Politica*, **25** (3).

D'Alimonte, Roberto and Bartolini, Stefano (1997a), *Maggioritario per caso: Le elezioni politiche del 1994 e del 1996 a confronto: il ruolo del sistema elettorale, le coalizioni, le scelte degli elettori*, Bologna: il Mulino.

D'Alimonte, Roberto and Bartolini, Stefano (1997b), 'Electoral Transition and Party System Change in Italy', in Martin Bull and Martin Rhodes (eds), *Crisis and Transition in Italian Politics*, London and Portland, OR: Frank Cass.

D'Alimonte, Roberto and Chiaramonte, Alessandro (1993), 'Il nuovo sistema elettorale italiano: quali opportunità?', *Rivista Italiana di Scienza Politica*, **22**.

D'Alimonte, Roberto and Nelken, David (1997), 'Introduction: A Year of Difficult Dialogue', in Roberto D'Alimonte and David Nelken (eds), *Italian Politics: The Centre-Left in Power*, Oxford and Boulder, CO: Westview Press.

Daniels, Philip A. (1988), 'The End of the Craxi Era? The Italian Parliamentary Elections of June 1987', *Parliamentary Affairs*, **41**.

Daniels, Philip A. (1993), 'L'Italia e il trattato di Maastricht', in Stephen Hellman and Gianfranco Pasquino (eds), *Politica in Italia: I fatti dell'anno e le interpretazioni*, Bologna: il Mulino.

Daniels, Philip A. (1999), 'Italy: Rupture and Regeneration?', in David Broughton and Mark Donovan (eds), *Changing Party Systems in Western Europe*, London and New York: Pinter.

De Fiores, Claudio (1995), 'Il presidente della repubblica nella transizione', *Democrazia e Diritto*, **35** (3–4).

della Cananea, Giacinto (1997), 'The Reform of Finance and Administration in Italy: Contrasting Achievements', in Martin Bull and Martin Rhodes (eds), *Crisis and Transition in Italian Politics*, London and Portland, OR: Frank Cass.

Della Porta, Donatella (1993), 'La capitale immorale: le tangenti di Milano', in Stephen Hellman and Gianfranco Pasquino (eds), *Politica in Italia: I fatti dell'anno e le interpretazioni*, Bologna: il Mulino.

Della Porta, Donatella (1996), 'Actors in Corruption: Business Politicians in Italy', *International Social Science Journal*, **149**, September.

Della Porta, Donatella (1998), 'A Judges' Revolution? Political Corruption and the Judiciary in Italy', paper presented to the workshop on 'Italy: Changes, Constraints and Choices' of the Joint Sessions of Workshops of the European Consortium for Political Research, University of Warwick, 23–28 March 1998.

Della Porta, Donatella and Vannucci, Alberto (1994), *Corruzzione politica e amministrazione pubblica: risorse, meccanismi, attori*, Bologna: il Mulino.

Della Porta, Donatella and Vannucci, Alberto (1997), 'The Resources of Corruption: Some Reflections from the Italian Case', *Crime, Law and Social Change*, **27** (3–4).

De Mauro, Tullio (1994), 'Lingua e dialetti', in Paul Ginsborg (ed.), *Stato dell'Italia*, Milano: il Saggiatore.

Dente, Bruno (1977), 'Sub-National Governments in the Long Italian Transition', in Martin Bull and Martin Rhodes (eds), *Crisis and Transition in Italian Politics*, London and Portland, OR: Frank Cass.

De Vito, F. (1996), 'Come si fa a fregare l'Umberto', *l'Espresso*, 17 May 1996, p.63.

di Federico, Giuseppe (1989), 'The Crisis of the Justice System and the Referendum on the Judiciary', in Robert Leonardi and Piergiorgio Corbetta (eds), *Italian Politics: A Review*, vol. 3, London and New York: Pinter.

Diamanti, Ilvo (1993), *La Lega: Geografia, storia e sociologia di un nuovo soggetto politico*, Roma: Donzelli.

Diamanti, Ilvo (1996), 'The Northern League: From Regional Party to Party of Government', in Stephen Gundle and Simon Parker (eds), *The New Italian Republic: From the Fall of the Berlin Wall to Berlusconi*, London and New York: Routledge.

Di Virgilio, Aldo (1994a), 'Elezioni locali e destrutturazione partitica. La nuova legge alla prova', *Rivista Italiana di Scienza Politica*, **24** (1), April.

Di Virgilio, Aldo (1994b), 'Dai partiti ai poli: la politica delle alleanze, *Rivista Italiana di Scienza Politica*, **24** (3), December.

Dogan, Mattei and Pelassy, Dominique (1990), *How to Compare Nations:*

*Strategies in Comparative Politics*, 2nd edition, Chatham, NJ: Chatham House.

Donovan, Mark (1995), 'The Politics of Electoral Reform in Italy', *International Political Science Review*, **16** (1).

Economist Intelligence Unit (1998), *EIU Country Report*, 2nd quarter 1998, London: Economist Intelligence Unit.

Farneti, Paolo (1985), *The Italian Party System (1945–1980)*, London: Pinter.

Ferraresi, Franco (1992), 'Una struttura segreta denominata Gladio', in Stephen Hellman and Gianfranco Pasquino (eds), *Politica in Italia: I fatti dell'anno e le interpretazioni*, Bologna: il Mulino.

Fiori, Giuseppe (1995), *Il Venditore: Storia di Silvio Berlusconi e della Fininvest*, Milano: Garzanti.

Flores d'Arcais, Paolo (1998a), 'Ma chi è l'eversore?', *la Repubblica*, 5 June 1998, p.13.

Flores d'Arcais, Paolo (1998b), 'Politici senza realismo', *Micro Mega*, **4**.

Foot, J.M. (1996), '"The Left Opposition" and the Crisis: Rifondazione Comunista and La Rete', in Stephen Gundle and Simon Parker (eds), *The New Italian Republic: From the Fall of the Berlin Wall to Berlusconi*, London: Routledge.

Follini, Marco (1996), 'L'Italia consociativa', *il Mulino*, **367**, September–October.

Follini, Marco (1997a), 'Il ritorno dei partiti', *il Mulino*, **370**, March–April.

Follini, Marco (1997b), 'Il sincretismo costituzionale. Se le regole non hanno un'idea', *il Mulino*, **372**, July–August.

Friedman, Alan (1996), 'The economic elites and the political system', in Stephen Grundle and Simon Parker (eds), *The New Italian Republic: From the Fall of the Berlin Wall to Berlusconi*, London and New York: Routledge.

Furlong, Paul (1990), 'Parliament in Italian Politics', *West European Politics*, **13** (3).

Furlong, Paul (1994), *Modern Italy: Representation and Reform*, London and New York: Routledge.

Fusaro, Carlo (1995), *Le regole della transizione: La nuova legislazione elettorale italiana*, Bologna: il Mulino.

Galli, Giorgio (1984), *Il bipartitismo imperfetto: Comunisti e Democristiani in Italia*, Milano: Mondadori.

Galli, Giorgio (1991), *I partiti politici italiani 1943–1991: dalla resistenza all'Europa integrata*, Milano: Rizzoli.

Geremicca, Federico (1992), '"De Michelis vattene" a Venezia il Psi si ribella', *la Repubblica*, 29 September 1992, p. 3.

Gilbert, Mark (1995), *The Italian Revolution: The End of Politics Italian Style?*, Boulder, CO and Oxford: Westview Press.

Gilbert, Mark (1996), 'L'Ulivo e la Quercia', in Mario Caciagli and David

I. Kertzer (eds), *Politica in Italia: I fatti dell'anno e le interpretazioni*, Bologna: il Mulino.

Ginsborg, Paul (1990), *A History of Contemporary Italy: Society and Politics 1943–1988*, London: Penguin.

Ginsborg, Paul (1994), 'L'Italia, l'Europa, il Mediterraneo', in Paul Ginsborg (ed.), *Stato dell'Italia*, Milano: il Saggiatore.

Ginsborg, Paul (1995), 'Italian Political Culture in Historical Perspective', *Modern Italy*, 1 (1), Autumn.

Ginsborg, Paul (1996), 'Explaining Italy's Crisis', in Stephen Gundle and Simon Parker (eds), *The New Italian Republic: From the Fall of the Berlin Wall to Berlusconi*, London and New York: Routledge.

Giuliani, Marco (1997), 'Measures of Consensual Law-Making: Italian "Consociativismo"', *South European Society and Politics*, 2 (1), Summer.

Graziano, Luigi (1973), 'Patron–Client Relationships in Southern Italy', *European Journal of Political Research*, (1).

Graziano, Luigi, Girotti, F. and Bonet, L. (1984), 'Coalition Politics at the Regional Level and Centre-Periphery Relationships', *International Political Science Review*, 5 (4), 1984.

Guarnieri, Carlo (1997), 'The Judiciary in the Italian Political Crisis', in Martin Bull and Martin Rhodes (eds), *Crisis and Transition in Italian Politics*, Portland, OR and London: Frank Cass.

Gundle, Stephen (1995), 'Rai e Fininvest nell'anno di Berlusconi', in Piero Ignazi and Richard Katz (eds), *Politica in Italia: I fatti dell'anno e le interpretazioni*, Bologna: il Mulino.

Gundle, Stephen and Parker, Simon (1996), 'Introduction: The New Italian Republic', in Stephen Gundle and Simon Parker (eds), *The New Italian Republic: From the Fall of the Berlin Wall to Berlusconi*, London and New York: Routledge.

Gusso, Massimo (1990), 'Da movimento-partito a partito-movimento: i radicali e il loro elettorato', in Mario Caciagli and Alberto Spreafico (eds), *Vent'anni di elezioni in Italia. 1968–1987*, Padova: Liviana Editrice.

Hellman, Stephen (1997), 'The Italian Left After the 1996 Elections', in Roberto D'Alimonte and David Nelken (eds), *Italian Politics: The Centre-Left in Power*, Oxford and Boulder, CO: Westview Press.

Hellman, Stephen and Pasquino, Gianfranco (1993), 'Introduzione' in Stephen Hellman and Gianfranco Pasquino (eds), *Politica in Italia: I fatti dell'anno e le interpretazioni*, Bologna: il Mulino.

Hine, David (1990), 'The Consolidation of Democracy in Post-War Italy', in Geoffrey Pridham (ed.), *Securing Democracy: Political Parties and Democratic Consolidation in Southern Europe*, London and New York: Routledge.

Hine, David (1993), *Governing Italy: The Politics of Bargained Pluralism*, Oxford: Clarendon Press.

Hine, David and Poli, Emanuela (1997), 'The Scalfaro Presidency in

1996: The Difficult Return to Normality', in Roberto D'Alimonte and David Nelken (eds), *Italian Politics: The Centre-Left in Power*, Oxford and Boulder, CO: Westview Press.

Ignazi, Piero (1994), 'Alleanza Nazionale', in Ilvo Diamanti and Renato Mannheimer (eds), *Milano a Roma: Guida all'Italia elettorale del 1994*, Roma: Donzelli.

Ignazi, Piero and Katz, Richard S. (1995), 'Introduzione. Ascesa e caduta del governo Berlusconi', in Piero Ignazi and Richard S. Katz (eds), *Politica in Italia: I fatti dell'anno e le interpretazioni*, Bologna: il Mulino.

Kalogeropoulou, Efthalia (1989), 'Election Promises and Government Performance in Greece: PASOK's Fulfilment of its 1981 Election Pledges', *European Journal of Political Research*, **17**.

Katz, Richard (1987), 'Party Government and its Alternatives', in Richard Katz (ed.), *Party Governments: European and American Experiences*, Berlin and New York: de Gruyter.

Katz, Richard (1996), 'Electoral Reform and the Transformation of Party Politics in Italy', *Party Politics*, **2** (1).

Keat, Russell and Urry, John (1975), *Social Theory as Science*, London: Routledge.

Lange, Peter (1980), 'Crisis and Consent, Change and Compromise: Dilemmas of Italian Communism in the 1970s', in Peter Lange and Sidney Tarrow (eds), *Italy in Transition: Conflict and Consensus*, London: Frank Cass.

LaPalombara, Joseph (1964), *Interest Groups in Italian Politics*, Princeton, NJ: Princeton University Press.

LaPalombara, Joseph (1987), *Democracy, Italian Style*, New Haven and London: Yale University Press.

Leonardi, Robert and Anderlini, Fausto (1991), 'Introduction', in Robert Leonardi and Fausto Anderlini (eds), *Italian Politics: A Review*, Vol. 6, London: Pinter.

Leonardi, Robert and Kovacs, Monique (1993), 'L'irresistibile ascesa della Lega Nord', in Stephen Hellman and Gianfranco Pasquino (eds), *Politica in Italia: I fatti dell'anno e le interpretazioni*, Bologna: il Mulino.

Leonardi, Robert and Wertman, Douglas A. (1989), *Italian Christian Democracy*, London: Macmillan.

Loosemore, J. and Hanby, V.J. (1971), 'The Theoretical Limits of Maximum Distortion: Some Analytic Expressions for Electoral Systems', *British Journal of Political Science*, **1**.

McCarthy, Patrick (1992), 'Il referendum del 9 giugno', in Stephen Hellman and Gianfranco Pasquino (eds), *Politica in Italia: I fatti dell'anno e le interpretazioni*, Bologna: il Mulino.

McCarthy, Patrick (1995), 'Forza Italia: nascita e sviluppo di un partito virtuale', in Piero Ignazi and Richard S. Katz (eds), *Politica in Italia: I fatti dell'anno e le interpretazioni*, Bologna: il Mulino.

McCarthy, Patrick (1996a), *La crisi dello Stato italiano: Costume e vita politica nell'Italia contemporanea*, Roma: Editori Riuniti.

McCarthy, Patrick (1996b), 'Forza Italia: The New Politics and Old Values of a Changing Italy', in Stephen Gundle and Simon Parker (eds), *The New Italian Republic: From the Fall of the Berlin Wall to Berlusconi*, London and New York: Routledge.

Magatti, Mauro (1996), 'Tangentopoli, una questione sociale', *il Mulino*, **368**, November–December.

Mannheimer, Renato and Sani Giacomo (eds) (1987), *Il Mercato Elettorale: Identikit dell'elettore italiano*, Bologna: il Mulino.

Marengo, Franco Damaso (1981), *Rules of the Italian Political Game*, Aldershot: Gower.

Mariotti, Cristina (1996), 'Santa Lucia del Miracolo', *L'Espresso*, 22 August 1996, pp. 4–6.

Mastropaolo, Alfio (1994a), 'Perché è entrata in crisi la democrazia italiana? Un'ipotesi sugli anni Ottanta', in M. Caciagli *et al.* (eds), *L'Italia fra crisi e transizione*, Roma: Bari.

Mastropaolo, Alfio (1994b), 'Le elezioni politiche del marzo 1994: Vecchio e nuovo nel Parlamento italiano', *Italia Contemporanea*, **196**, September.

Mastropaolo, Alfio (1996), 'La classe politica parlamentare tra rivoluzione e restaurazione', *Italia Contemporanea*, **204**, September.

Merkel, Wolfgang (1987), *Prima e dopo Craxi: Le trasformazioni del PSI*, Padova: Liviana.

Morlino, Leonardo (1996), 'Crisis of Parties and Change of Party System in Italy', *Party Politics*, **2** (1).

Morlino, Leonardo and Tarchi, Marco (1996), 'The Dissatisfied Society: The Roots of Political Change in Italy', *European Journal of Political Research*, **30**, July.

Natale, Paolo (1994), 'C'era una volta l'elettore socialista', in Renato Mannheimer and Giacomo Sani (eds), *La Rivoluzione Elettorale: L'Italia tra la prima e la seconda repubblica*, Milano: Anabasi.

Nelken, David (1996), 'The Judges and Political Corruption in Italy', *Journal of Law and Society*, **23** (1), March.

Neppi Modona, Guido *et al.* (1995), *Stato della Costituzione: Principi, regole, equilibri. Le ragioni della storia, i compiti di oggi*, Milano: Il Saggiatore.

Newell, James (1994), 'The Scottish National Party and the Italian *Lega Nord*: A Lesson for their Rivals?', *European Journal of Political Research*, **26** (2).

Newell, James (1995), 'Electoral Behaviour and Political Change: Recent Italian Elections in their Postwar Context', *European Studies Research Institute Working Papers in Contemporary History and Politics no. 4*, University of Salford, April.

Newell, James (1998), 'At the Start of a Journey: Steps on the Road to

Decentralisation', in Luciano Bardi and Martin Rhodes (eds), *Italian Politics: Mapping the Future*, Oxford and Boulder, CO: Westview Press.

Newell, James and Bull, Martin J. (1993), 'The Italian Referenda of April 1993: Real Change at Last?', *West European Politics*, **16** (4), October.

Newell, James and Bull, Martin J. (1996), 'The Italian General Election of 1996: The Left on Top or on Tap?', *Parliamentary Affairs*, **49** (4), October.

Newell, James and Bull, Martin J. (1997), 'Party Organisations and Alliances in Italy in the 1990s: A Revolution of Sorts', in Martin Bull and Martin Rhodes (eds), *Crisis and Transition in Italian Politics*, Portland, OR and London: Frank Cass.

Nuvoli, Paolo and Spreafico, Alberto (1990), 'Il partito del non voto', in Mario Caciagli and Alberto Spreafico (eds), *Vent'anni di elezioni in Italia. 1968–1987*, Padova: Liviana.

Padellaro, Antonio (1996), 'I boiardi dell'Ulivo', *L'Espresso*, July, pp. 53–5.

Padellaro, Antonio (1997), 'Lottizzare e salvarsi l'anima', *L'Espresso*, 11 December, pp. 69–70.

Pansa, Giampaolo (1996), 'Illazioni su una direttora', *L'Espresso*, 22 August, pp. 42–3.

Pappalardo, Adriano (1994), 'La nuova legge elettorale in parlamento: Chi, come e perché', *Rivista Italiana di Scienza Politica*, **24** (2), August.

Pappalardo, Adriano (1996), 'Dal pluralismo polarizzato al pluralismo moderato. Il modello di Sartori e la transizione italiana', *Rivista Italiana di Scienza Politica*, **26** (1), April.

Parisi, Arturo and Pasquino, Gianfranco (eds) (1977), *Continuità e mutamento elettorale in Italia*, Bologna: il Mulino.

Pasquino, Gianfranco (1989), 'The Obscure Object of Desire: A New Electoral Law for Italy', *West European Politics*, **12** (3).

Pasquino, Gianfranco (1991a), 'La promozione dei referendum elettorali', in Fausto Anderlini and Robert Leonardi (eds), *Politica in Italia: I fatti dell'anno e le interpretazioni*, Bologna: il Mulino.

Pasquino, Gianfranco (1991b), 'The De Mita Government Crisis and the Powers of the President of the Republic: Which Form of Government?', in Filippo Sabetti and Raimondo Catanzaro (eds), *Italian Politics: A Review*, vol. 5, London and New York: Pinter.

Pasquino, Gianfranco (1996), 'Il governo di Lamberto Dini', in Mario Caciagli and David I. Kertzer (eds), *Politica in Italia: I fatti dell'anno e le interpretazioni*, Bologna: il Mulino.

Pasquino, Gianfranco (1997), 'No Longer a "Party State"? Institutions, Power and the Problem of Italian Reform', in Martin J. Bull and Martin Rhodes (eds), *Crisis and Transition in Italian Politics*, London and Portland, OR: Frank Cass.

Pasquino, Gianfranco and Hellman, Stephen (1993), 'Introduzione', in

Gianfranco Pasquino and Stephen Hellman (eds), *Politica in Italia: I fatti dell'anno e le interpretazioni*, Bologna: il Mulino.

Pasquino, Gianfranco and Vassallo, Salvatore (1994), 'Il governo di Carlo Azeglio Ciampi', in Carol Mershon and Gianfranco Pasquino (eds), *Politica in Italia: I fatti dell'anno e le interpretazioni*, Bologna: il Mulino.

Pederson, Mogens, N. (1979), 'The Dynamics of European Party Systems: Changing Patterns of Electoral Volatility', *European Journal of Political Research*, **7** (1).

Pitruzzella, G. (1994), 'I poteri locali: Tra autonomia e federalismo', in Paul Ginsborg (ed.), *Stato dell'Italia*, Milano: Il Saggiatore.

Pridham, Geoffrey (1983), 'Party Politics and Coalition Government in Italy', in Vernon Bogdanor (ed.), *Coalition Government in Western Europe*, London: Heinemann.

Pridham, Geoffrey (1988), 'Two Roads of Italian Liberalism: The Partito Repubblicano Italiano (PRI) and the Partito Liberale Italiano (PLI)', in Emil J. Kirchner (ed.), *Liberal Parties in Western Europe*, Cambridge: Cambridge University Press.

Rallings, Colin (1987), 'The Influence of Election Programmes: Britain and Canada 1956–1979', in Ian Budge *et al.* (eds), *Ideology, Strategy and Party Change: A Spatial Analysis of Postwar Election Programmes in Nineteen Democracies*, Cambridge: Cambridge University Press.

Rhodes, Martin (1994), 'Reinventing the Left: The Origins of Italy's Progressive Alliance', in Carol Mershon and Gianfranco Pasquino (eds), *Italian Politics: A Review*, Vol. 9, London: Pinter.

Rhodes, Martin (1996), 'The Italian Left between Crisis and Renewal', in R. Leonardi, and R.Y. Nanetti (eds), *Italy: Politics and Policy*, Vol. 1, Aldershot: Dartmouth.

Rhodes, Martin (1997), 'Financing Party Politics in Italy: A Case of Systemic Corruption', in Martin J. Bull and Martin Rhodes (eds), *Crisis and Transition in Italian Politics*, London and Portland, OR: Frank Cass.

Rinaldi, Claudio (1996), 'Se Ciampi prende ordini', *L'Espresso*, 4 July, p. 53.

Rinaldi, Claudio (1998) 'Storia di una tentata circonvenzione d'incapace', *L'Espresso*, 11 June, pp. 54–6.

Rodotà, Stefano (1988), 'Grande rifroma senza qualità', *la Repubblica*, 7 May, p. 15.

Romano, Sara (1992), 'Appendice documentaria', in Stephen Hellman and Gianfranco Pasquino (eds), *Politica in Italia: I fatti dell'anno e le interpretazioni*, Bologna: il Mulino.

Rose, Richard (1984), *Do Parties Make a Difference?*, 2nd edition, London: Macmillan.

Ruggeri, Giovanni (1994), *Berlusconi: Gli affari del Presidente*, Milano: Kaos Edizioni.

Ruzza, Carlo and Oliver Schmidtke (1996), 'Towards a Modern Right. Alleanza Nazionale and the "Italian Revolution"', in Stephen Gundle and Simon Parker (eds), *The New Italian Republic: From the Fall of the Berlin Wall to Berlusconi*, London and New York: Routledge.

Sabetti, Filippo (1992), 'Emergenza criminalità', in Stephen Hellman and Gianfranco Pasquino (eds), *Politica in Italia: I fatti dell'anno e le interpretazioni*, Bologna: il Mulino.

Salvadori, Massimo L. (1994), *Storia d'Italia e crisi di regime: Alle radici della politica italiana*, Bologna: il Mulino.

Sani, Giacomo and Segatti, Paolo (1997), 'Programmi. media e opinione pubblica', in Stefano Bartolini and Roberto D'Alimonte (eds), *Maggioritario per caso. Le elezioni politiche del 1996*, Bologna: il Mulino.

Sartori, Giovanni (1966), 'European Political Parties: The Case of Polarized Pluralism', in Joseph LaPalombara and Myron Weiner (eds), *Political Parties and Political Development*, Princeton, NJ: Princeton University Press.

Sartori, Giovanni (1974), 'Rivisitando il pluralismo polarizzato', in Fabio Luca Cavazza and Stephen R. Graubard (eds), *Il caso italiano*, Milano: Garzanti.

Sartori, Giovanni (1976), *Parties and Party Systems: A Framework for Analysis*, Cambridge: Cambridge University Press.

Sartori, Giovanni (1986), 'The Influence of Electoral Systems: Faulty Laws or Faulty Method?', in Bernard Grofman and Arend Lijphart (eds), *Electoral Laws and their Political Consequences*, New York: Agathon Press.

Sartori, Giovanni (1995), *Come sbagliare le riforme*, Bologna: il Mulino.

Scheuch, Erwin (1967), 'Society as a Context in Cross-Cultural Comparisons', *Social Science Information*, **6** (5), October.

Segatti, Paolo (1995), 'I programmi elettorali e il ruolo dei mass media', in Stefano Bartolini and Roberto D'Alimonte (eds), *Maggioritario ma non troppo. Le elezioni politiche del 1994*, Bologna: il Mulino.

Smith, Gordon (1989), 'A System Perpective on Party System Change', *Journal of Theoretical Politics*, **1** (3).

Tarrow, Sidney (1977), *Between Center and Periphery: Grassroots Politicians in Italy and France*, New Haven and London: Yale University Press.

Trigilia, Carlo (1986), *Grandi partiti e piccole imprese. Comunisti e democristiani nelle regioni a economia diffusa*, Bologna: il Mulino.

Trigilia, Carlo (1994), 'I paradossi di un capitalismo leggero', in Paul Ginsborg (ed.), *Stato dell'Italia*, Milano: il Saggiatore.

Uleri, Pier Vincenzo (1994), 'The Referendum Phenomenon in Italy: From the Beginnings to the Crisis of a Democratic System (1946–1993)', paper presented to the workshop on The Referendum Experience in Europe of the Joint Sessions of Workshops of the European Consortium for Political Research, Madrid, 17–22 April.

Valentini, Giovanni (1999), 'Una legge per due poli', *la Repubblica*, 20 January, pp. 1 and 18.

Vassallo, Salvatore (1995), 'La politica delle coalizioni. Da un sistema partitica all'altro', in Gianfranco Pasquino (ed.), *L'Alternanza Inattesa: Le elezioni del 27 marzo e le loro conseguenze*, Soveria Mannelli (Catanzaro): Rubbettino.

Vassallo, Salvatore (1998), 'The Third *Bicamerale*', in Luciano Bardi and Martin Rhodes (eds), *Italian Politics: Mapping the Future*, Oxford and Boulder, CO: Westview Press.

Verzichelli, Luca (1994), 'Gli eletti', *Rivista Italiana di Scienza Politica*, **24** (3), December.

Verzichelli, Luca (1995), 'I nuovi parlamentari', in Piero Ignazi and Richard S. Katz (eds), *Politica in Italia: I fatti dell'anno e le interpretazioni*, Bologna: il Mulino.

Verzichelli, Luca (1997a), 'The Majoritarian System Act II: Parliament and Parliamentarians in 1996', in Roberto D'Alimonte and David Nelken (eds), *Italian Politics: The Centre-Left in Power*, Oxford and Boulder, CO: Westview Press.

Verzichelli, Luca (1997b), 'La classe politica della transizione', in Roberto D'Alimonte and Stefano Bartolini (eds), *Maggioritario per caso*, Bologna: il Mulino.

Waters, Sarah (1994), '"Tangentopoli" and the Emergence of a New Political Order in Italy', *West European Politics*, **17** (1), January.

Wertman, Douglas A. (1994), 'L'ultimo anno di vita della Democrazia cristiana', in Carol Mershon and Gianfranco Pasquino (eds), *Politica in Italia: I fatti dell'anno e le interpretazioni*, Bologna: il Mulino.

Woods, Dwayne (1992a), 'The Centre No Longer Holds: The Rise of the Regional Leagues in Italian Politics', *West European Politics*, **15**.

Woods, Dwayne (1992b), 'La questione dell'immigrazione in Italia', in Stephen Hellman and Gianfranco Pasquino (eds), *Politica in Italia: I fatti dell'anno e le interpretazioni*, Bologna: il Mulino.

Wright, Erik Olin (1985), *Classes*, London: Verso.

# Glossary of Parties, Political Movements and Electoral Alliances

**AD    Democratic Alliance (*Alleanza Democratica*)**

A grouping born in the aftermath of the 1992 general election following the call of a number of prominent individuals, including the editor of *la Repubblica* newspaper, Eugenio Scalfari, for the formation of a broad-based national-level alliance to oppose the traditional parties of government, and especially the DC and the PSI.

**teanza Nord    Northern Alliance**

A confederation of the *Lega Lombarda* and five other formations (the *Liga Veneta*, *Piemont Autonomista*, and the leagues of Liguria, Emilia Romagna and Tuscany) and the label used by the common slate of candidates which they presented at the European Parliament elections of 1989. The Northern Alliance was the prelude to the establishment of a unitary federation of the six, later that year, in the shape of the *Lega Nord*.

**Alliance for Good Government    *Polo del buon governo***

The name given to the coalition of parties presenting common candidates in the single-member districts of the southern regions at the general election of 1994. It consisted of *Forza Italia* and the MSI-*Alleanza Nazionale* along with three minor formations, namely, the *Unione di Centro*, the *Centro Cristiano Democratico* and the *Polo liberaldemocratico*.

**AN    National Alliance (*Alleanza Nazionale*)**

The formation announced by the leader of the *Movimento Sociale Italiano*, Gianfranco Fini, in the wake of his party's success in the communal elections of November 1993. Designed to further the party's growing legitimacy, it was supposedly a confederation of forces of the right, but in fact almost totally dominated by the MSI. The MSI itself merged its identity totally with AN when, at its Fiuggi congress in February 1995, it formally dissolved itself.

## CCD    Christian Democratic Centre (*Centro Cristiano Democratico*)

One of the two main successor parties arising from the split in the DC which took place in January 1994 when the other, and larger, successor party – the *Partito Popolare Italiano* was founded. Bringing together part of the ex-doroteo faction of the DC, and including politicians such as D'Onofrio and Casini, the CCD took 29 Chamber of Deputies seats in 1994 and 19 in 1996.

## CDU    Christian Democratic Union (*Cristiani Democratici Uniti*)

Formally established on 23 July 1995, the CDU was in fact born in March of that year as the result of a split in the *Partito Popolare Italiano* provoked by its general secretary, Rocco Buttiglione. Buttiglione wanted to ally his party with *Forza Italia* while a majority of National Committee members remained opposed. The CDU joined forces with the CCD at the 1996 election when the two parties presented a common slate of candidates for the proportionally distributed seats (and when the CDU took a total of 11 Chamber seats).

## *Craxiani*

Followers of PSI leader, Bettino Craxi. Upon the latter's enforced resignation as general secretary in 1993, the *Craxiani* distinguished themselves by their attempts to resist efforts to reform the party. Most joined the *'federazione dei socialisti'* at the end of 1993 before coming under the aegis of Silvio Berlusconi and the Freedom Alliance immediately thereafter.

## C-S    Social Christians (*Cristiano-sociali*)

A small grouping born as the result of a meeting in June 1993 when trade unionist members of ACLI and other exponents of the world of Catholic associationism decided to establish a federation that would be inspired by the ideals of social Catholicism and would seek to form part of the emerging Progressive Alliance. As a result principally of the initiative of the PDS leader, Massimo D'Alema, in February 1998, the C-S joined Spini's *Laburisti*, Crucianelli's *Comunisti Unitari* and Bogi's left Republicans in a merger with the PDS to form a new party called the *Democratici di Sinistra*.

## CU    United Communists (*Comunisti Unitari*)

A small grouping surrounding Sergio Garavini and Famiano Crucianelli born in March 1995 as the result of the split in *Rifondazione Comunista* caused by the refusal of a majority of the latter's deputies to vote in favour of the finance law then being piloted through parliament by the Dini government.

## DC Christian Democratic Party (*Democrazia Cristiana*)

The Christian Democratic Party was founded in Milan in September 1942 by anti-fascist Catholics and ex-leaders of the pre-fascist *Partito Popolare Italiano*. From the beginning, the DC's programmes were founded on explicitly cross-class appeals designed to allow the party to pursue a catch-all strategy that would reach beyond the ranks of the Catholic faithful and allow it successfully to act as the main bulwark against communism. Ever the largest party in post-war Italy, the DC was the mainstay of every governing coalition from the end of the War until the resignation of the Amato government in 1993.

## *Democratici*

A parliamentary group, born in early 1995, bringing together parliamentarians belonging to the *Patto Segni, Alleanza Democratica* and the *Socialisti Italiani*.

## DP Proletarian Democracy (*Democrazia Proletaria*)

A 'far left' grouping which emerged from PDUP in 1976. Its appeal was based on an eclectic mixture. It had a workerist tendency in the north but also included greens, libertarians and feminists. It was always deeply critical of the PCI and the Soviet Union. Its vote averaged 1.6 per cent at the elections it fought in the 1970s and 1980s. On the emergence of *Rifondazione Comunista* it decided to disband and join the latter formation.

## DS Left Democrats (*Democratici di Sinistra*)

The official name of the PDS following the Florence congress of 12–14 February 1998 which saw the party joined by Spini's *Laburisti*, Carniti's *Cristiano-sociali*, Crucianelli's *Comunisti Unitari* and Bogi's left Republicans. The idea of such an amalgamation had first been publicly aired by PDS leader, D'Alema, in June 1996. It was envisaged as a means of creating a new democratic socialist party as an alternative to the idea of a centre-left 'Democratic Party' (viewed with sympathy by those around Walter Veltroni in the PDS) which would bring together the components of the *Ulivo* within one organization.

## FDS 'federation of socialists' (*'federazione dei socialisti'*)

A loosely organized grouping formed in late 1993 by Socialist parliamentarians who had been allies of Bettino Craxi and who were opposed to the moves of the then PSI general secretary, Ottaviano Del Turco, to locate the party within the framework of the Progressive Alliance.

### Fed. Lib.   Liberal Federation (*Federazione dei Liberali*)

Political grouping surrounding ex-Liberal Valerio Zanone, set up in 1994, in opposition to the other main 'successor' formation to the old PLI, the *Unione di Centro*, perceived by Zanone and his followers as being too rightist.

### Federalists

Grouping of parliamentarians with origins in the Northern League who switched their allegiances to Silvio Berlusconi during the course of the twelfth legislature. Allocated ten of the single-member Chamber seats in the negotiations leading to the formation of the Freedom Alliance in 1996 they managed to secure the election of five Deputies.

### FI   Go Italy! (*Forza Italia*)

The name given to the organization established by Silvio Berlusconi, in January 1994, as a means of bringing together, in one coalition, the forces of the right in view of the upcoming general election of that year. Less a mass-membership organization than a tightly controlled marketing entity designed to further the political ambitions of its leader, from the beginning the most salient themes of FI's appeal were individualism, free markets and traditional values.

### *Fiamma/Fiamma Tricolore*

see: 'MSFT'

### Freedom Alliance

The name given to the coalition of parties presenting common candidates in the single-member districts of the northern regions at the general election of 1994. It consisted of *Forza Italia* and the Northern League along with three minor formations, namely, the *Unione di Centro*, the *Centro Cristiano Democratico* and the *Polo liberaldemocratico*. 'Freedom Alliance' was also the name given to the electoral cartel formed by the parties of the right (FI and AN together with the CCD-CDU and Federalists) for the general election of 1996.

### *Fronte dell'Uomo Qualunque*   The Common Man's Front

Organization founded by Neapolitan playwright, Guglielmo Giannini, in 1945. Designed to combat anything perceived as threatening the ordinary Italian (hence the name, 'Common Man's Front'), it took 5.3 per cent of the vote and thirty seats in the Constituent Assembly elections of 1946 but had collapsed by the time of the first post-war general election in 1948.

## *Laburisti*    Labour

Political grouping surrounding ex-Socialist Valdo Spini. At the 1996 election it formed part of the *Sinistra Europea* securing the election of six deputies. In February 1998 it joined the *Democratici di Sinistra*.

## *Lega Autonomista Veneta*    Venetian Automomist League

Regional autonomy grouping, independent of the Northern League, whose candidates for the 1996 election were included in the *Ulivo* coalition running under the label '*l'Ulivo-Lav*'.

## *Lega d'Azione Meridionale*    League of Southern Action

Regional autonomy grouping. It put up seven candidates for single-member Chamber seats in 1996 and got one elected.

## *Lega Lombarda*    Lombard League

The name of the organization founded by Umberto Bossi in 1984 (originally as the *Lega Autonomista Lombarda*) to campaign for autonomy for the region of Lombardy through a federal reform of the state. The *Lega Lombarda* would from 1989 be the most significant constituent element of the Northern League to which it would lend both its leader and its highly centralized style of organization.

## *Lega Nord*    Northern League

The name of the organization founded in December 1989 by the leader of the *Lega Lombarda*, Umberto Bossi, as a means of bringing together a number of northern regional autonomy leagues under one umbrella. The Northern League combines a rigidly centralized form of organization with an appeal based on a unique blend of populism and 'ethno-regionalism'.

## *Liga Veneta*    Venetian League

The name of the organization founded in 1979 by Franco Rochetta after his encounter with the ideas of Bruno Salvadori of the Union Valdotaîne. The *Liga Veneta* was the first of the regional autonomy leagues to be founded and initially the most successful. Later, however, it would be eclipsed by Bossi's *Lega Lombarda*.

### *Lista Dini*    Dini List

The formation surrounding the outgoing premier, Lamberto Dini, the Dini List was one of the four components of the *Ulivo* each of which presented a common slate of candidates for the proportionally distributed seats at the election of 1996. It was composed of four separate parties: Boselli's *Socialisti Italiani*, Dini's own *Rinnovamento Italiano*, the *Patto Segni* and Sergio Berlinguer's *Movimento Italiano Democratico*.

### *l'Ulivo*    The Olive-tree Alliance

The name given to the electoral alliance, headed by Romano Prodi, which at the general election of 1996 brought together the parties of the centre-left.

### 'Mayors' Party'

A loosely organized entity surrounding Massimo Cacciari, mayor of Venice, whose aim has been to try to cut the ground from under the feet of the Northern League by campaigning for decentralizing reform on an explicitly cross-party basis.

### MID    Italian Democratic Movement (*Movimento Italiano Democratico*)

Organization founded by Sergio Berlinguer, one-time minister in the Berlusconi government. One of the four components making up the *Lista Dini* at the general election of 1996.

### MSFT    Social Movement-Tricoloured Flame (*Movimento Sociale-Fiamma Tricolore*)

Neo-fascist party founded in 1995 by ex-members of the Italian Social Movement unable to accept the decision of the latter party to consolidate its new-found political legitimacy by submerging its identity with the less ideologically distinct *Alleanza Nazionale*. At the 1996 election, votes won by *Fiamma Tricolore* candidates played a significant part in the victory of *Ulivo* candidates at the expense of Freedom Alliance candidates in a number of districts, especially in the South.

### MSI    Italian Social Movement (*Movimento Sociale Italiano*)

Party founded in December 1946 by a number of former officers in Mussolini's Repubblica di Salò. Though careful to avoid explicit statements of a desire to restore fascism (reconstitution of the Fascist Party being banned by the post-war Constitution) the MSI's nationalism and authoritarianism marked it out clearly as a party of the neo-fascist variety.

## Pact for Italy

The name given to the electoral alliance formed, for the general election of 1994, by Martinazzoli's *Partito Popolare Italiano* and Segni's Pact for National Renewal as a coalition of forces of the centre.

## Pact for National Renewal

The name given to the coagulation of forces surrounding ex-Christian Democrat Mario Segni which in 1994 formed an electoral alliance, the Pact for Italy, with Martinazzoli's PPI. Popularly known as the 'Segni Pact', in 1994 the Pact for National Renewal included what was left of the *Partito Repubblicano* surrounding its leader La Malfa, ex-Socialists surrounding Amato, and ex-Liberals surrounding Zanone.

## *Pannella*

The name given to the forces surrounding the charismatic ex-leader of the Radical Party, Marco Pannella. At the 1994 election Pannella's followers presented their own slate of candidates, the *Lista Pannella*, for the proportionally distributed Chamber seats. For the seats distributed according to the plurality formula, they took the name *Riformatori* and ran under the *Forza Italia* label.

## *Pannella-Sgarbi*

The name taken by followers of Marco Pannella standing as parliamentary candidates at the 1996 election. Dissatisfied with negotiations surrounding the distribution of the Freedom Alliance's candidatures prior to the election, Pannella had announced that he would field his own candidates for 29 and 122 of the Chamber and Senate plurality seats respectively. He then managed to secure an eleventh-hour agreement with Berlusconi whereby he agreed to invite his candidates to withdraw from the contest in exchange for an appeal by Berlusconi to Freedom Alliance voters to support *Pannella-Sgarbi* candidates running for the proportionally distributed seats.

## *Partito Sardo d'Azione*    Sardinian Party of Action

Party originally founded in the post-World War One period to campaign for Sardinian autonomy and then reconstituted after the fall of fascism. It wants official recognition of the Sardinian language and ultimately, independence within the European Union. Its candidates for the 1996 election were included in the *Ulivo* coalition running under the label 'l'*Ulivo-Psd'a*'.

*Patto Segni*

see: 'Pact for National Renewal'

## PCI     Italian Communist Party (*Partito Comunista Italiano*)

Italy's principal party of the left during the period spanning the Second World War and the party's transformation and change of name, in 1990–91, to the *Partito Democratico della Sinistra*. Consistently the second-largest party in terms of votes and seats, the PCI was kept permanently in opposition as a result of the so-called *conventio ad excludendum*, the agreement between the DC and its allies never to admit it to government because of its presumed anti-system nature.

## PDS     Democratic Party of the Left (*Partito Democratico della Sinistra*)

The larger of the two main successor parties to the pre-1990s PCI. The PDS was born when the PCI underwent a split following the collapse of the Berlin Wall. This led the PCI's leader, Occhetto, to conclude that the disintegration of the East European regimes required that the party be transformed into a non-communist party, the Democratic Party of the Left.

## PDUP     Party of Proletarian Unity for Communism (*Partito di Unità Proletaria per il Comunismo*)

Party born out of the collapse of the PSIUP in 1972. Its founding members consisted of those who were unwilling to respond to the failure of the PSIUP by joining either the PSI or the PCI and who were critical both of the PCI's growing moderation and its continuing (if decreasingly fervent) willingness to defend the policies of the Soviet Union.

## Pld     Liberal-Democratic Alliance (*Polo Liberaldemocratico*)

A small grouping of 'Patto Segni dissidents' surrounding Teso and Usiglio who transferred their allegiance to Silvio Berlusconi in the months prior to the 1994 election. Like the UdC, the Pld was not strong enough to demand an independent voice in the negotiations leading to the formation of the alliances of the right and was merely allocated a small number of candidacies by *Forza Italia* as part of its own quota.

## PLI     Italian Liberal Party (*Partito Liberale Italiano*)

Party formally constituted in 1922 but with organizational and political roots in the ruling élites which governed Italy following unification. The traditional defender of the interests of the employing class, the PLI was unable to turn this to its advantage in the post-war world in competition with a DC whose understanding of the need for an appeal to a wider audience than the urban bourgeoisie offered to big business greater electoral guarantees. Espousing a doctrinaire combination of free-market liberalism and political authoritarianism, the PLI was one of the three smaller parties of the secular democratic centre that traditionally formed the DC's minor coalition allies – the other two being the PRI and the PSDI. Its vote averaged 3.5 per cent at elections between 1948 and 1992.

### *Polo*

see: 'Freedom Alliance'

### *Polo delle Libertà*

see: 'Freedom Alliance'

### *Polo per le Libertà*

see: 'Freedom Alliance'

### *Popolari*

Often used as a shorthand term for the *Partito Popolare Italiano*, it refers here to one of the four constituent parts of the *Ulivo* that each presented a common slate of candidates for the proportionally distributed seats at the 1996 election. Headed by the PPI, it also included the followers of Prodi, Maccanico's UD, and the SVP.

### PPI     Italian Popular Party (*Partito Popolare Italiano*)

Recalling the name of the pre-fascist Catholic party, *Partito Popolare Italiano* was the name chosen by the largest of the two 'successor parties' to the DC when the latter split in January 1994.

### PR     Radical Party (*Partito Radicale*)

A party which found its origins in a split in the PLI in 1955, the PR was always characterized less by an easily definable ideology than by a distinct *style* of politics: flamboyant, individualistic, participatory. The party's concerns were above all with civil rights issues, peace, and the denunciation of abuses of power of whatever form. Always eschewing formal party organization, at its congress in January 1988, the PR decided to discontinue fighting elections *as* the PR, devoting its energies instead to the creation of a 'transnational radical party' that would be concerned with issues, such as pollution, military defence and European integration, which went beyond national boundaries. The PR's tradition continued to be represented at elections

– by the *Lista Pannella* in 1992 and 1994, and by the *Lista Pannella-Sgarbi* in 1996.

### PRI    Italian Republican Party (*Partito Repubblicano Italiano*)

Party founded in 1895. When it re-emerged after the fall of fascism it expressed an outlook combining anti-monarchism, anti-clericalism and anti-fascism together with a pro-market and trans-Atlantic stand. One of the three smaller parties of the secular democratic centre that traditionally formed the DC's minor coalition allies – the other two being the PLI and the PSDI – the PRI's vote averaged 2.8 per cent at elections between 1948 and 1992.

### Prodi

In the 1996 general election, Romano Prodi, besides being the *Ulivo's* prime ministerial candidate also had his own small group of followers whose parliamentary candidates were organized, under the aegis of the *Popolari*, as the *Comitati per l'Italia che vogliamo* (literally, 'Committees for the Italy that we want').

### *Progressisti*

see: 'Progressive Alliance'

### *Progressisti 1996*

The label used by those candidates belonging to *Rifondazione Comunista* who, as part of the stand-down arrangement reached with the *Ulivo* for the 1996 election, were running for one of the seats distributed according to the plurality formula.

### Progressive Alliance

The name given to the electoral cartel formed by the parties of the left (the PDS, RC, the *Rete*, the Greens, RS, the PSI, AD, and the C-S) for the general election of 1994.

### Progressive Federation

The parliamentary group formed in the aftermath of the 1994 election which brought together parliamentarians belonging to the PDS, the Greens, the C-S and the *Rete*.

### PSDI    Italian Social Democratic Party (*Partito Socialista Democratico Italiano*)

Party born, in 1947, of a split in the Socialist Party as a consequence of the latter's 'Unity of Action' pact with the PCI. While lending to

DC-based governments of the 1950s a reformist, socialist colouring, the PSDI was virulently anti-communist and rapidly became a party of mere power-brokers and clientelistic interests. One of the three smaller parties of the secular democratic centre that traditionally formed the DC's minor coalition allies – the other two being the PLI and the PRI – the PSDI's vote averaged 4.4 per cent at elections between 1948 and 1992. Swept away by *Tangentopoli* it had all but ceased to exist by the end of 1993. Some of its parliamentarians, led by the MEP Enrico Ferri, were included, under the name *Unione dei Democratici e dei Socialisti* (Union of Democrats and Socialists), in the Alliance for Good Government. However, it failed to secure the election of a single candidate in 1994.

### PSI    Italian Socialist Party (*Partito Socialista Italiano*)

Party founded in 1892. The loss of its position as the principal party of the left in the immediate aftermath of the fall of fascism, created for the PSI a fundamental strategic dilemma that it would have to face throughout the fifty-year period separating the armistice from the party's effective collapse in 1993, namely, that it could only escape subordination to the PCI at the cost of subordination to the DC and vice versa. It appeared to have found an independent role for itself in the 1980s when its indispensability in coalition formation allowed it to set the agenda of political debate, but precisely because this drew it ever more closely into the web of power-broking and corruption woven by the DC, it would prove ultimately to be the cause of the party's demise.

### PSIUP    Italian Socialist Party of Proletarian Unity (*Partito Socialista Italiano di Unità Proletaria*)

Party formed in 1964 by left-wing members of the PSI opposed to the latter party's entry into government the previous year. Obtaining 4.5 per cent of the vote and the election of 23 deputies at the general election of 1968, the party collapsed in 1972 when its vote fell to 1.9 per cent and it failed to elect a single deputy.

### PVA    Valle d'Aosta List (*Pour la Vallée d'Aoste*)

see: '*Union Valdôtaine*'

### RC    Communist Refoundation (*Rifondazione Comunista*)

Party formed in December 1991 following the decision of the PCI to transform itself into a non-communist party with a new name. RC founding members fell into two basic groups: former adherents of the old, 'pro-Soviet' wing of the PCI and others who wished to keep alive the traditions of Italian communism, and on the other hand, heirs to the 'new politics'/'student protest' tradition of the 1960s and 1970s. Despite its eclecticism, RC has managed to maintain a respectable electoral performance, for example, taking 8.6 per cent of the Chamber of Deputies proportional vote at the election of 1996.

## *Rete*   Network

Political grouping surrounding ex-Christian Democratic mayor of Palermo, Leoluca Orlando, set up in 1990–91 to campaign against the *Mafia* and against corruption in public life. Taking 1.9 per cent of the vote and 12 Chamber seats in 1992, the *Rete* was one of the minor formations belonging to the Progressive Alliance in 1994 and to the *Ulivo* in 1996.

## RI   Italian Renewal (*Rinnovamento Italiano*)

Political grouping established by ex-prime minister Lamberto Dini in February 1996 when he decided to continue his political career under the aegis of the *Ulivo*. Describing itself at its founding as a 'new, moderate and reformist political formation of the centre', RI was able to gather round it three other minor formations – the MID, the SI and the *Patto Segni* – to construct the *Lista Dini*, one of the four slates of candidates put up by the *Ulivo* for the proportionally distributed seats at the 1996 election.

## *Riformatori*

see: '*Pannella*'

## RS   Socialist Renewal (*Rinascita Socialista*)

Political group surrounding Giorgio Benvenuto which followed him out of the PSI when he resigned as the latter's general secretary in May 1993. Was one of the eight formations making up the Progressive Alliance at the 1994 elections.

## Segni Pact

see: 'Pact for National Renewal'

## SI   Italian Socialists (*Socialisti Italiani*)

Political grouping surrounding ex-Socialist Boselli. It formed part of the *Lista Dini* at the 1996 election. In February 1998 the SI came together with Schietroma's Social Democrats and Intini's Socialist Party (PS) to form the *Socialisti Democratici Italiani* (Italian Democratic Socialists, SDI), aiming to reunite the heirs of the PSI within a single organization of a weight sufficient to be able to engage profitably with D'Alema's *Cosa Due* (literally, 'Second Thing', recalling the term *'Cosa'* used to refer to the PDS in 1990 before it had been given a name), namely, the *Democratici di Sinistra.*

## *Sinistra Europea*    European Left

The name given to one of the four components of the *Ulivo* presenting a common slate of candidates for the proportionally distributed seats at the election of 1996. It was composed of the PDS, the C-S, the *Comunisti Unitari,* the *Laburisti, Unità riformista* and Schietroma's Social Democrats.

## SVP    South Tyrolese People's Party (*Südtirolervolkspartei*)

Political party formed in 1945 to further the political and socio-economic interests of the German- and Ladin-speaking peoples of South Tyrol in opposition to central government in Rome. The party's hegemonic status in South Tyrol has assured it the election of a handful of Deputies to every parliament despite its miniscule size on a national level.

## UD    Democratic Union (*Unione Democratica*)

Political formation of the centre surrounding Antonio Maccanico and created early in 1996 with the specific aim of participating in the general election of that year. UD was a confederation of a number of minor groupings, namely, AD, the PRI, ex-Liberals and some dissident followers of the SI. UD in turn formed part of the *Popolari* component of the *Ulivo.*

## UdC    Union of the Centre (*Unione di Centro*)

Grouping surrounding ex-Liberals Raffaele Costa and Alfredo Biondi which in the 1994 election was included in the Freedom Alliance and the Alliance for Good Government. The UdC was not strong enough to demand an independent voice in the negotiations leading to the formation of the alliances and was merely allocated a small number of candidacies by *Forza Italia* as part of its own quota. Costa and Biondi now sit as representatives of *Forza Italia* in the Chamber of Deputies.

## UDR    Democratic Union for the Republic (*Unione Democratica per la Repubblica*)

Political formation surrounding ex-President Francesco Cossiga, formed in February 1998 with the aim of re-building the fortunes of the centre-right and isolating the left by acting as a 'pole of attraction' for 'moderate' forces within the *Ulivo.* Within days of its birth it had gained the support of 51 parliamentarians and provoked major splits within the CCD and CDU.

### Union Valdôtaine

Party founded in 1945 to further the political and socio-economic interests of the French-speaking peoples of the Valle d'Aosta against central government in Rome. In both 1994 and 1996 it secured the election of one Deputy and one Senator.

### Unità rif.     Reformist unity (*Unità riformista*)

Political grouping surrounding ex-Socialist Giorgio Ruffolo. In the 1996 election it formed part of the *Sinistra Europea*.

### *Verdi*     Greens

Though 'Green Lists' were presented at elections from 1978 onwards, an organization resembling a 'Green *party*' – the *Federazione Nazionale delle Liste Verdi* (National Federation of Green Lists) – did not emerge until 1986. A 'new politics' party appealing above all to the young, 'post-material' generation, the Greens have seen their support average 2.6 per cent at general elections since the mid 1980s.

# Index